LAY DOWN YOUR HEART

GEORGE TARDIOS

Lay Down Your Heart

Bagamoyo to Lake Tanganyika:
Retracing Stanley's journey of 1871
in search of Dr Livingstone

Copyright © 2025 Christine Tardios

Sketchmap on page xxii-xxiii by James Nunn after the author's rough,
Copyright © Christine Tardios 2025

The moral right of the author has been asserted.

Apart from any fair dealing for the purposes of research or private study, or criticism or review, as permitted under the Copyright, Designs and Patents Act 1988, this publication may only be reproduced, stored or transmitted, in any form or by any means, with the prior permission in writing of the publishers, or in the case of reprographic reproduction in accordance with the terms of licences issued by the Copyright Licensing Agency. Enquiries concerning reproduction outside those terms should be sent to the publishers.

The manufacturer's authorised representative in the EU for product safety is Authorised Rep Compliance Ltd, 71 Lower Baggot Street, Dublin D02 P593 Ireland (www.arccompliance.com).

Troubador Publishing Ltd
Unit E2 Airfield Business Park
Harrison Road, Market Harborough
Leicestershire LE16 7UL
Tel: 0116 279 2299
Email: books@troubador.co.uk
Web: www.troubador.co.uk

ISBN 978-1-83628-257-0

British Library Cataloguing in Publication Data.
A catalogue record for this book is available from the British Library.

Printed and bound in Great Britain by 4edge Limited
Typeset in 12pt Minion Pro by Troubador Publishing Ltd, Leicester, UK

To my wonderful wife, Christine, who walked with me.
Without her help and companionship, I could never have
made this journey. She is an angel.

'Africa, unless you know what you are about, is a damned good place to keep out of. We old hands, who have been in Africa for over half a century, would strongly advise you to drop the whole idea of an expedition on foot... Sleeping sickness from tsetse fly is rife. You will also need tins of DDT to spread around your sleeping bags or blankets to keep off millions of ants, cockroaches etc. And you will have to take care the rats do not bite your feet off at night and that snakes do not curl up on your chests for warmth and that hyenas do not sneak in and take off a foot or an arm or a piece of your face...'

From a Sunday Telegraph *reader's letter to the author received shortly before the expedition's departure for Cairo in March 1984*

Contents

List of Illustrations   xi
Author's Preface   xiii
Preface by Christine Tardios   xix
Map: Our Jouney from Bagamoyo to Ujiji   xxii

PART ONE – BEGINNINGS
1. The Idea   3

PART TWO – GOING DOWN: FROM CAIRO TO BAGAMOYO
2. Following the River Nile through Egypt, Sudan and into Kenya   25
3. Dar es Salaam: Haven of Peace   58
4. From Zanzibar to Bagamoyo   74

PART THREE – DEPARTURE
5. Uzaramo: Land of the Tree that Gives Salt   101
6. Ukwere: Land of the Millet Stalks   111
7. Uluguru: Land of the Withered Leg   137
8. Ukami: Land of Waste   150

9	Uzigua: Land of the Diviners	168
10	Morogoro: Searching for the Old Walled City	176
11	Mkata Swamp – and Bush Fire!	190

PART FOUR – FINALLY FREE FROM GAME SCOUTS

12	Usagara: Land that Spread	207
13	Mpwapwa: How Stanley's Man Farquhar Met His End	219
14	Dodoma: Idodomera ('To be stuck')	237
15	From Uyanzi to Unyambwa: Land of the Flies to Land of the Dog	242
16	Unyaturu: Land of Here – and a Queen of the Bees	249
17	Ukimbu: Land of the Beginning – and an Ambush	256
18	Unyamwezi: Land of the Moon – and the Tembe of Livingstone	272
19	Tabora: the Sleepy Town	282

PART FIVE – INTO THE LAND OF SLEEPING SICKNESS

20	Ugunda: Land of Deserted Villages	301
21	Ukonongo: Land of Iron Hoes	315
22	Onward to Mpanda – Through the Land of the Hunters	330
23	Uvinza: Land of the Dried Pumpkins	350
24	Uhha: This Land	366
25	The Final Push – Ukaranga to Ujiji: Land of the Small Village	378

| 26 | Arrival in Ujiji | 384 |

Epilogue 401
Glossary of Terms in Swahili 417
Abbeviations in English 422
Bibliography 423

List of Illustrations

Between pages 136 and 137
1. The author's inspiration for the expedition acoss Tanzania
2. The expedition team on Zanzibar before crossing to Bagamoyo
3. Reception in front of the Livingstone Tower, Bagamoyo, to mark the start of our expedition
4. The expedition is seen off by people of Bagamoyo
5. Helping Burton over a wooden bridge
6. George and Andy have to carry panniers across the Usigara
7. We're equipped for all seasons
8. George with villagers reviews our camp area at Masimbu ravaged by a bush fire
9. George prepares to inject a blood-stained Stanley with antibiotics after an assault by hyenas

Between pages 328 and 329
10. A man collecting wood appears and encourages us
11. George, Ruger always to hand, has studied his map and insists we complete Stanley's route to the end

12. Christine cleans a cormorant for supper
13. Unfinished carving of our names on a large rock at Mpwapwa
14. The treacherous Bahi Swamp, now like a sandy seashore when the tide is out
15. Recent lion footprints at Mpwapwa
16. Journey's end; in Ujiji
17. The donkeys have been well trained for the journey by air to their new home in Nairobi

Author's Preface

In 1871 the Welsh-American journalist and explorer Henry Morton Stanley set out on an expedition to find Dr Livingstone, who had attempted to find the source of the Nile and disappeared completely in the African interior more than five years before. Stanley set out with 153 bearers, four chiefs, four personal assistants, twenty-three soldiers, two white men, twenty-seven donkeys and one cart, two horses, one dog and two dismantled three-foot-wide boats capable of carrying twenty-six persons between them. Stanley's team also carried a silver tea service, potted meats and pastes, wine and champagne, and was sponsored to the princely sum of $4,000 from the *New York Herald*, with more if he wanted.

From schooldays, ever since reading a treatment of Stanley's account of his expedition, *How I Found Livingstone in Central Africa*, in an illustrated comic series, I had identified with Stanley's life and adventures: a brash, self-made man of simple origins, opportunistic, used to relying on himself and not averse to banging heads to get his way.

I left school early and didn't settle to any lasting career

path, at first existing on sundry casual work and then turning to schoolteaching and coaching creative writing, finally taking an advanced adventure education course in the Lake District. This was the moment, pressing forty years of age, when I finally decided what to do with myself.

I decided to follow Stanley's footsteps in his search for Dr Livingstone. To sail by traditional dhow from Zanzibar to Bagamoyo on the mainland of Tanzania and walk on foot, without the advantage of the technological aids we now have, all the way to the village of Ujiji on Lake Tanganyika where Stanley and Livingstone met, a very approximate distance of 1,200 miles. Although I had never been to Africa, I felt this would be a very worthwhile quest. I would lead an expedition with my wife and three friends, carrying everything in rucksacks, with our only modern advantage being to take up-to-date anti-malarial drugs and other medicines. Basically, however, I had very little idea what I was doing. For a start, the three friends quickly became just one other besides my wife and myself.

Anyway, it seemed to us that our expedition would be important in allowing us to touch hands with the past. And this we certainly did. We travelled through the region that had recently become Tanzania at the end of the colonial era, moving from tribal area to tribal area. Many of Stanley's villages lived on only in old men's memories, and the tribal histories handed down orally within each tribe had already begun to pass away too. Practically all historical documents were destroyed after Independence by over-zealous officials not wanting to be reminded of German and British colonial rule. Tanzanian bush villages, however, even though the populations had inevitably grown, were still much the same as they had long been.

But the way the classic explorers and adventurers witnessed the real Africa was on the wane when we saw it in the mid-1980s – at a time when the tech giants were investing billions of dollars into delivering internet service to rural and remote areas, opening up Africa as never before.

The title of this book is a translation of the Swahili saying 'Bagamoyo', meaning 'Lay down your heart', i.e. 'Take off your load and rest' – used by and of caravan porters on arriving at Zanzibar after a gruelling journey on foot through east-central Africa. In the eighteenth century Bagamoyo became the name of the chief trading town in the region of Zanzibar.

The book should have been written many years ago. But it was to be a long time before I was in a position or a fit state of mind to begin writing it; to take up, later in life, the daily diary I had kept throughout the expedition and revisit the whole experience. For a start, after the rather more than two-year expedition had been accomplished, it took us eight and a half years to leave Africa. We had to arrange a permanent home for the three surviving donkeys and then prepare reports we had undertaken to deliver to the Tanzanian Government by way of return for help and advice they had given us when we had started our journey. Among the matters on which we had collected information were the site of the exact location of the nineteenth-century fortified town of Morogoro which had disappeared after a flood; an explanation as to why fishermen were not catching more fish in Lake Tanganyika; and information leading to the reduction of the slaughter of elephants by poachers. After we had completed these and other tasks, the local press and the Tanzania Tourist Corporation provided income for us for descriptive articles, and we found ourselves caught in a time warp that kept us trapped in Africa as the years went by.

By the time we eventually returned home it took us further years not only to acclimatise back to life in England but to recover, in my case at least, from the mental condition resulting from the expedition itself. Ever since we had reached our goal in Ujiji I had remained in a condition which not until our return to England was diagnosed by a specialist as post-traumatic stress, resulting from prolonged day-to-day pressure in order to survive. Back to what was supposed to be normal life in England I experienced blocked breathing problems, an adrelaline count way off the chart, highly disturbing dreams, and continual emotional and spiritual numbness, as if I didn't exist. I too light-heartedly declined any sort of dedicated mental health care – which my wife didn't need as much as I did – and we settled back in our ramshackle house in Camden, north London and set about doing what we could to reinvent ourselves. Perhaps writing this book has been my final cure.

Our unawareness led us to make our expedition. If we had not been so naive and idealistic, innocent of the ways of Africa, we would have realised how near impossible was the task we were attempting. Above all, it was a personal journey. We did it for ourselves and nobody else. Most Europeans we met in Kenya and Tanzania thought our journey laughable, foolhardy. I suppose it was a search for

Author's Preface

honour which moved further away from us the more we travelled towards it. And having started something, we felt we had to finish it.

I have never felt in step with the metropolitan way of life. At the time of our expedition, for the sake of my shrinking soul I desperately needed to find a niche where human beings were still human and practised the old-fashioned virtues of generosity, truth and loyalty. Somewhere they had to exist – in Africa as much as anywhere. For me, our expedition was undertaken in the spirit of a mad, jubilant, impossible quest for my ideals – which I believe to have been shared at least to some extent by my companions. It seems inseparable from a state of mind which remains with me to this day, in which in my indoor existence I still imagine the shimmer of endless tawny plains stretching and entering the room, the heart-cracking sizzle of cicadas, and smell the baked, hot breath of Africa.

George Tardios

Preface by Christine Tardios

This book should have seen the light of day many years ago. Only since George recently died at the age of seventy-nine has his account of our expedition across a newly independent Tanzania been put in hand for publication.

My husband and I and a young friend completed our two-year expedition in 1986. It was another five years before we returned to England, as various matters had first to be brought to a satisfactory conclusion, most urgently finding a permanent home for three donkeys. Also George had undertaken, in return for a guarantee of safe passage throughout our time in the country, to write and deliver some reports for the Tanzanian Prime Minister based on our experience on the expedition, from the changed location of a historic site to a possible reason for a disappointing recent fishing yield by newly equipped boats supplied by the government on Lake Tanganyika.

The main reason, however, why George was not in a frame of mind to write of our experience for some time to come was that he was recovering from physical and mental stress. Villagers we met had called him 'Mr Buffalo' in Swahili for his physical strength and toughness. But even some time after our return to England in 1991 he was diagnosed with PTSD, which took several more years to disappear.

When we eventually felt 'normal' again, George took up acting for a (?) livelihood and attended the Actors Centre, which offered a creative home for actors with continuous acting training. Once we went to LA to make an award-winning short film with George as one of the two actors.

Back in England I personally felt pleased with myself. I love to see new places and learn new things, and I had played my part in the story. It was George on whose shoulders the full and awesome weight of responsibility had always fallen, and on whom the whole experience had taken most toll.

Eventually, George got down to writing an account of our expedition based on the daily diary he faithfully kept up at a time that has now passed firmly into history. Paradoxical as it may seem, it took him just three months.

Those who gave us generous help in Tanzania are too numerous to name, but special acknowledgement should be made to two persons who provided us with historical information we should otherwise never have been able to come by. Chairman Kingo of the village of Kingolwira Misongeni gave us biographical details about his ancestor Chief Kisabengo, founder of the modern city of Morogoro, drawn upon in Chapter 10. In Morogoro Father Canute of the Holy Ghost Fathers showed us a description of Kisabengo's walled town compiled in Kiswahili by a visiting Holy Ghost missionary in 1881 and preserved in the Missionary archives in Bagamoyo, quoted in translation in

Chapter 9; this helped us solve the longstanding mystery of the location of the original fortified settlement, which was moved in the nineteenth century after destruction by a catastrophic flood.

George's knowledge of Africa's history is based on the authorities most accepted around the time of our expedition nearly half a century ago, and he got to know his way about south-east Africa in the immediate post-colonial era against a background of information and ideas derived from an even earlier period of his own life. After leaving Africa, while his experience of the expedition remained firmly in his mind thanks to his daily diary of the time, he lost touch with currently held conclusions on matters such as ethnic history, and his personal account sometimes brings up generalisations and ideas on the wider plane that may have been revised by later authorities unfamiliar to him.

Christine Tardios

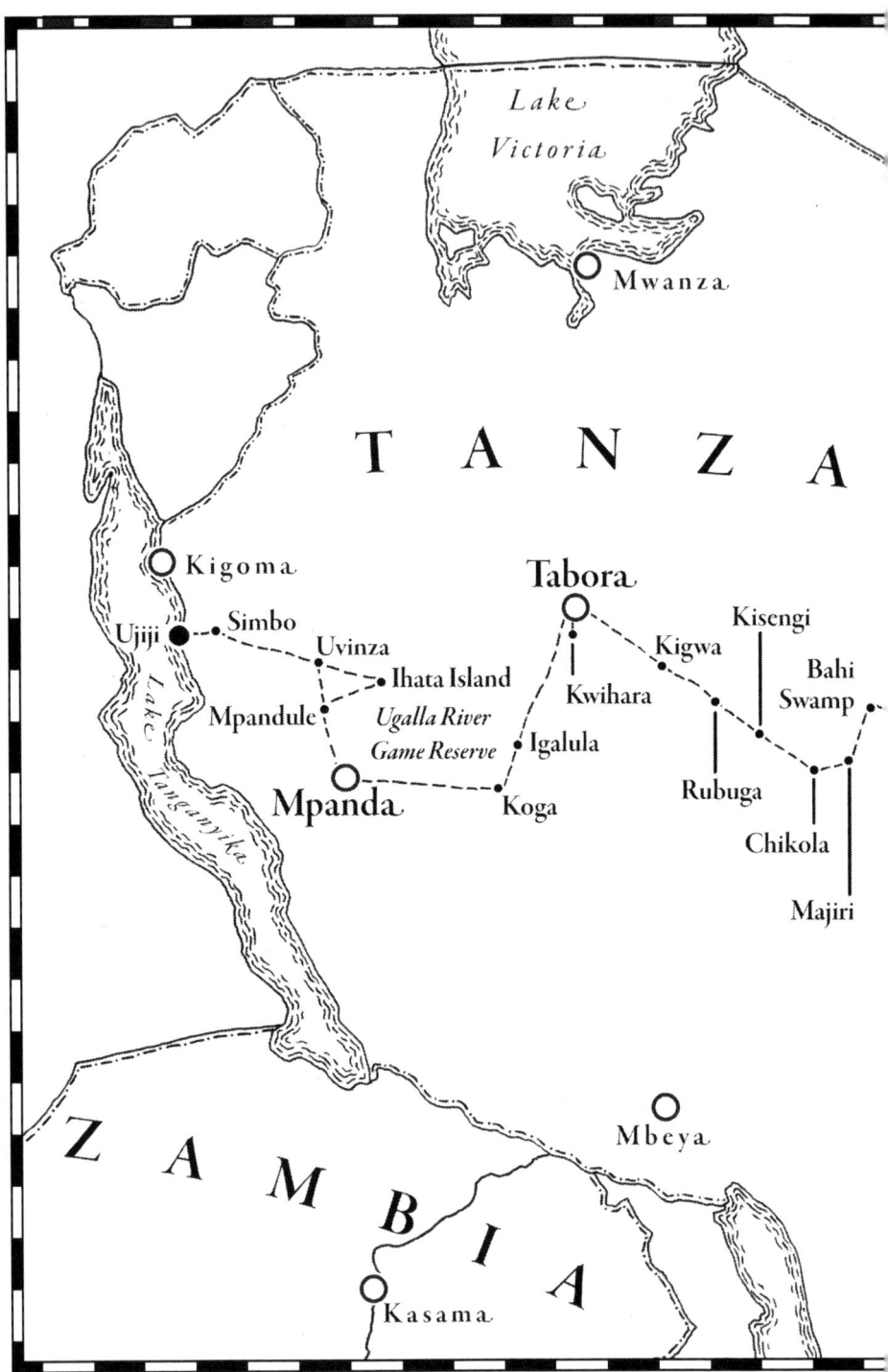

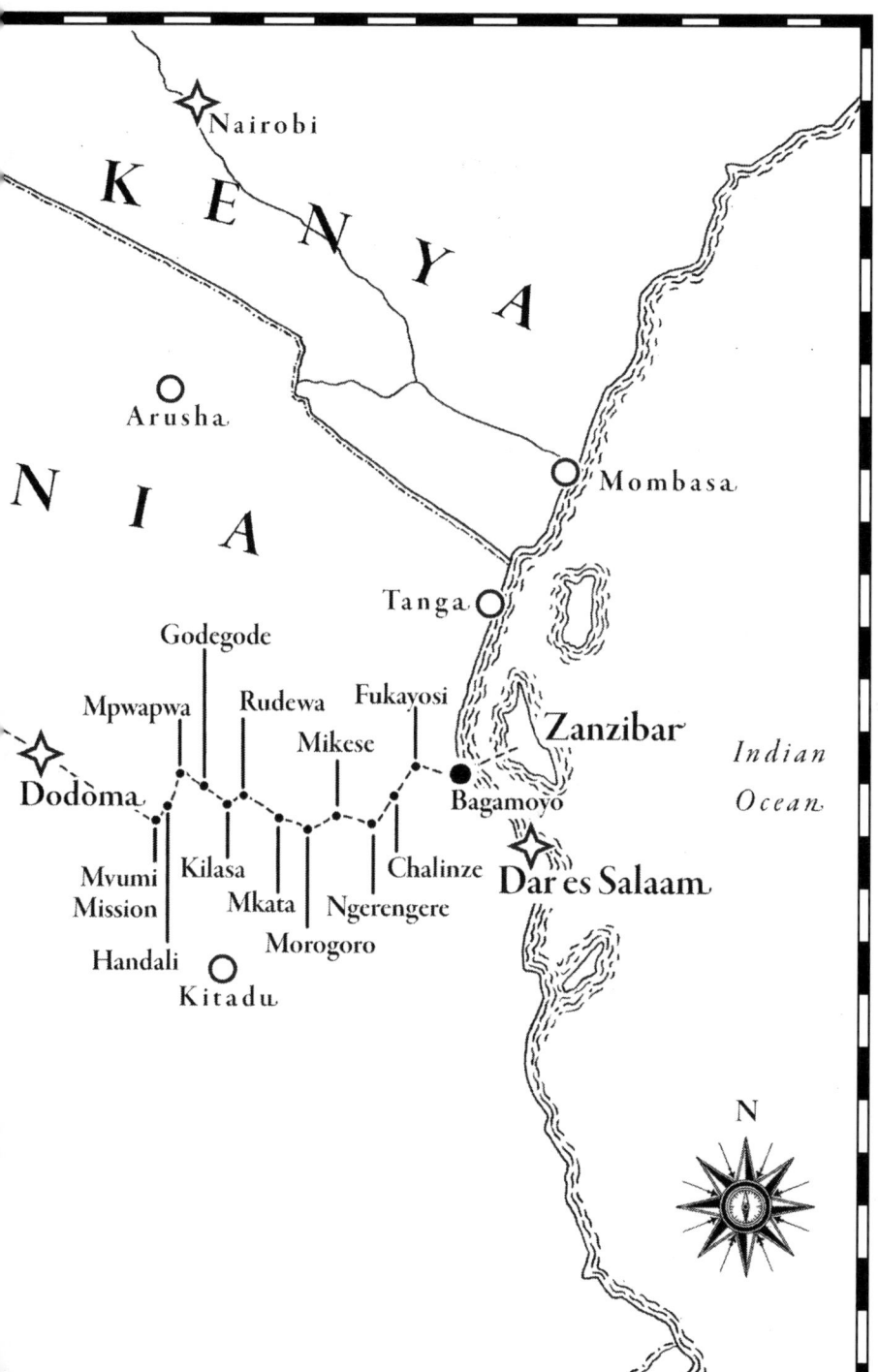

PART ONE –

BEGINNINGS

1
The Idea

Frosty London threatening to break through the window panes. I cuddled closer to the sizzling gas fire dressed in multilayered, suffocating clothing, the heat only penetrating certain front parts of my body. My back remained chilled and I turned my bottom to the gas fire's warmth.

As a result of a mad whim of mine, my wife Christine and I had spent the last year in wintry Ambleside up in Cumbria, living in a caravan, on a University of Lancaster 'Advanced Adventure Education Course', training to be instructors in river and sea kayaking, rock climbing, potholing, fell walking, and snow and ice mountaineering. We had been sent down a river in pairs for two weeks, with everything we needed to be self-sufficient stuffed into our kayaks. We froze! Rivers were naturally full after winter rain, or when snow had melted in the hills – the best time to kayak. Our instructor had specified there was no such thing as bad weather, only bad choice in clothing. On kayaking nights we would leave our soaked wetsuits and thermal underwear hanging on bushes outside our tiny tents to dry, and in the morning have to crack the iced forms into wearable shape.

PART ONE – BEGINNINGS

Back home in London, I desperately needed to comfortably stretch my bones out under a warming sun. I needed an *adventure*, a quest to break the dull repetitive cycle of sleep, work, eat, sleep, work… I lectured in English and General Studies at Paddington FE College during the week, worked nights as a security guard and cleaned a West End cinema at weekends. I had never earned so much in my life, yet after paying off the regular instalment to the bank for our mortgage we were left with only £15 a week to live off. Since being spat out by school I had done so many dull jobs: window cleaner on cradles, postman, telephone enquiry clerk. I had worked as a salesman for most of the Oxford Street stores and hated it so much I had been sacked from all of them for lateness. I was disillusioned with routine, with being used and blocked from what I should be doing – writing.

Born of immigrant Greek-Cypriot parents who arrived in London in 1935 (there were only a handful of Cypriots in England at the time) and brought up by my mother (my father left when I was two), I was used to doing things the hard way. I took what should have been my father's place, and by the time I was sixteen had skipped childhood and had a large and heavy chip on my shoulder. I was also largely self-educated. The school I attended produced predominantly machine workers. I had always come first in English because of my composition prowess and had numerous stories printed in the school magazine. I had wanted to write, to be a journalist, so at the school-leaving age of fifteen I had told all this to the interviewing Youth Employment Officer attached to our school.

'Look, son, you can either study for a City & Guilds to

The Idea

become a tool-maker, or work for Dunn's Hat Company in Kentish Town – "If you want to get ahead, get a hat". That's all I can do, I'm afraid.'

I insisted on journalism. This was not just a dream!

'OK, son.' He rifled through his index cards. 'If you wanna write, I'll find something here with writing. Here you go.' He lifted out a scribbled card. 'Best I can do, I'm afraid. Take it or leave it!'

'What's the job?'

'A clerk in an estate agents' office.'

'Where's the writing?'

'You'll be writing letters…'

I had walked out.

But I persisted. At the grand old age of twenty-five (as a mature student at college) I stunned the drama tutor by composing music for the Caucasian Chalk Circle and a modern version of a druggy production of *Hamlet*. I was writing songs and poetry. Then out of the blue I was awarded a writing scholarship by two poets who visited the college. I had never realised my writing had value. £10 per week and living in an isolated thatched farmhouse – Totleigh Barton Manor – in order to produce poetry.

I couldn't do it! The beams and wooden floors creaked; sheep and bullocks were bleating and coughing in the surrounding fields. I missed the sounds of traffic. I phoned up the funder, John Moat, and said I was wasting his money. He drove down to see me and proposed I work at running the house as a residential creative writing centre, an idea he and a colleague had been toying with for some time. The Devon farmhouse became the Arvon Foundation's first centre; a second owned by poet Ted Hughes followed up in Yorkshire. It was an achievement I felt very proud to be part of. I also began writing again! And later I became involved with setting up the Arvon Foundation/*Observer* poetry competition, then the BBC TV Poetry Society.

I counted myself extremely fortunate to have met my wife, Christine. We married when I was twenty-five and working in clubs in London's Finchley Road – 'La Cage D'Or', 'The Europa' and 'The Alpine Tavern'. Christine was a part-time waitress at weekends, teaching primary school children during weekdays, and I was a doorman. The Kray brothers used to drink at the latter club, exploring the possibility of us giving them protection money, but we were already paying West Hampstead Police Station for security. When I was threatened with having my legs shot off Christine sheltered me in her bedsit in Swiss Cottage, and actively helped me to pass super-speed 'A' levels (we picked the questions from old exam papers) and gain a teacher training place in Rolle College, Exmouth, Devon where we fled.

Christine was born in Leicestershire and brought up in Guernsey but had then travelled to the mainland to study at Portsmouth and had been teaching in Brixton and Islington. She had also worked as a project leader in various summer camps, was an ILEA-approved part-time tutor for recreational institutes and youth centres, had helped supervise an adventure playground, been a house manager at the Arvon Foundation, assisted me in judging the LWTV *South Bank Show* poetry competition, and completed a training course in movement and dance at the Laban Centre, Goldsmiths College. She held a brown belt in Shotokan karate.

She was most definitely *not* a muscle-bound Amazon but was slim and blue-eyed, full of curiosity and practical enthusiasm. On our course in the Lake District, when potholing deep underground she had patiently and calmly talked me through my rigid panic while I was being squashed in the Cheese Press. And I don't really think I could have completed the African expedition without the help of my wife, just as I don't think I could get through life without her.

Now, in London, I felt like I needed a new adventure – and my boyhood fascination with Stanley's expedition came back into my mind. I began to busy myself finding out about the early Nile explorers and the route he had followed.

*

A little history here.

Two hundred million years ago the continent of Africa was merely one of many joined land masses, part of Gondwanaland, the southernmost of two supercontinents. By the late Stone Age, this area was sparsely populated by groups of hunter-gatherers who then intermarried with other groups and, over time, became more settled communities. Developments included the cultivation of plants and domestication of animals as well as the construction of a sophisticated irrigation system.

Around 4,000 years BCE, merchant sailors from India, the Persian Gulf and eastern Mediterranean utilised the trade winds to reach east Africa, carrying with them goods to barter. Tribal chiefs would have casually offered conquered 'men' to the Arab traders to carry the heavy goods exchanged back to the coast. There, these men were sold on.

Egypt fell to Alexander the Great in 332 BCE – and the first question he asked when he came to Luxor was, 'What causes the Nile to rise?' For the Nile swept southward through Nubia ('Sudan') and Egypt to spill into the Mediterranean. In the desert countries through which it flowed the river was life itself. It rose and flooded the Nile valley every summer and locals wondered why the river would swell during their hottest and driest time of the year. If it failed to flow even one year, then Egypt would perish! This led naturally to question where the Nile originated. Not to know the river's source was to live in a state of insecurity. Thus, varied expeditions, by both Alexander and Caesar, were dispatched into the interior – all failures, blocked by swamps or with those travelling simply disappearing. The Dark Continent was keeping its secret.

And so it remained. By the nineteenth century in Europe, adventurers had travelled to both America and Australia, China was now known, and land masses and oceans of the world were being mapped and charted much as they are today. But the source of the Nile remained a puzzle. It was the greatest geographical mystery.

In 1856 the Royal Geographical Society sent two explorers – Burton and Speke – to Africa to settle the matter. A mismatched pair, they were both continually ill with fevers on the expedition. Burton suffered from an ulcerated jaw and could only take liquid food. His legs were so swollen he was almost paralysed. Speke was so blind he could hardly see Lake Tanganyika when they reached it. He also became somewhat deaf when a beetle crawled into his ear and he made matters worse by attempting to remove the insect with a small penknife! So ill were they it was decided to return to *Kazeh* (Tabora) for recuperation. Having made an early recovery, Speke asked Burton's permission to continue alone further north toward another Arab-reported lake. With thirty-five followers and supplies for six weeks he set off and after twenty-five days arrived at the southernmost point of a great lake, which he named in honour of Queen Victoria – 'the Victoria Nyanza'. He believed this lake to be the source of the Nile, but Burton disagreed with his conclusions since he felt, quite correctly, that Speke had not sufficiently explored the lake.

In 1860 Speke attempted to resolve the matter once and for all by leading another expedition with James Grant, an old friend. When they reached present-day Uganda Speke headed west to properly explore the lake, only to find a large river (the Nile) flowing from it in the north at what he named 'Ripon Falls'. Tribal warfare forced him to abandon his journey further, but when he reached Gondokoro in Southern Sudan he came upon Samuel Baker, an enthusiastic amateur adventurer and explorer, and his second wife, Florence, and together they were to discover and name 'Lake Albert' (1864) and 'Murchison Falls'. They later claimed both Albert and Victoria lakes were the source of the Nile. Speke sent a short telegram to the Royal Geographical Society: 'The Nile is settled.'

But Burton still disagreed. How did Speke know, viewing the lake from the north in Buganda (Uganda), that this was the very same lake as seen from the south in their previous expedition? No one had yet mapped the lakes or river or followed the river all the way to the Mediterranean. It was decided there should be a public debate to settle the matter, but then Speke died, apparently by accidentally shooting himself while climbing over a stone wall, though Burton definitely considered it a suicide.

On hearing of Speke's death he commented drily, 'There is a time to leave the Dark Continent. Madness springs from Africa.'

With myriad lakes now to contend with, controversy over the question of the Nile was kept alive. And the Royal Geographical Society turned to the dependable Dr David Livingstone, a medical missionary who had on and off spent almost twenty-five years in Africa. They persuaded him to return and settle the matter.

Livingstone was both a qualified doctor and an ordained minister. His aim was to be a medical missionary in China, but the Opium Wars blocked his passage there and, inspired by a speech on the abolition of slavery, he had turned in 1841 to Africa. He was the first white man to open up southern central Africa, map uncharted spaces of Africa, cross the Kalahari Desert, cross the African continent from east to west, follow the course of the Zambezi River, and discover Lake Nyasa, Murchison Falls (before Baker) and Victoria Falls. As an explorer he had walked 29,000 miles of Africa and laid open nearly one million square miles of new country. Basically, he and other explorers of the time unwittingly helped open up Africa to European colonialism.

Now Livingstone was tempted by the crucial idea of discovering the source of the Nile and making final sense of the Burton and Speke dispute. At this time he was fifty-two years of age.

The Idea

Now in 1865 he was again swallowed by the African interior, completely disappearing from civilisation. By 1869 he had not been seen by any white man for four years! In England there was a public outcry to 'Find Livingstone!' although little was done, except by the young American owner of the *New York Herald*, James (Jamie) Gordon Bennett, who knew that if his newspaper found Livingstone there would be a huge rise in circulation. He immediately sent a telegram to his favourite twenty-eight-year-old reporter, Henry Morton Stanley, who was covering the Civil War in Spain.

Stanley had had a difficult childhood. An illegitimate son of a farmer known as a drunkard and a local butcher's daughter, he was raised by his retired grandfather, being placed into a workhouse when the grandfather died. Here his life was a misery and at the age of eighteen he sailed to America as a cabin boy (£1 and a uniform). In America he was fortunate enough to be adopted and educated by the wealthy cotton merchant Henry Hope Stanley and to be given his new name. He moved to freelance journalism in New York after the American Civil War.

Now his task was to track down Dr Livingstone. By 1870 the Germans were already occupying the coastline of present-day Tanzania and attempting to create a German East Africa with Bagamoyo as its capital. While staying here – the end of the main trade route before one set sail for Zanzibar – as a guest of the Germans, Stanley learned from Arab caravans that Livingstone had fallen ill with malaria and had his medical supplies stolen. He was therefore nursed and forced to travel with Arab slave caravans for four years until, suffering severely from foot ulcers, dysentery, pneumonia and rotting teeth, he had to be left to recover if at all in the village of Ujiji on Lake Tanganyika.

And so, in 1871 Stanley set off on his expedition. Despite his vast entourage travelling on a recognised Arab caravan route akin to a motorway of its time, his tin bath, bearskin rug, bottle of Worcestershire sauce, silver tea service and gentlemen's pâtés, by the time he reached Tabora (roughly two-thirds of the way) he had lost to disease and hardship two soldiers, eight porters and twenty-five of his twenty-seven donkeys. His two horses and Omar the dog had died earlier. The remaining two donkeys soon followed, as did eventually his two white assistants, Farquhar from alleged elephantiasis and Shaw from alleged malaria.

We would walk faithfully in Stanley's footsteps, trek every detour he made when lost and use his meticulous written account as our guide and yardstick, then write a comparison between Stanley's time and our own. We would begin our walk in the infamous coastal village of Bagamoyo, Tanzania, opposite the island of Zanzibar. Bagamoyo was the start and terminus of the old slave trade, and for past explorers it was the entry point into the 'Dark Continent' of Africa. For our expedition very many miles away from any kind of help against diseases and wild animals, the Tanzanian bush would remain the 'Dark Continent', for this part of Tanzania had actually regressed: the main trade/slave route Stanley had begun on had now disappeared. Setting out from Bagamoyo following this well-used track, Stanley had immediately met the first of many an approaching Arab caravan; we would not. Only a third of the villages Stanley passed through now existed;

impenetrable thickets had grown in many places; man-eating lions raided the isolated villages preying on elderly inhabitants and young children. If I could bring Stanley back to life, fly him in a helicopter and drop him down into his familiar parts of Tanzania he would today become completely lost.

As, most likely, would we.

Stanley did, of course, find Livingstone, and the older man, when finally found, then became a father figure to Stanley. In his own account, a full ten pages is taken up with Stanley being over-effusive in his praise of Livingstone after their meeting at Ujiji on 10 November 1871: 'Livingstone's was a character that I venerated, that called forth all my enthusiasm, that evoked nothing but sincerest admiration… when I fell sick with the remittent fever, hovering between life and death, he attended me like a father.'

Livingstone in letters home wrote of Stanley: 'He behaved as a son to a father – truly overflowing in kindness… He laid all he had at my service, divided his clothes into two heaps and pressed one heap upon me; then his medicine chest; then his goods and everything he had; and to coax my appetite often cooked dainty dishes with his own hand. He came with true American generosity. The tears often started into my eyes on each proof of kindness.'

But by then Livingstone was fifty-nine years of age and close to death, suffering from myriad African afflictions: recurring dysentery, colitis, malarial and other fevers, foot sores and loose teeth. He died a year later of internal bleeding, still haunted by thoughts of the failed missionary work which he had seen as his main occupation. The slave trade still flourished, plans to establish a mission on the banks of the River Shire had been proved impractical, his wife had died of fever attempting to follow him and most importantly there was not a single convert.

I was not to be deterred by these accounts of the past. I put aside all adverse stories I was told and just beavered away ensuring the basics were covered: the route, food and shelter. And our little party was put together. Myself and Christine, of course. And then Andy Graham, an affable, tall, gangly, giraffe-like twenty-one-year-old with long straggly legs. He was freckled, with a blaze of distinctive red hair and a frequent easy-going hearty laugh. I had met him in the Lake District College where he had calmly climbed alongside my frozen body on the cliff-face and rescued me from an imminent rock-climbing accident. Andy came from a sheltered and polite Norfolk army family and as a boy had been sent to board at a public school where he had been expected to do well in all things. Consequently, Andy had incredible 'front confidence' and was able to ingratiate himself with most people by just asking them numerous questions about themselves. He had worked at a survival school in Scotland, spent a year as the mate on a fifty-seven-foot ketch cruising between the Faroes, St Kilda and the Outer Hebrides, was an experienced walker and had trekked in the Alps and elsewhere. I liked his sense of humour. He was easy-going and had definite practical skills that I lacked: namely ropework, shelter construction and fire lighting. His practicality and common sense would prove useful.

Alongside the three of us were also Bob Lawson from Newcastle, more Norse-looking than English with the famed Geordie capacity for alcohol and mad behaviour.

We had met at the Arvon Foundation. His girlfriend Sue, also from Newcastle, was small and petite but had great strength of character.

I had prepared by thoroughly absorbing Stanley's life from many books such as *Henry M. Stanley: The Enigma* by Emyr Wyn Jones as well as his own account, *How I Found Livingstone* and visited the Royal Geographical Society to retrace his route onto the very few modern maps available. We were told we could only purchase the detailed maps we desperately needed after having first procured Tanzanian permission in the Dar es Salaam Map Office. Once in Tanzania, I consoled myself, we would also learn about the country and gain an understanding of Africa.

In the 1980s most of Africa, particularly Tanzania, was without technology and classed as a deprived third world country, depending on its crumbling and underworked rural economy and on foreign aid for its survival. With its aspirations and all the Western interferences, how had Tanzania changed within the last hundred years? It was interesting for us too to see how such a society functioned, as it would provide living and unique pointers as to how Britain must have been before the Industrial Revolution changed so much with the new technology.

I was asked the question repeatedly, so let me put the personal reason for our expedition this way. Well, slowly approaching the age of forty, I had been haunted by hearing the crashing sound of waves roaring, voices screaming, the earth crying, sizzling, and the buzzing of the solar system – the utter chaos of creation! Most of us in truth are deep down aware of the dichotomy of being drawn to the wild and to Nature but with a simultaneous terror of it. We have learned to repress emotions, to close the door on our true self… and become lost. And when we are 'out of sorts', we stay home to 'recover', to become whole and normal. In other words, to once again clothe our nakedness with suppression. I decided to break away, to embrace and dig myself deep into Nature to truly discover what could come out of it. I needed, it seemed, to be able to depend on myself, to be inspired, to be immersed in wild Nature and to experience a simpler, more instinctual way of living.

On this expedition, we would sleep in dome tents. Cooking was to be on wood fires or kerosene stoves. Military millbank bags would be used to purify water.

But we were not planning to disavow ourselves of modern medicine. Stanley had travelled with calomel, which in the nineteenth century was used to treat everything from TB and parasites to toothaches and constipation. And many diseases were prevalent in outback Tanzania. I had therefore spoken with the St Pancras Hospital for Tropical Diseases in London and the Liverpool School of Tropical Medicine about diseases we could suffer from and what medicine to take. A helpful GP arranged for us to carry appropriate first aid for afflictions such as amoebic dysentery and also ensured we were protected against typhoid, TB, polio, malaria, dengue fever, hepatitis, rabies, cholera, yellow fever and typhus. We even had someone arrive by motorbike with innoculations against anthrax! We all took a preventative anti-malarial drug, maloprim. As buffers we had chloroquine and fansidar – as well as Stanley's quinine to treat malaria.

What we could not prepare for was bilharzia –

schistosomiasis or 'snail fever' – parasitic larvae that use snails as a host in African freshwater lakes and rivers and are capable of burrowing into human flesh and becoming mature egg-laying worms. The worms could live in the body for three to five years, infecting the urinary tract and eventually causing kidney failure and liver damage. Other diseases were leprosy, bubonic plague, elephantiasis, hookworm, trichinosis, sleeping sickness and AIDS. Also, we were understandably concerned about snakebites. To carry active anti-venom it would have to be refrigerated, and even if we could carry a small fridge in the bush, we could not plug it into trees!

People have since asked, 'Why did you not make a film of your expedition?' The problem then was we would have had to carry an extremely cumbersome video camera on our shoulders and have a suitcase-sized battery pack to recharge the camera and no means to charge the battery itself. Instead, we kept a notebook and asked every chief and village chairman to sign it, proving we had passed through their territory. Otherwise, we would be armed only with detailed maps and a Silva compass.

My initial plan was that we would fly direct to Tanzania, that the whole expedition would take us a year to complete. With five of us I realised we would require some kind of financial sponsorship (air flights to Tanzania, for example), so I blithely wrote to the Royal Geographical Society. Feeling well prepared with budget sheets and all expedition details neatly down on paper I set out to be interviewed for sponsorship by them. This, on reflection, was a mistake: I should have sent Andy in my stead; unlike myself, he was noticeably English, had attended public

PART ONE – BEGINNINGS

school and was well able to cope with such situations. He would have spoken the correct and expected words. Nevertheless, it was I who entered the hallowed portals of the Royal Geographical Society.

Outside, high up in the brickwork was a life-sized statue of Livingstone peering out into Kensington Gardens and the distant Serpentine. Inside on display was Livingstone's portable chair and writing table next to an aged Arctic kayak made of wood and skins. The society possessed a painted portrait and bust of Livingstone, his cap with gold band, collar and pen, a magnifying glass, sextant, original copies of his expedition fieldwork and the slave chains he brought back from Africa. If Livingstone was such an important figure to them, then surely they would look kindly at our expedition…

Feeling somewhat overawed I sat and waited. Summoned to the interview room upstairs, I distributed my handouts and sat down to absolute silence as a panel slowly perused my budget sheets and expedition details.

Suddenly, thank God, a clearing of a throat.

'Mr Tardios, there seems to be some disparity in your budget figures.'

Time passed as they all now discussed the budget among themselves.

Finally, the first person again: 'No, no, all correct, my mistake. Your figures are fine, Mr Tardios.'

Someone else piped up, 'We see you intend to fly to Cairo in Egypt, then cross to Sudan, travel through the Sudd Swamp on paddle steamers to Juba, trek into Kenya and then Tanzania. Why this prolonged and roundabout route, Mr Tardios?'

I explained that this route followed the River Nile, which was why renowned explorers went there in the first place. And this was only if we did not receive sponsorship. With sponsorship we would fly direct to Tanzania.

'Ah, I see. But if you did take this route, how do you propose to cross the Sudan-Kenya border? You are aware of Shifta bandits frequenting this area, are you not?'

'The Shifta are a Somali band and are situated more north-eastward, so not really a problem,' I replied. 'What I do worry about is the warlike Toposa tribe, who are in constant battle with Turkana cattle raiders. I know that they could possibly be near the border.'

'Toposa? No, no, it's Shifta on the border…' A few more minor questions and I was dismissed. I should have kept my well-informed, proud, secondary-modern mouth shut!

They turned us down for sponsorship, or even for their recommendation on the grounds we were being naive, wouldn't be able to cross the Sudan–Kenya border and would most probably be killed by Shifta bandits. This was a Catch 22 situation, since with sponsorship we wouldn't need to cross the blasted border!

Without sponsorship, I knew that two of our group – impoverished Bob and Susie – would now drop out. Christine was agreeable that we should go ahead. Egyptair would fly us to Cairo cheaply and I would have £1,500 in travellers' cheques. Andy, it transpired, was still keen to accompany us. He owned a Barclaycard which he would drain to death.

I also subsequently discovered that there are no Shifta on the Sudan–Kenya border.

Our expedition featured in a number of national

newspapers. We had also been interviewed on the Jimmy Mac Show in Cumbria and Thames TV in London.

An unsolicited airmail letter from a Mr E.T. Brown, Umtali, Zimbabwe (our expedition had been reported in the *Sunday Telegraph*, which had also covered Stanley's search) was short and to the point:

'Africa, unless you know what you are about, is a damned good place to keep out of. We old hands, who have been in Africa for over half a century, would strongly advise you to drop the whole idea of an expedition on foot. Apart from all the diseases you can catch: malaria of every sort, dysentery of two kinds; one can be fatal in twenty-four hours, the other can maim for life. Bilharzia in rivers is easy to get and difficult to clear out of one's system. Sleeping sickness from tsetse fly is rife. You will also need tins of DDT to spread around your sleeping bags or blankets to keep off millions of ants, cockroaches etc. And you will have to take care the rats do not bite your feet off at night and that snakes do not curl up on your chests for warmth and that hyenas do not sneak in and take off a foot or an arm or a piece of your face...'

Burton and Speke's 1856 expedition comprised thirty-six porters, ten gun-carrying slaves, four guides and a posse of Indian/Pakistani soldiers for protection. According to Stanley, Burton and Speke lost all their donkeys to illness. Men died of disease or deserted. Dr Livingstone originally had twelve Indian soldiers, two servants, Susi and Chuma, and a team of freed slaves – fifty-nine followers in all. Stanley himself had his party reduced from close on 200 to under a dozen during his highly circuitous route to reach Ujiji.

The Idea

We were merely three innocent individuals without modern technological aid, hoping with humble dome tents, rucksacks, meagre maps and a Silva compass to walk approximately 1,200 miles through a now relapsed and broken-down country infested with disease and wild animals.

We planned to leave there for the interior on 21 March 1984, the same day and month as Stanley but 113 years later.

On the day we left, the *Times* (Diary Section) covered our departure:

'One of the most ambitious, if not foolhardy, expeditions of the new year begins today: an attempt to retrace Stanley's quest for Dr Livingstone in "the dark continent"... While the expedition will confront many of the same hazards that faced Stanley in 1871 – being attacked by animals; stricken by illness; stung and bitten by a multiplicity of insects and snakes – there is also apparently some risk of being mugged by marauding gangs of bandits. The expedition will also lack some of Stanley's advantages – namely 153 bearers, four chiefs, four assistants, 23 soldiers, 27 donkeys and two horses. By comparison, rucksacks, lightweight tents and three pairs of feet hardly seem up to the task.'

PART TWO –

GOING DOWN: FROM CAIRO TO BAGAMOYO

2

Following the River Nile through Egypt, Sudan and into Kenya

In Cairo, through a giant loudspeaker we were greeted with an ear-splitting call to prayer – '*Allahu Ekber... Allaaaah...*' It was evening; a red sinking sun and we speedily made our way to Talaat Harb Street and the Pension Oxford, our accommodation found in the *Africa on the Cheap* guide. Talaat Harb was a busy main road in the centre of town teeming with shops and restaurants.

We trekked exhaustingly around, wearing fully loaded rucksacks, and eventually found accommodation. Our room at Pension Oxford was a basic paint-peeling shell, three simple beds overlaid with misshapen foam mattresses. I was thankful for a large window even though it opened out over noisy car-honking Talaat Harb. There were no locks on the door. The toilet and washing facilities were shared among all the residents – exposed plumbing, cobwebbed walls and indeterminate puddles. But it was cheap. With a swagger of self-satisfaction we screwed our 'prepared-ahead' hasps onto our room door, inside and out, then gladly left our rucksacks with a large locked padlock on the door as we raced excitedly up to the flat roof, soaking in the exoticism, the steaming foreign night sounds, the men in the street – we noticed there were no local women – dressed in white shifts (gellabias). Then we saw the women up high hanging out washing, cooking on open fires, and living in makeshift huts on layer after layer of flat roof.

The next morning, after a breakfast of stale rice cake and watery tea, a besuited journalist appeared, soaked and panting after a four-flight climb, mopping sweat with a new white handkerchief. He wanted to interview us for the newspaper *Al Ahram*. We then hit the streets of tall concrete buildings or, that is, the streets hit us. No sooner were we outside the doors of Pension Oxford than the cries of '*Baksheesh? Baksheesh?*' began. The loudspeakered din of the off-key call to prayer froze our thoughts. The *Ezan* sung with devotion was spine-tingling, but the muezzin's call (repeated five times a day) was a gargling frog-swallowed hawk, accompanied by carbon monoxide fumes and the constant hooting of cars. Young men would block our path – 'You want my sister, my brother, mother…?' Groups would deliberately cross the traffic-infested street and attempt to pinch Christine's behind.

Talaat Harb wore us down.

'My friends, you are from where?' Wherever in the world you said, a relative would immediately be manufactured living or studying in that very same area. 'Do you know my brother Rashid? He is studying at the university there. My friends, we have much in common. I would like to buy you tea. Please do not refuse, my friends, I would like to welcome you to Egypt.' Having been hooked, always willing to believe the best, we were then walked through the hot, honking streets.

'Where are we going?'

'Not far, not far, my friends. It is my uncle's house. We have real Egyptian tea.'

Inevitably, however many times we wanted to trust in a genuine offer of hospitality we would end up in a perfume-making shop and the 'hard sell' would begin. Bottles of perfume dramatically shrank in size and price as we refused to purchase. We always got our tea.

On the strength of the *Al Ahram* interview, Egyptian TV now wanted us for *In Town Tonight*. The owner of Pension Oxford, a shuffling, dribbly-nosed old man with a flesh-wobbling wife, was ecstatic as he grandly informed us of this invitation which could possibly publicise his establishment, though the TV programme was to take place by the banks of the Nile.

Ramadan, a fellow resident, pushed himself upon us. 'I will guide you to the place. I know it, my friends.'

The most glamorous female interviewer had been chosen judging by the crushing crowd of men waiting near the river. Ramadan fought to be in front beside the interviewer, interrupting her questions with advice until she sharply told him, 'Close your mouth!' She couldn't help showing off her charms to the camera, smiling widely and waving her hands around like an amateur belly dancer until the muffler on her microphone flew off and flopped into the Nile. Immediately all the men (Ramadan amongst them) struggled with each other to be the first to dive into the Nile and retrieve it.

The Hilton Hotel coffee bar and garden became a welcome refuge. Here we planned how to speedily get our visas in order to leave Egypt and enter Sudan. Having visited the relevant dusty office numerous times either to find it closed or gaping open with countless sleepy promises that were never kept, we gradually realised through our naively befogged minds that they were waiting for a bribe. But we weren't prepared to pay. This situation could last forever.

I telephoned them. 'This is the British High Commission here. We have three British expeditioners who need visas to enter Sudan in order to carry out an expedition in Africa which we'd like them speedily to do. We would appreciate any help you can offer them.'

We were handed a prompt note by the owner of Pension Oxford who was so overawed by this piece of officialdom his nose had ceased dripping. We were to collect our visas in a week.

We decided to use this week to do two things: to see the pyramids and, if possible, to travel up the Nile to Aswan by felucca. Andy said Ramadan had already intimated he knew where the feluccas and their owners were moored. Soon we were sitting on a small floating raft on which a wooden shelter had been built. In the corner the felucca owner (with little English), wreathed in clouds of smoke, puffed at a small pipe. He looked half asleep. He talked in grunts and throat-clearing croaks which all of us found hard to understand. I was beginning to feel seasick as the raft bobbed up and down. Christine said her stomach was also acting up.

Andy asked us, 'D'you think he's smoking hash?'

The felucca captain considered our clearly enunciated

river proposal, stood up, weaved drunkenly to the door, hawked and spat into the Nile. Picking up a metal kettle he dipped it into the river, filled it and put it onto a small lit portable gas stove. Christine was horrified. The captain was about to offer us tea. The Nile was teeming with bilharzia and other diseases.

'No worries,' Andy said, taking out his Puritabs.

The captain attempted to explain as he poured us liberal amounts of tea that the river was very low this time of year, so it would be impossible to sail upriver. We in turn attempted to understand his broken mumbles while Andy carefully, so as not to offend the captain's hospitality, slipped Puritabs into our cups. Unfortunately, the Puritabs did not dissolve as we had hoped (we realised later that Puritabs do not dissolve immediately in hot liquid); instead they effervesced and spun around our cups like furious spermatozoa. Andy could not hide all the cups. We just stared at the racing Puritabs.

The captain's eyes seemed to bulge out of his head. '*Hamdillah* (Praise be to God)!' he cried and miraculously ejected himself out of the hut to disappear from our sight.

'I told you he was smoking hash,' Andy said.

On we went through aromatic streets of dust to the unique and puzzling pyramids. To our left was a perfect picture-postcard view of these triangular shapes floating on endless miles of Saharan sand, camels slowly tiptoeing past, horses' heads drooping in bright sun, their riders dressed in flowing white gellabias. To our right, almost encroaching on the sands, were concrete buildings and tarmacadam: the city of Cairo – a view kept out of postcards. It was almost impossible to perceive any clear link between the population of modern Cairo and the magical builders of these pyramids.

We kept looking to the left.

Beside the great Pyramid of Cheops, a spidery Egyptian guide and guard of ancient monuments, garbed in what once had been white, informed us there was no electricity. There was no point in entering the pyramid unless we bought a candle from him to light our way. This candle was a stub guaranteed to drip melted wax onto fingers – and cost one Egyptian pound!

'And after, my friends,' said our expensive preserver of antiques, 'you can climb pyramid with me to see the sun set. Or you want to climb Sphinxi? All very cheap.'

From the wandering desert touts: *'Baksheesh? Baksheesh? You ride horse?'*

As far as we were concerned that was it. We had to get away from Cairo.

Hurghada, we were told, was a small, peaceful tourist resort on the Red Sea. We would go there until our visas were ready.

We literally had to fight our way onto the old bus standing in a line of anonymous buses (all looking broken down) until it started its engine. People began charging on, pulling and punching others away; babies were being handed in through windows. There were no queues, no official to enforce good behaviour. Inside there was only crushed standing room, face to stink-breathing face with gellabia-shrouded, grinning passengers. We hung from bouncing straps for five and a half hours. Every so often men beside me would hawk endlessly deep in their throats and spit. The road was uneven and potholed, the bus leaping and swaying as if in a storm. A woman was vomiting copiously among the seats and her vomit had run down the bus floor entering every crevice.

The centre of Hurghada was milling with young men patiently waiting for the passengers to alight: 'You want room? Room? You want room?' We were pushed and pulled in all directions. 'Please, please, my friends, I have clean room.' Above these voices: 'Come to Captain Mohammed's Happy Home, where you will be happy. Cheap room, clean. Captain Mohammed's Happy Home.' The originality did it.

Captain Mohammed was plonked regally in a plastic circular chair. He held out his hand. 'Welcome, my friends. Welcome to Captain Mohammed's Home. I hope you will be comfortable.' He didn't say 'happy'. He clapped his hands and women appeared. 'You must have tea, my friends. You have had a long journey.'

The captain was tubby, a small pot edging over his belt, and a tiny blackened moustache precariously balanced on his top lip. He said he was a real captain and owned a boat.

'My friends, I am a lover of the sea. I peer into its depths and see myriad multicoloured fishes wriggling among the pearly bubbles. I am a conservationist. I wish with my last breath to protect all creatures great and small. Yes, my friends, I am a man of vision.'

We were amazed at his thoughts and diction, though later we were to discover that he had large coloured albums written by a true conservator of the sea – Jacques Cousteau – and he had simply liberally quoted him, as if the words were his own.

'What is that mound tied with string to your front

gate, Captain Mohammed?' Christine asked. We could just make out a shape in the light-bending sun.

'Oh, that is a sea turtle. We shall eat it!'

We went closer. There was sand in its eyes, tossed there by Mohammed's small children who were now busily prodding the punch-drunk turtle with a stick.

'It will make good soup,' added Captain Mohammed, oblivious to our horrified faces.

Well, we decided to rescue the turtle. This could only be done when everyone was fast asleep. Four in the morning, Andy woke me. He was already dressed; I was groggily naked having just been pulled out of a warm bed. We crept out to the gate and untied the turtle leaving behind the string. We dragged it slowly into our lobby (it was too heavy to lift) and washed the sand out of its eyes. We could hear Mohammed snoring. Other guests were fast asleep. We tossed a coin. Andy lost. We decided because of the turtle's weight Andy would have to carry it to the nearby sea in a rucksack. With great difficulty we struggled to slide the turtle into the rucksack, stopping after every slither-sound to check for sleeping residents. Finally, only just fitting in the turtle – its head and one flipper poked out cheekily from the top – Andy got down on his knees while I fitted the rucksack over his arms. He stood upright very slowly.

The light cut off. The street was empty as expected at this time, just barking stray dogs, the sizzle and spark of electric power lines as light went on and off like strobes. Striding bravely on, looking over our shoulders for any onlookers, one minute we were shrouded in darkness, the next was revealed a stark-naked figure walking beside a tall humpbacked person with a turtle's head and flipper sticking out of his neck. Andy continued alone to the sea, placed the turtle in the water and after a heart-stopping moment as the turtle stayed immobile, stunned by its tragic adventures, it swam slowly away.

The next morning as we lay in bed we were besieged by cries of '*Hamdillah! Hamdillah!*' and incomprehensible Arabic comments. At breakfast, 'Oh, my friends, my friends. They have stolen my turtle!' He pointed to the gate where the lonely piece of string dribbled sadly downward. 'I have many, many enemies in this town. You see how they insult me by leaving the string?'

*

We left three days later, taking a stormy ferry from Aswan to Wadi Halfa. Over jostling tea and rice cakes we fell into conversation with a Sudanese involved with business in Egypt. He suddenly interjected mid-conversation, 'We must leave now to make space. Others need to sit and take tea!'

We were amazed at such unselfish courtesy. Then at the cash desk I discovered we owed nothing. He had already paid for the tea and cakes! Andy, Christine and I exchanged incredulous glances.

Wadi Halfa was just brown sun-scorched desert with a railway line running through, a scene from the old Wild West. The train would take us to Khartoum, the capital of Sudan.

We found the thin-as-a-kipper station master in a nearby wooden hut. 'Ah, you are *khawajas* [foreigners], you will travel first class! No need to pay extra. We have a first-class carriage specially for Europeans. There are four more Sons of John [shades of the legendary Prester John] who will journey with you to Khartoum.' He led us through the sand to a waiting train carriage and a tiny huddle of Europeans. There was no engine.

'The train will come. Please take your seats. You will be comfortable here.' We sat and waited. For a long time. Eventually the engine and normal carriages materialised, joined themselves to our first-class compartment and we set off.

Our basic carriage didn't appear plush, but after we clambered through to the normal passenger compartments and viewed overcrowded wooden benches, passengers lying on the ground between benches and entwined in old-fashioned luggage racks trying to sleep, clay urns filled with soiled thirst-relieving water, toilet facilities a mere hole in the wooden floor, we were glad for our practically empty carriage.

Night fell, and being in a desert the temperature dropped dramatically. There were no windows! We couldn't close out the cold! Whipped up by the speeding train the desert sands began to whirl into the carriage and sting our faces. There was no light!

We could only just make out the position of the other passengers if they smoked. We spent the hours until morning shivering, our heads and faces wrapped in spare jumpers and shirts. Sand was everywhere. It was a relief when the alternately rapid and then snail-moving train entered the outskirts of a village and stopped for a while amongst yellow-lit braziers for passengers to spit out the grit, stretch frozen legs and purchase fruit, roasted corn and rice cakes from the many yelling hawkers that inevitably appeared.

Our first-class experience ended at Khartoum in the very early morning. It was still desert – only with buildings. We were led through whirling-dust-laden streets past open sewers by a young lad who claimed he knew of a cheap lodging house – 'El Koubani'. We finally arrived, wilting under our heavy rucksacks, at a wooden makeshift compound painted blue. We looked to the lad expecting him to hiss, '*Baksheesh?*' Instead, he had turned away, sweating in the oppressive heat, and was about to trudge his long way back.

'Thank you!' we shouted out.

He replied with a phrase we were to hear again and again in Sudan: 'No thanks for duty.' We never again heard the hated word *baksheesh*.

Inside the compound the rickety rooms were put together with plywood and chicken wire. The floor was earth. Taking a good look at us, Mohamed, the slow-moving, gangly manager in a thin suit who looked as if he could die at any second, issued orders. And his minion from the south, tall, black-as-ebony Saidi, immediately ejected two Egyptians from their room.

'This will be more private for you and your wife,' Mohamed said. 'The *Misri* will have a smaller room.' A single room was found for Andy.

The word *Misri* is used for an Egyptian in Sudan with great contempt, although it was originally the name of one of Egypt's greatest scholars of Islam – Shaykh Muhammed al-Hafizi-al-Misri. The Sudanese men, caring and thoughtful, viewed Egyptians as grasping and dishonourable.

'If towels are stolen from the line,' Mohamed said, 'you can be sure it is the *Misri*. They are not good men.'

Toilet and shower were outside in a separate compartment. Mohamed and Saidi scattered away the other residents and stood guard while Christine, the only woman in the lodging house, showered. Having not slept on the freezing train we fell into a heavy slumber, our last view being of the chicken wire and blue sky at the high apex of our room.

*

The next morning we woke to melody: Saidi playing a sad lament on his home-made flute – a hollow metal pipe with holes. Saidi missed his life and family in the Southern Dinka tribe, but he could only find paid work in Khartoum. He sent most of his meagre salary home. I liked Saidi and Mohamed so much I felt as if we'd known each other for years. I wanted them both to accompany us on our expedition in Tanzania. Perhaps we could help them enrich themselves. But they were proud Sudanese and wanted to stay in their own country.

After our epic train journey we were extremely hungry for breakfast. A man in sparkling gellabia outside El Koubani's said he would guide us to an eating house. He did for what seemed an hour through sun-bubbling streets. I noticed he kept to the shadows. A wooden-fronted shop served breakfast: rice cakes and cinnamon tea.

The man entered with us and sat at an adjoining table. 'In case you wish translation or wish to order further food.'

'He's after a free meal,' whispered Andy. 'Would you like to join us?' he loudly invited.

'No, no, my friends, I am sitting here to help you with translation in case you wish anything more.'

'D'you think he means it,' said Christine, 'and is just being extra courteous?'

'We'll see...'

On going to settle up we found he had already paid. Shamefaced we informed him, 'Tomorrow we shall take you out for supper.'

'No, my friends. It is not necessary. Tomorrow I leave for business in Egypt.'

'Well, we thank you. You are a good man.'

'No thanks for duty, my friends.' I melted each time I heard this comment.

We were visited by Mr Khalafalla, a jolly man who was head of Sudanese Radio and TV. He wished to interview us. It would be a one-hour programme. Christine was worried. When nervous she stammered, and this long programme would certainly make her nervous. A Korean acupuncturist we had happened to meet at El Koubani's, and whom we'd successfully treated for malaria, volunteered to deal with the nerves.

'There will be no stammer!' he prophesied.

We called on Idris Jack, a Sudanese with twinkling eyes and a small moustache whom we had met on the train to Khartoum. He lived in Elafoun in a mud-brick house within a mud-walled compound. The area was exquisitely clean, swept perfectly clear of dust. His women lived in another mud-brick house. They had prepared a Sudanese supper, many small dishes like tapas. But we didn't see the women who had cooked the food at all. Friends of Idris Jack dressed in blinding white *gellabias* served us, trekking to and from the women's house with platters. They were amazingly caring of our well-being. The food was delicious. We tasted *kissera* and *weka* for the first time. *Kissera* was a thin sour pancake which mopped up sour-sweet *weka* – the clear but sticky juice of boiled-up okra. We became addicted.

Idris Jack told us that his favourite wife could not have children and he may have to divorce her. The Sudanese prized offspring. It struck us that the fault may be his. He was almost fifty, but he would never admit to this or visit a doctor. Before we left, the women finally presented themselves for compliments and took Christine off with them to their house. She was greatly privileged, we realised, to have been allowed to eat with the men in the men's house. Christine returned giggling with tales of henna'd hands and various perfumes used on different parts of the body in order to please men. One of Idris Jack's friends (they are all civil servants) requested our company on Tutti Island.

'My friends, we shall drink *Aragi* and dance under the stars on the island where the Blue and White Niles meet.' They actually do talk like this. And they also mean it.

The night before the TV interview we ate at a proper restaurant with the Korean. Christine, to the waiter's alarm, was sporting protruding needles in her ears and forehead like a porcupine.

They didn't work. She stammered throughout her TV questions. We watched the programme with Idris Jack. It was so interminably slow we almost fell asleep. The interviewer painfully enunciated every English word and got a lot wrong: 'Andrew Graham experienced sailing on a forty-foot sketch…' she began.

'This interviewer is terrible,' Andy stated. 'She should be sacked!'

Abdul later informed us that this was impossible as she was the President's mistress.

On tiny Tutti Island, where the Blue and White Niles met, we watched our tall thin friends in spotless white *gellabias* drink a little *Aragi*, listen to Sudanese music on their portable radio and then, arms outstretched, spin like innocent dervishes under the stars. I shall never forget this wonderful moment.

Further south in the busy marketplace of Kosti, following advice we stocked up on chunks of dried hippo meat (*sharmout*) sold from open sacks to last us our two-week paddle steamer journey up the Nile to Juba, today the capital of *South* Sudan.

We paid for our incredibly cheap steamer tickets in Sudanese pounds.

'There are two other *khawajas* travelling deck class. You are the only ones in first class cabins. You will like them,' the ticket inspector said. 'And because you are first class, you can be allowed on first.'

We had already learned our lesson from the 'first class' train journey. Our expectations were nil.

We anticipated correctly. The wooden paddle steamers were lined up in the water behind a gated compound. They were cannibalised wrecks dating from Victorian times. The gates were specially unpadlocked for us and we stepped into a land of sad ghost ships, the steamers actually rotting in the sun. The first class cabins were absolutely filthy, the walls besmeared with unidentifiable traces which we would have to scrub clean and dubious-looking bunk beds.

There were no locks on the doors and the main toilet was a cabin a few doors away – a hole in the warped floor.

Thank God we had been allowed to board early, for next morning, sustained on tea boiled up on our Trangia stoves (water purified through Millbank bags), we watched four barges being towed across the water and tied with ropes on either side of our steamer and at the front and the back! They were obviously awaiting a large number of passengers and expecting heroic service from this frail little steamer.

The gates were unpadlocked and an unholy shouting, rushing crowd immediately charged the steamer, people struggling with each other, laying down clothes on steamer and barge floors to claim ground. These had to be the deck passengers. Most of them were Southern Sudanese. There were no other cabin-class passengers and we realised why the cabins had been so run down: unused for centuries. Families unpacked bedding and cooking utensils and begun boiling up *assida*, a translucent pink porridge made from sorghum, their staple diet. Andy, caught up in this hysteria, accidentally emptied his bagged portion of hippo meat over the side. I was horrified! Our three-load portions of wind-dried meat together with rice was the only protein we had to survive on for the next two weeks! And we had *karkaday* (dried fuchsia leaves) to boil up for vitamin-C-saturated tea. The paddle wheel close to our cabins began churning the water, small puffs of smoke erupted out of a chimney on the roof and our steamer slowly began to push the attached barges forward. We saw the other two *khawajas* on the deck of one of the barges. They were Dutch.

Andy and I explored the many spaces, leaping from

barge to barge and being careful, as the steamer rounded a bend, not to jump when the barges began to stretch out their rope tethers. When they hit the bank they banged together with ferocious speed. Greetings were called out as we passed and many invitations to sit and eat *assida*. Andy, less his hippo meat, was tempted. Sorghum, we were told, is the one and only indigenous crop of mainland Africa. Everything else – mangos, bananas, coconuts, corn etc. – was introduced from other countries. Andy succumbed and found the *assida* watery and tasteless.

On the decks we noticed that many babies were ill with swollen stomachs, flies in their eyes, hair turning red. They were listless, lacking in energy. The parents asked us for medical help. Andy and I stared blankly at each other. We had a paperback book which we treated like our bible: *Where There Is No Doctor* – a compendium of African illnesses, their symptoms and simple treatment. It was invaluable. Andy read out directions while I observed symptoms, counting beats between the children's breathing. Was it fever? There were so many types and causes. Malnutrition? Worms? Whatever other illnesses they had we decided these children were also suffering from simple dehydration. We made rehydration drinks, passed them around and the babies perked up. From then on, despite our protestations we were known as 'The Doctors'. We wandered the decks in our new roles passing out paracetamol, chloroquine (careful not to deplete our personal supply) and generally healing the sick. In return Andy was fully fed, making up for his lost meat.

Sitting close to the churning paddle I drifted through the Southern Sudanese pastoral tribes on land as we moved through villages upriver. In the day, tall, thin, high-cheekboned Dinka women smoked intricately carved tiny pipes, lavishing massive attention on their herds of groomed cows for whom they composed praise-songs. At night the river banks were alive with leaping fires, frantic drumming agitating the dark.

I studied flat-faced round-headed Nuer – peaceful strict traditionalists who when aroused fought to the death; Shilluk tribesmen (violent killers) armed with spears and clubs, nakedly striding the banks, perfectly muscled specimens with biceps honed by life, covered from head to foot in ghostly white ash to ward off mosquitoes; Atwet-Dinka rich in cattle, but greedy and grasping; Moundari, friendly and generous, with sculptured bodies; some were nomadic fisherfolk living on papyrus platforms sailing downstream in dug-out canoes to sell their catch.

An inquisitive Shilluk tribesman with a gigantic war club over his shoulder stepped onto our steamer at one of the many village stops we made. This giant strode about proudly nodding to some of the terrified passengers sitting on the deck floor. He had deep scars cut into his face, hair shorn very close to his large ugly head, his features creased into a warlike expression. He was forbidding. Not someone you'd want to meet anywhere on a dark night. Without warning (this was usual) the steamer puffed away from the bank. Seized with sudden panic the Shilluk begun racing around the steamer decks shouldering people out of his way as if they were ants, searching for a way off the steamer. He was terrified of the water. Eventually he calmed and stayed meekly on board, well-behaved until the next village two river bends away.

We entered the Sudd, a vast swampy wetland, a mosquito-infested area the size of England. In Arabic Sudd means 'barrier' and it certainly proved to be so for early explorers who got lost or died here from malaria. There were many passages around floating islands of reeds and papyrus a hundred metres in diameter. Here families of natives lived in small huts on floating rafts all constructed from papyrus. They caught fish that feed on aquatic plants. On the sandbars they grew corn and grazed livestock.

'The wetlands are our life source,' said sixty-year-old Achiek Mayaw, lying on the barge floor shrouded in a chequered sheet. 'Generations of my ancestors lived in the same place for hundreds of years.'

Sadly, as I write in 2014, this lifestyle is threatened *again* by plans to work once more on the notorious Jonglei Canal. This was begun in 1978. It was meant to cut a 350-kilometre swathe through the wetlands, south to north from Bor to Malakal channelling water usually lost in evaporation into Northern Sudan and mostly *into* Egypt for use in agriculture. Egypt obviously strongly supported the scheme.

When we passed through the work was ongoing. We saw helicopters busily zipping back and forth and heard mostly loud American voices involved in its construction. Southern Sudanese passengers told us that oil had been discovered. Unofficially America seemed also to be involved. But who would get the oil? It was becoming increasingly clear to us that the Jonglei Canal would only benefit the speedier carriage of oil out of the inhospitable Sudd to the north and further afield. A way of pastoral life would be lost. The Sudd would be drained. Four hundred species of bird life would disappear, elephants, countless hippo and crocodiles. Reducing evaporation would likely lessen rainfall in this area. Draining marshes would alter fisheries and grasslands, a delicate eco-system on which the Dinka, Nuer and Shilluk had come to depend.

A recommencement of the Civil War (in 1983, after we passed through) completely halted the project. But then the South achieved its long-sought independence in 2011, and since then have begun fighting amongst themselves, a tribal war, while the canal project has recommenced. Progress, going forward, was held as something desirable. Yet it was abundantly clear that as goods and technology had progressed, we as human beings had not. If anything we had regressed.

Our journey proceeded in stops and starts. The river was low and the steamer had to travel slowly, taking care not to ground itself. We awoke one morning in the Sudd Swamp to find our cabin at a strange angle, a papyrus reed poking through our open window. I called to Andy and jumped out of bed. There was no noise from the paddle. The steamer was absolutely still. On deck we found we were listing to one side. We were the only ones on board. Deck-class passengers had vanished. The barges had all been cut loose and were floating a hundred yards away with the evacuated staring in our direction. We realised they were waiting for us to sink!

Our steamer had drifted into a bed of firm papyrus reeds which were holding it up. After some hours when it was obviously clear we would not submerge, the barges were propelled toward us and staff dived underwater to ascertain the damage. There was a small hole which may have occurred from collision with shallow rocks during the night. The hole was speedily fixed by sailors diving down in relays with improvised melted bars of soap! The soap would hold until Juba.

The university students had run out of food. The journey because of the shallow river was taking much longer than they had anticipated. They called on the captain to move faster. He said he could not. We would be mired on sandbanks and it would endanger and further delay everyone. They threatened him with mutiny to no effect.

Finally they told him they would kill the first-class passengers. That was us! The captain generously relayed this information and he knew these Southern Sudanese students meant what they said. We had thought these students our friends. We'd had many rambling philosophical and political conversations together on the steamer roof. We had even asked them about the Black Stone.

'Yes, we have heard of this stone for the snakebite. It is called the Congo Stone. You must get it.'

'From where?'

'We do not know, brother.'

Frightened out of our skins we decided to padlock the cabin doors and fight to the last breath. Christine and I sat on the lower bunk and laid out knives and all the damaging cutting tools we had in our possession. Andy did the same in his cabin. This was all we could do. Eventually they came. They began banging loudly on the cabin doors urging us to open up, then hacking at the doors with cleavers and machetes. Andy told me they were practically through his door. Knives clenched in our palms, Christine and I stood before our besieged door. They would soon break in and we would die…

Then everything stopped! We heard the captain's voice in conversation with theirs. He asked us to open our doors. Only the captain was outside. It was all over! He told us privately that he had agreed to their demands, but in reality would go no faster. He could not afford to have the steamer and barges grounded. And he could not guarantee that this would not occur again. We would have to wait and see.

We knew that we could never again look at those students in the same way.

By now the river water was extremely low and as we unexpectedly approached Juba after two languorous weeks on the Nile, our steamer scratched over pebbles and sandy ground before it moored in a small concrete man-made harbour. In the blink of an eye most everyone had abandoned the decks heading for the delights of town.

Juba at the end of the sailable Nile seemed to be at the complete end of nowhere. It was a tight-packed, humid village with low mud houses and a central dusty road linking homes and aid services; we referred to it as the 'arsehole of the world'. Only backpackers and aid personnel seemed to inhabit the hot street. It was close to the site of what was earlier known as Gondokoro, where all early explorers of the Nile stayed. The water here, we were told, was definitely tainted and undrinkable, and we had also to be careful of 'green monkey disease', prevalent in Juba. We eventually discovered this was Marburg virus disease caught through contact with infected green monkeys, a viral haemorrhagic fever in human and non-human primates indistinguishable from Ebola. In the Congo they ate green monkey meat! Much later in Tanzania we discovered that 'green monkey disease' was also a reference to AIDS, which at that time did not have a medical name. And AIDS was known on the continent of Africa solely as a homosexual disease.

The owner of our lodge was in hospital. He had been stabbed the week before and his two Sudanese sons were in charge. There were no private rooms, only shared toilets and washing facilities and beds lined up in long corridors. Andy could not knock a nail into the hard wall for his mosquito net, so he attached it to a tall antique wooden hat stand which he positioned beside his bed. Stealing was rife! At night we slept under our mosquito nets covered by thin sheets, money belts strapped to our thighs, our hands tightly gripping knives.

Lines of lorries queued up outside a hut on the outskirts of Juba, seeking permits to trade. Lorry drivers lounged for hours in shadows thirstily drinking fresh coconut juice (*madafu*). They brought loads of Sportsman cigarettes into Sudan from Kenya and illegally smuggled out gold panned from Sudanese rivers. We needed a lift extremely quickly and would have to pay for our passage. The long monsoon rains were due soon making crossing rivers impossible for a period of three months. No one would then be on the bush roads until well after the monsoon had ended. We managed to agree a lift and our driver took us to the edge of town where he purchased a lamb.

This was slaughtered and barbecued for supper. Locals in a nearby house urged us to sleep on the earth floor of a disused mud-built bakery for safety. In the morning we found we had been abandoned. The lorry had gone! Apparently the driver had decided to go to Uganda instead of Kenya, so he drove off in the early hours.

We were stuck! We had little chance of hailing another lift in the area we now found ourselves. Also, we had no food and nothing was being sold in the locality. The locals, wanting to help, excitedly flagged down an Encounter Overland lorry but could not understand why the driver – an Englishman like us – wouldn't take us because we were not 'original' paying passengers. And the rains were coming!

We ate fried termites like oily, crunchy shrimps for breakfast and drank milky tea without sugar, as young kids ran around catching flying termites and stuffing them raw, wings and all into their eager mouths. Another lorry lumbered past and thankfully stopped for water. On the back were fourteen Eritrean refugees travelling to Kenya. One of the fat Indian drivers agreed our price, and we slung our rucksacks onto the back.

We spent the next ten days bouncing over rough ground and across river beds, clouds of dust rising up from the rear of the vehicle and completely covering us in a grainy red. Our drivers were in a hurry to beat the rains. We could not lie or sit because of the potholed earth roads. We were easily tossed into the air. Over time we were forced to hang onto overhead metal rails that usually supported a canvas canopy in order to avoid the huge bumps. We just wanted to lie down and sleep. By the end our inside organs crashing against each other were agonisingly painful. We hugged our stomachs, holding ourselves together. The two drivers taking it in turn to drive chewed twigs of *miraa* (a mood-enhancing plant) until their teeth were green to keep themselves alert. At night we slept under the lorry, all huddled together for safety.

In torrential rains which thankfully washed off the thick dust which had become a fixed mask on our faces we came upon the Encounter Overland lorry – stuck in a riverbed! Ignoring it, our driver stood on our bonnet to better survey his own proposed route across the speedily rising water. Encounter Overland tipped slowly over, rucksacks floated away, there were screams for help and bodies in the water. Our driver simply climbed back into his cab, successfully crossed the river, and drove sedately away.

By the time we reached the Kenyan border town of Lokichoggio, apart from looking like unidentified objects, unwashed and thirsty, we and the refugees were literally starving. On the way there was nothing for sale. The drivers had their own stash of food; we were not a priority.

The town was just a collection of a very few ramshackle wooden huts set in a clumsy line on only one side of the dried red-mud road. Very Wild West again. But there was one shop! Because we arrived in the early hours we tiredly ignored the lorry's underside and slept on the road just outside the anticipated opening of the shop. In the morning we were licked awake by stray dogs.

The dark interior of the shop eventually revealed there was nothing inside. The Indian owner listening to our tale of woe interrupted to say, 'I have a chapati I have not eaten and I think I may have an old tin of baked beans. I shall have to look. Will that do?' Of course, of course, these were treasures! We ate our cold chapati and congealed baked beans from the rusty tin, sitting outside on the corrugated hard road, waving away the hungry dogs. The refugees would have to wait until they reached Nairobi.

But we were now in Kenya. First Egypt, then the Sudan, and now Kenya. We were moving further towards our goal of reaching Bagamoyo in Tanzania, Stanley's starting point for his expedition.

Our ruthless driver suddenly ejected us outside a lodging house at night. Not in Nairobi, the capital, but in Eldoret, a large town in the highlands of Kenya. The lodging house was extremely gaudy but clean and comfortable and could be rented by the hour. Our bedroom was Hollywood pink with a gigantic luxurious bed taking up the room. Inscribed on the headboard was '*Lala Salaama*' ('Peaceful Sleep'). Andy also had a double bed. These were good signs, we agreed, until our sleep was disturbed by grunts and screeches of pleasure and we realised we were in a Kenyan brothel!

Christine was feeling weak and suffering from persistent diarrhoea. Next morning she practically collapsed in a full-of-goods supermarket frequented by Europeans (it really was a surprise to see so many white faces), and as Andy and I held her up, a large, beetroot-coloured English lady rushed over to help and immediately phoned her doctor.

Dr Oganda was a chubby, ever-smiling, kindly man. He referred Christine to a local hospital. 'She has amoebic dysentery,' he pronounced, 'and needs to be on a drip as soon as possible.'

'What are you doing in Kenya?' he asked. 'Are you carrying appropriate medicines?'

He reviewed our expedition first aid supplies and replaced most of the drugs, in particular the antibiotics Septrin and Talpen, the only ones we had been given.

'You Europeans don't realise how easy it is to die in Africa. These antibiotics are useless here,' he told us. 'The choice is either suffer the possible side effects of strong and effective antibiotics, or die!'

Christine spent a week in a private room in the hospital being rehydrated. Meanwhile Andy and I went to stay with Luce, the English lady who had called the doctor for us, and her husband, Reg. The couple lived very comfortably in a spacious red-roofed house beside a sprawling campus of which Reg was the headmaster – the Africanised Hill Secondary School, which once had an excellent reputation. Reg confessed he was just a junior school teacher in England and didn't really know why he was accepted as a headmaster in Kenya, but it didn't take us long to understand that Reg was the 'token whitey', a mere figurehead chosen by black parents to head the school – very common in Kenya and some other African countries where putting a white man in charge, albeit without power, was almost a 'good housekeeping' sign of 'approval', a symbol of respectability. Reg definitely had no power!

We learned much about Kenya from their visitors: an army officer discussing how much land he would obtain once it was confiscated from white farmers; the land distributor who parcelled out the confiscated land. Originally two and a half acres per family, it had now risen to five acres, so he had to reluctantly take away from some African families in order to give the required portion to others. His work was made more difficult when he received official notes on his car windscreen ordering him to give twenty acres to a major who had just received a short posting to Nairobi.

PART TWO – GOING DOWN: FROM CAIRO TO BAGAMOYO

The land distributor invited us to his house for dinner. It was a confiscated English farmhouse comprising darkened, empty rooms with no furniture, no decoration and agricultural land stretching as far as the eye could see turned to scrub and ruin. Inside the house was a scene from feudal England. Walls and ceilings were black and grimy with soot and grease. People squatted on hard earth in the darkness. His welcoming wife with pots bubbling and smoke enveloping the room was cooking our supper over a crackling wood fire on the floor of her sitting room.

Reg took us out often, always to drinking clubs. We were sitting with an enormous American officer when we heard on the radio a loud report of an attempted Kenya Air Force coup against President Moi. Apparently the President was rethinking allowing the Americans to use Mombasa as an Indian Ocean base for their aircraft carriers and this was a planned rap on the knuckles; coups were regular occurrences. The American officer smugly revealed he'd heard of the Black Stone, only he called it the Belgian Stone. And then faltered in confidence when we asked where we could get it. It remained a mystery.

The plot was foiled! We were told that the SAS had retrieved Moi by helicopter and American troops were mopping up the remains of the attempt. The frustrated air force then turned about and expelled their venom on a common enemy, the hated Indian population! We were told this was very normal.

We planned to visit the famous explorer Wilfred Thesiger who lived in Maralal, Samburu-land with his adopted son Lawi. We were hoping for expedition advice. That is, of course, if he would deign to see us.

Wilfred Thesiger was extremely welcoming. He had an office at the top of an old garage where he was busily writing his autobiography. Expedition advice, though, was difficult:

'In my day,' he said, 'I could send a telegram to a district commissioner stating my needs, and when I arrived awaiting me would be the camels and goods I required. I don't suppose you can do that now?' He had no knowledge whatsoever of the famed Black Stone but said, 'Don't worry. Snakes will be more afraid of you and will keep well away.'

Thesiger kindly invited us to Samburu ceremonies taking place in the Maralal hills where he lived. The Samburu encampment was a sharp contrast to Maralal. This was African country: humpy green hills stretching to the horizon; Samburu enclaves of low mud huts like those of the Maasai, and young tribesmen in scarlet robes, spears clasped at their sides leaping higher and higher on the peaks. These young warriors were recruited and, we were told, were trained by the SAS as an elite army unit, the GSU (General Service Unit) which also guarded the President. Thesiger's spacious house looked like a log cabin. He had a machete (*panga*) beside his bed. 'There was recently an attempt on my life,' he admitted. The parents of his adopted son, Lawi, lived here. Their *boma* (an enclosed home-space) was a thorn-fence surrounding a low curved-roof stick-framed hut smeared with ashes and clay and masses of cow dung. Inside it was dark and much less than a studio apartment size, with the smoking sheep-droppings-fuelled fire (to deter mosquitoes) taking up most of the space. It was claustrophobic and we were glad to get out.

We stayed in Maralal for two weeks, eating overcooked goat meat (all that existed) at our lodging house, and it became increasingly apparent that the reason Thesiger preferred to always live in the back of beyond was primarily because of his love and admiration for young men, Lawi being his latest paramour. My respect for Thesiger, his generous kindness and many adventures, remained undimmed. During our stay in Kenya we had met many supposed bush experts, recommended white hunters dressed in pristine safari gear, zebra bands around their bush hats, hugging gleaming rifles and eagerly providing unsolicited advice – nullified by the fact that they had never walked in the bush. They had always been strapped into four-wheel-drive vehicles. Thesiger was the closest we had come to the 'real' traditional explorer, now misplaced in time. But Lawi's parents clearly now expected Lawi to marry and enter a heterosexual relationship. Thesiger was old and had outgrown his use. Thus the attempt on his life...

We left by *matatu*, a covered pick-up with benches fitted on either side for passengers. A long rough journey over potholed earth roads but extremely cheap. I should mention that Kenyan whites never ever travelled on native transport, so an unofficial colour bar existed.

We headed for the Nairobi Youth Hostel where there was a crazed dictator in charge. 'No room! No room!' he chanted. But when offered a few Kenyan shillings he changed his mind – 'OK, three bunks. Go there now. Go!'

We met other travellers who were free with their invaluable advice. I had only £500 left in travellers' cheques having spent £1,000 on the journey so far and was a mite worried as we had not yet reached Tanzania. Following advice given, Andy and I rolled around in the dust and looking dishevelled ran to the local police station to report we'd been mugged and my cheques stolen. Nairobi was full of thieves, so the police promptly supplied me with a theft report which I took to the bank, which then gave me new travellers' cheques. I now had new viable cheques and £500 in dud ones, cancelled due to having been 'stolen'. On the proceeds, we booked three first class sleepers on the train to Mombasa.

All of us disliked Nairobi and couldn't wait to leave. Muggings and killings were a daily occurrence. If you were in a car, some ragamuffin would bang on the passenger side and point at the tyre. While you were peering out the open window another thief would be helping himself to your goods on the other side of the car. We were told stories of thieves who boldly fished for goods with a fishing line and hook through slightly open bedroom windows while people slept. Should the sleepers awake and attempt to grab their disappearing goods they would find countless razor blades attached to the line. You ultimately couldn't trust anyone and had to look over both shoulders before discussing political corruption in Kenya. Even shoeshine boys were listening and would not hesitate to report you for a small reward. Many people who spoke out of turn regularly disappeared.

In Egypt we couldn't cope with the Egyptians. Now we definitely abhorred the white Kenyans and weren't too sure about generally trusting the black population either. What the hell was going on with us? In England, we had thought we were measured in our views and extremely tolerant of other races. Definitely anti-apartheid. Christine was brought up in Guernsey, Andy was originally Scottish and I was of Cypriot blood. Why were we changing?

The sleeper train and excellent dining car were pure luxury like a murderless episode from an Agatha Christie novel. We just had to ensure the windows were tightly closed when pulling into stops. We then took a ferry to Diani Beach, the nearest location to the Kenya–Tanzania border, and tramped in blood-boiling heat (not forgetting the draining rucksacks) to the lounging border guard in his Kenyan sentry box. We handed over our border-crossing permissions originally sent to London by the Ministry of Information in Tanzania which he attempted to read upside down. He told us the border was closed by Tanzania because of increased smuggling. He laughed, 'Tanzania has no goods at all in their country.' But he could not tell us when the border would open again.

So we tramped our interminable way back to the sands. Diani was a long beach of *Treasure Island* white sands and coconut trees lapped by the clear Indian Ocean, interspersed with foliage-hidden heavily guarded tourist hotels. From these hotels we sent a telex to Tanzania informing them of our plight. There was no answer.

While we waited, we rented a small cottage and stayed on this idyllic beach, making regular trips to the border and sending countless telexes to no avail.

*

The border reopened! We were on our way again. We set off on a heat-captured overcrowded local bus to Tanzania. It made many stops and we stood the whole way, we

Europeans towering above Tanzanian tribespeople, our noses level with their heads. For seven hours we breathed in the combined aromas of sweat, ash and cow dung (rubbed into hair to repel mosquitoes). My soaking thigh stuck firmly onto a plump lady's buttocks which were squashed against me. Her dress and my trouser leg were wringing wet and at one stop we had to gracefully and politely peel ourselves apart.

One man got on the overcrowded bus and was a shilling short in his fare. The conductor, who had to clamber over passengers to collect money, sometimes having to hold onto ceiling struts and crawl spider-like over our heads, ordered him in Kiswahili to get off the bus. The person refused. And so the conductor, without warning, hit him hard on the face with his solid ticket rack. Then the whole bus erupted, punching and kicking the man (we dodged the blows) until he was either unconscious or dead. His body was then manipulated over our heads and between the spaces of standing passengers. The bus was still speeding along, but the doors were ordered open. And he was bundled out. We saw his senseless body bouncing off the potholed tarmac.

Andy leaned over and whispered, 'Where have you brought me?'

Tanzania was the answer; the border was approaching. We would soon be in Dar es Salaam.

3

Dar es Salaam: Haven of Peace

Active colonisation of the East African coast began in the eighth century AD when Arab settlers built towns on Zanzibar, Mafia and Kilwa. In around 1200 a group of Shirazi (people who traced their ancestry to Shiraz in Persia) settled and founded new dynasties. Many of the immigrants intermarried with the locals and their descendants became known as the 'Swahili'. The coastline of Tanzania is known as *Uswahili* – Land of the Swahili people. The greatest compliment paid in Tanzania is to be referred to as an *Mswahili* – '*Wewe ni Mswahili, kweli* (You are a Swahili, truly)'. This means not only are you fluent in the language but more importantly that you are cunning and crafty like a fox, prepared to cross the law in pursuit of profit. These are much admired attributes.

We were staying in the dust-laden Indian section of Dar es Salaam, a miserable nondescript grey of crumbling buildings. We had to enter our simple lodging house by climbing over fallen debris and through a literal hole in the wall. Despite the delights of local Indian food and euphoria-inducing *pan* (shavings of betel nut, smear of tobacco and sweet spices wrapped in a betel leaf, left to soak and dematerialise in the mouth) we only stayed for two nights before booking into the Lutheran Hostel in the centre of town, around the corner from the modern Kilimanjaro Hotel.

The Kilimanjaro Hotel sat many miles away from that snow-capped mountain. It was the most modern building in Dar with a lengthy lukewarm swimming pool steaming in the humidity and a cafe serving welcome cold beers. Also, dodgy plumbing . . . This area of Dar es Salaam was comprised of colonially impressive German-built government buildings, and imported peacocks weaving over watered grassy patches, their bleating calls haunting the night. *Askaris* (private and government guards/soldiers) lounged everywhere armed with AK-47s. The small darkened Indian-owned shops were all empty of goods except for green packet after green packet of identical China tea.

This was part of a reciprocal deal for the Chinese building in 1976 of the TAN-ZAM railway, running from Dar es Salaam to Zambia. Tanzania and Zambia had combined forces to eliminate copper-rich but landlocked Zambia's economic dependence on Rhodesia and South Africa, both then ruled by white-minority governments. With this railway Zambia's copper could reach the sea at Dar es Salaam. After failing to obtain Western support they turned to the People's Republic of China for help. At a cost of US$500 million, this was China's largest foreign aid project.

We ate at the Kilimanjaro Summit Restaurant on the roof, catching sea breezes. The waiter brought us a very full leather-covered menu. Andy ordered steak.

'*Hamna*,' barked the waiter.

'Pardon?'
'I'm sorry, sir. There is none.'
'OK then, I'll have the pork chop?'
'*Hamna.*'
We didn't need a translation. 'OK, the burger.'
'*Hamna.*'
'The fish!'
'*Hamna.*'
'What then do you have on the menu?'
'Only chicken, sir.'
'Only chicken?'
'Yes sir.'
'If you knew that, why did you give us the full menu?'
'I thought you would like to read it, sir.'

On our first night in the hotel we were shown to our room by the porter. From the large windows there was a beautiful view of the harbour. I decided to take a photo.

'No, no, sir, please! It is forbidden.'
'What is forbidden?' asked Andy.
'To see the harbour.'
'But everyone can see the harbour from their windows,' interjected Christine.
'No, it is forbidden to see it in your machine.'
'Ah, so I cannot take a photograph of the harbour,' I clarified.
'No, no, it is forbidden to see it from your window. I am sorry.'

I knew there was a much better view from the rooftop restaurant. 'I will not see it from my room then.'
'Thank you.'
'I will see it from the rooftop with my machine.'

'Yes, yes, this is good. Welcome, sir.'

Another morning we ate outside at the nearby Embassy Hotel, the sun sitting in our eyes.

We were interrupted by loud cries from the street: '*Mwizi! Mwizi!*'

'Does that mean "moon"?' Christine asked, showing off her knowledge.

'No, that is *mwezi*,' corrected Nikitas, '*mwizi* means thief!'

Naked from the waist up an individual appeared, weaving past people at speed. They tried to grab at him. The cries increased. Someone tripped him up. Suddenly from nowhere a large crowd formed. They had machetes and club-like sticks. After punching him to the ground they chopped at him with machetes. Blood spurted in fountains. They beat him with clubs. His body and face were covered with blood and dust. He was not moving.

Men poured out of offices in three-piece suits and ties and began kicking his inert body, snatching clubs out of others' hands and beating his head. With each hard blow the battered body seemed to levitate off the pavement. We watched the body reverberating on the ground throwing up dust. Finally, the excited crowd dowsed him with gasoline and set him alight.

'What did he steal?' Christine asked.

'Perhaps he did not steal anything and is not a thief,' we were told. 'Someone pointed at him, called "thief" and so he had no option but to run for his life. This happens often. It settles old scores.'

Permissions were needed to embark on our journey and we visited the Ministry of Information. Surprisingly, they had on file all correspondence from London and our desperate telexes from Kenya.

'But you didn't answer!'

'No. But we knew you would come,' said a smiling Willie Mbunga, who with his friendly wife ran this careful department as if involved in discovering anti-government spies.

*

Tanzania has an area half the size of Western Europe. Situated just below the Equator, temperatures can reach well into the 100º Fahrenheit. Bordered by clear lakes and 500 miles of tropical coastline sloping into the Indian Ocean, its landscape varies from the beige, arid semi-desert of the central plateau known in Kiswahili as *nyika* (as in *Tanganyika*, meaning, we were told, 'a walk in the wasteland'), to the snow of the northern mountains. The interior is part of a vast highland extending from South Africa to Ethiopia. The country also embraces the islands of Zanzibar, Pemba and Mafia.

The country today contains the biggest game parks in the world: the Serengeti Plains, Ngorongoro Crater, Lake Manyara and the Selous Game Reserve. Mount Kilimanjaro, at 19,340 feet, is the highest mountain in Africa. A north-east monsoon blows from October to February (utilised by past Arab traders to sail their dhows to India) and a south-east monsoon for the rest of the year. The long rains are from March to April and the short rains from October to November. In the scrubby central plains the sparse woodland and sunburnt savannah grass are harsh and unwelcoming, and there is only one combined rainy season from November to May. This quite often does not occur, causing crop failure and widespread starvation. Where poverty was rife, daughters were often sold in exchange for livestock, a girl fetching from five to twenty cows. Two out of five were married before they turned eighteen, some even as young as seven years old.

Most Tanzanians we saw lived in rectangular-built mud houses with corrugated-iron roofs. The inhabitants spent most of their lives outside, sitting on tiny stools around a fire, the women sprawled on straw mats twining each other's hair. Even so they were not immune to thefts. My taxi-driving mate Shadrak informed me that while his family were fast asleep, thieves patiently dug down and burrowed under his mud walls in order to enter and steal the family's clothes. The height of luxury in a Tanzanian house was the nail on which to hang your clothes!

The staple diet was *ugali*, a maize-flour tasteless porridge similar to the original Sudanese *assida*. This was boiled up and heavily stirred until so thick you had to cut it into chunky white portions with a knife. It was everywhere we went. Shadrak explained the necessity of *ugali*: 'You can invite me to your house for dinner and I will eat everything – meat, vegetables, potatoes. I will even have seconds. But when I leave I will feel hungry, because I have not eaten *ugali*.'

The local population were incredibly inventive at scavenging tin cans, bottles and cardboard which could all be put to use in building houses or in constructing intricate toys/sculptures for sale to tourists. There were no dustbins or rubbish collectors; everything that was not immediately grabbed was burned outside houses, causing acrid smoke. Car mechanics used ingenious methods to keep broken-down vehicles moving. We were in a taxi one day when, stopped at traffic lights, the pothole-shaken heavy engine quietly dropped out onto the road.

Tanzania became an independent black African country, a one-party state, in 1961 and from that very moment held out its upturned palm and became dependent on foreign aid. Soon after, President Nyerere introduced his *Ujamaa* policies to the country.

Ujamaa meant familyhood or pulling together. These socialist ideas were welcome and workable in theory, but in practice became ineffective. Nyerere wanted the scattered inhabitants of Tanzania moved to central locations where there were excellent roads. This way agricultural produce by collective effort could be easily redistributed. Central schools could be established providing education for all and dispensaries sited with trained staff and proper drugs. First off, people refused to move from their villages even when they inhabited drought-stricken areas. This was the land of their ancestors, whose spirits (*mizimu*) were in the soil, in the rivers, in the trees. Nyerere was forced to use armed soldiers to crowd them onto the backs of lorries and impel them off their tribal land. Next, they refused to work with each other on the new communal farmland. They pointed out that if a person did very little work they would receive the very same pay as those that worked diligently. This was unfair.

Because political besuited officials from Dar es Salaam would be arriving to inspect the farms it was necessary for *someone* to cultivate the fields. So schoolchildren with hoes on their shoulders were marched off before school commenced to work on land their parents had spurned. Their education inevitably suffered. Although officially a free health service was now meant to exist, in reality corruption led to a thriving black market in medicines.

In East Africa we white people were referred to as *wazungu*, which may be derived from the experience of a past chief in the Usambara Mountains who, discovering that his lands had been gradually surrounded by unwanted white settlers, quizzed people in all directions for confirmation and finally exclaimed, '*Wanazunguka sisi* (They have surrounded us).' *Kizunguzungu* is a children's game and another word from which *wazungu* could be derived. You run fast in a circle until you drop to the floor from giddiness. The word also means 'not to deal straightforwardly, to act deviously'.

The White Fathers – one of the first groups of missionaries to visit Tanzania in the 1800s – now lived in an imposing centrally situated property. We had been permitted to ask them for historical information, but instead finally resolved the mystery of the Black Stone. An elderly Father asked us, 'What do you intend doing about wild animals?' and we explained that the only matter we had not prepared for was snakebite.

'We keep hearing of a Black Stone, Congo Stone, Belgian Stone, but have come to the conclusion that it's just a legend. It doesn't exist,' I blurted.

'Oh, how many do you want?' he said. 'We just had a consignment sent in from Belgium.'

It transpired that the Belgian White Fathers, the first arrivals in the Belgian Congo, came upon the stone there and carried it with them for protection.

'We'll have three, please,' I said weakly.

The Black Stone was just that – a black piece of stone looking like charcoal. Later, I had it checked at the main pharmacist in Dar es Salaam owned by Mansoor Daya, who told me that it was made up of carbonised cow bone and masses of compressed vegetable matter. It was used thus. If bitten, you placed the stone on the bite, which had to be seeping. It would stick and suck out the poison but not the blood. When the stone fell off it was placed in an alkaline solution – milk, or chalk in water – to disperse the poison. Then it was again placed back on the bite. If it no longer adhered, then it had successfully sucked out all the poison. A miracle! Magic!

First aid sorted, now we needed to sort out how to transport our goods across Tanzania since we were incapable in this sweaty heat of carrying in rucksacks enough supplies to sustain us until we reached villages in the bush.

'Porters! Porters! Porters is what you need! Porters every time. Donkeys? Useless beasts! Dead before you know it...' So pronounced Alan Rodgers – pointed out to us as a wildlife expert amongst the European community.

We were in favour of donkeys – instinctively against the idea of using porters because of the colonial overtones. Also, we did not want to be encumbered by other people on the march, and a donkey could carry a load of 140 pounds and fend for itself while the porter's load included his own goods, utensils and food. Our donkeys, we decided, would also survive.

For Stanley in 1871, the issue had at first appeared clear: 'The African Traveller can hire neither waggon nor camels, neither horses nor mules, to proceed with him into the interior. His means of conveyance are limited to black and naked men, who demand at least 15 dollars a head for every 70lbs weight carried only as far as *Unyanyembe*.' (That was a distance of approximately 650 miles.) Ultimately, however, Stanley hedged his bets and was privileged to be able to afford the luxury of both porters *and* donkeys. As it turned out all twenty-seven of his donkeys, which he bought for $20 apiece, eventually died from drinking polluted water, worms and overwork, and he had to recruit extra porters. But they also fell ill and died or malingered or deserted…

'Donkeys? They'll attract lion and hyena for miles around. You'd be fools, fools!' exclaimed Rodgers.

We stuck with donkeys and our hunt began. A donkey saga. We were told by government veterinarians that there were donkeys we should investigate in the city stadium. We could have them for 'Very cheap price…' The donkeys, left over from a disastrous aid project, sadly were crippled.

We decided it could be advantageous to meet with the Prime Minister, Edward Sokoine, a Maasai who was supposedly extremely helpful and honest, loved by the ordinary people whom he attempted to assist. I telephoned, explained who we were and made an appointment, amazed at how easy it was. Andy phoned the local press and invited them along too.

On the day, we were led in to the Prime Minister, and not knowing what he looked like I respectfully shook the hand of his assistant standing beside him.

Sokoine laughed. 'Who are all these people?' he asked.

'Publicity,' Andy said.

'Good for both of us,' I added.

The Prime Minister laughed again and waved us all to seats around a large polished table. Local Africafe instant coffee, water, milk, sugar and biscuits had been laid out. 'Help yourselves,' he invited and quizzically but good humouredly inspected the group, some armed with flash cameras. Although he'd been briefed, he politely asked about our proposed expedition. And immediately made up his mind.

'An excellent idea,' he said, 'but we need to help you practically. While here in Dar es Salaam you will work together with the Tanzania Tourist Corporation' – I wrote numerous articles for them. 'They will arrange for you to stay in the Kilimanjaro Hotel.' (Oh, no!) 'On your expedition should you need food, the regional trading companies will be wholly available to you. You definitely need to learn Kiswahili and we will also provide an intensive course at Mweka Wildlife College on wild animals you may encounter. I can supply you with scouts, but I insist you carry firearms.'

'Well, we don't have any,' said Andy.

'I didn't think Tanzania would look kindly on us having firearms,' I confessed.

'You must have them,' Sokoine repeated. 'One day's walk from Dar es Salaam you will be alone in the bush and my presence and protection will end. You may have a scout with you' – he turned to me – 'but only *you* can protect your wife! If you don't have any firearms we'll give you them, and Mweka College will teach you how to shoot.'

His assistant was speedily writing everything down and soon we were armed with a Ruger .357 Magnum revolver, an automatic shotgun, a Mauser 9.3 x 62 rifle, a gas pistol, flares and sufficient ammunition.

The Ruger we eventually discovered was useful for close work, handy to have in the tent and worn in a holster while walking; the shotgun was invaluable; we could shoot to eat. The rifle was old; any shot over distance was highly inaccurate as the bullet would almost plop out of the barrel and fall to the ground. The gas pistol was most useful if we wanted to ward off violent human beings who we didn't want to permanently damage. And should we get lost in the extensive *miombo* woodland (our compasses having failed), flares, since there was no one around to spot them, would prove useless. They were discarded.

According to the police, who were issuing our firearms certificates, we now merely needed a short note from our British High Commission stating our names, that we were a British expedition and required firearms' certificates.

The BHC, however, gave letters to Christine and Andy but inexplicably not to me.

'Were you imprisoned in England?' the police inspector asked. After much discussion he concluded, 'We just don't understand you people. Your commission hardly offers any assistance to the British here . . .'

Drowning our sorrows by the hotel's unrefreshing swimming pool, we were approached by one of the BHC staff. 'Oh, my dears,' she said, 'I'm so sorry. I know why they won't give you a third letter and I think they're wrong... You see, they don't know that you're married. They think Andy and Christine are together and that you and Christine will have a wild affair in the bush, Andy will intervene and you being a passionate foreigner armed with a gun will shoot him.'

I was stunned listening to this projected, twisted

melodrama of my life. I immediately phoned the BHC from Reception and kept my message short: 'My name is George Tardios. I feel I should let you know that Christine and I have been married for fifteen years.'

Within ten minutes I received a call telling me to go and collect my letter.

Fulfilling our agreement with Sokoine we travelled towards cool-weather Arusha to learn Kiswahili at the Danish Volunteer Training Centre. There were more than 120 tribes in Tanzania with their own tribal languages, and one of the notable achievements of President Julius Nyerere had been that he managed to unite them together with this one language, Kiswahili, which he decreed a national language. This was to our advantage. Unlike Stanley who had to rely on inadequate interpreters and mere gestures, we learnt basic Kiswahili over three weeks there. All of us became quite proficient as it was not a difficult language to learn.

Mweka Wildlife College was down the road in Moshi, situated in the foothills of Mount Kilimanjaro. At Mweka Christine proved to be a markswoman. She did not possess and so did not depend on over-large shoulder muscles, whereas we men unconsciously flexed our muscles when shooting and occasionally went 'off target'. But more than that she was a woman, and I had noticed at the Lake District College that females had more survival sense and stamina than men.

We voluntarily agreed to keep notes and compile reports for various Tanzanian institutions on our journey: the exact location of Kisabengo's lost city of Morogoro, which Stanley named Simbamweni (for the University of Dar es

Salaam); changes in ecology, crops grown and reasons why fishermen were not catching more fish on Lake Tanganyika (for the Ministry of Agriculture); location of any genetic mutants seen, poaching trails and caches of buried elephant tusks (for the Game Department); plus successful *Ujamaa* villages (for the Prime Minister's Office). We agreed to do this readily, little realising at this stage that the work would prove to be onerous.

We were rescued from the miserable Lutheran Hostel where we had been staying by a Norwegian aid expert we met, so didn't experience the failed plumbing, lack of toilet rolls and air conditioning in the atrociously expensive Kilimanjaro Hotel.

Andy had the bright idea now we had to purchase donkeys that we should be seeking sponsorship from the aid agencies. Without success, that is, until we met smiling Olaf from NORAD who listened attentively to our pleas, laughed genuinely at all our jokes and offered us shared accommodation with his family in his house by the sea.

Olaf and his wife Marit wanted to accompany Christine and myself to Bagamoyo where we hoped to meet the Holy Ghost Father at the famous mission and check out the donkey situation. I explained to Olaf that we had to take our own guns and also ask for an armed police escort from the sinister old Arab Fort just before the large Arab village. For Bagamoyo was filled with crooks fleeing capture in Dar es Salaam. They had all come together like the 'Hole-in-the-Wall Gang' to prey on hapless visitors. They sat in coconut trees and signalled to each other with whistles.

Arriving at the forbidding old Arab Fort looking like a stage set from the *Count of Monte Cristo* and a large warning sign in English requesting people to ask for an armed police escort, we were surprisingly shown upstairs to the police inspector's room.

He immediately left his desk and paced the room like a lion. 'When we have prisoners we know how to treat them.' He demonstrated strangulation bent low to the ground. 'You must kill them. It is the only way.' Changing tack he began to berate colonialists. 'We Africans do not have it easy like the colonialist whites! But we know what to do. Oh, yes.' He ran up and down in a frenzy in front of his large desk, his hands manipulating tortuous shapes in the air.

We left without a police escort.

Near the mission's coconut plantations the whistles began. On foot we peered high into the palm fronds but saw no one. Trudging on, Christine nudged me. I stopped and looked behind. Four men were closely following us. We continued. More men joined them.

I took my revolver out of its holster and handed Olaf the gas pistol. 'You will have to shoot if they attempt anything.'

Olaf – tight, white-faced – refused to take the pistol. All the time we were moving forward on the track in a single line.

'Olaf, they will cut us to pieces and rape our wives if we do nothing.'

Still Olaf refused. 'I cannot, George.'

Exasperated I handed the pistol to Christine who willingly took it. Marit was trembling. There was a wire-fenced electricity compound ahead of us with a Kalashnikov-armed guard. I asked him to open the padlock. He did nothing. The group behind us was only twenty feet away approaching stiffly toward us like zombies. I pointed my revolver at the guard and pulled back the hammer. He opened and we rushed in.

'Close it!' I ordered.

The large gang outside the compound fingered the fence and smiled at us menacingly.

'You are a warrior, George,' Marit whispered. If she only knew how my knees were knocking.

The guard surprisingly had a phone in his hut. I phoned the mission. Father Frits (the *only* Father) drove over to collect us. The group of crooks dispersed when they saw him.

'This is always happening,' Father Frits said. 'Why did you not get a police escort?'

4
From Zanzibar to Bagamoyo

When Zanzibar was an uninhabited tropical island fishermen sailed there from the mainland during certain seasons, taking advantage of the deep water. They took food and fruit and spent several days on the island. The seeds they left behind speedily germinated and on returning, amazed at this fruitfulness, they exclaimed, '*Mungu umejaa.*' ('God, you have filled this place with your overflowing presence.') This was later shortened to *Unguja*, and elders still know Zanzibar by this name. *Zanguebar* was an overall name in the first century AD – *Zangh* or *Zenj* meaning Negro, and *bar* (coast).

Stanley's 1871 Zanzibar was a pleasing active island: 'Crooked narrow lanes, white-washed houses, mortar plastered streets... alcoves on each side with deep recesses, with a foreground of red-turbaned Banyans, and a background of flimsy cottons, prints, calicoes... floors crowded with ivory tusks; dark corners with a pile of unginned and loose cotton; stores of crockery, nails, cheap ware, tools...'

Stanley described seeing Bishop Tozer, head of the Universities Mission to Central Africa, in the street haggling at a tinker's stall dressed in crimson robes of office and the 'queerest' headdress. The inception of this mission was in response to a dramatic appeal Livingstone made at Cambridge University in 1857. He invited Oxford and Cambridge to plant a mission in Central Africa. 'I go back to Africa,' he said, 'to try and make an open path for commerce and Christianity. Do you carry out the work which I have begun? I leave it with you.'

Bishop Tozer and his successor, Bishop Steere, therefore began this work in Zanzibar in 1864. Later the Cathedral Church of Christ was intentionally built by Bishop Steere on the site of the last great slave market at Mkunazini in 1873, the year in which the slave market was legally closed. The altar stands where the whipping post existed. On a pillar above the pulpit there hangs a crucifix made of wood taken from the tree at Chitambo, Zambia, under which Livingstone's heart was buried on his death in 1873.

Throughout this period American, German, French and English vessels arrived bringing cotton cloth, brandy, gunpowder, muskets, beads, brass wire and chinaware – the currency of the time – and left taking back to their own countries ivory, gum copal, cloves, hides, cowries, sesame, pepper and coconut oil. Slave labour on Zanzibar and Pemba islands produced ninety-five per cent of the world's cloves, and Stanley estimated the value of exports from Zanzibar at $3 million.

With the exception of a few wealthy Arabs, traders were dependent upon loans from the Banyans (Indians) in order to travel into the interior for ivory and slaves. The Banyans and Mohammedan Hindus, together with the Arabs, represented the upper and middle classes owning the large estates and trading ships. The Africans on the island comprised Waswahili, Somali, Comorines and Wanyamwezi, probably numbering two-thirds of the entire population and providing the labour force either as slaves or free-men. They worked on plantations, or on estates and gardens of the landed proprietors, or performed the work of *hamals* (carriers/porters). The Africans lived not in Stone Town but in the area known as *ngambo* (the other side), referring to the other side of the swampy creek which seeped south and ended just 250 yards short of the sea.

Zanzibar lost its independence in 1890 and became a British Protectorate. The swamp was reclaimed, roads were built, a museum, post office, golf course, government hospital, power station and cable and wireless established; a new bridge and wharf completed. Across the creek in *ngambo*, new roads and drainage were constructed and local huts replaced by houses with cement pillars and coral in the traditional style. The British returned ownership to the Sultan of Zanzibar in December 1963 and one month later the Sultan was deposed in a three-hour bloodbath of a revolution. Zanzibar was declared a republic under a Mswahili, Sheikh Abeid Karume. On 29 October 1964 Zanzibar and Tanzania were declared the United Republic of Tanzania. Although Stanley would still recognise the old Stone Town, there had definitely been changes, transfer of ownership being the most prominent. For instance, since the 1964 revolution, squatters have understandably taken over the solid coral-built houses previously occupied by Omani Arabs in Stone Town.

Whereas Stanley in 1871 sailed from Bombay, India, via Mauritius and the Seychelles to Zanzibar, we flew there for free on Air Tanzania from Dar es Salaam to the island.

It was much easier. And from Zanzibar, we would take a dhow along the coast to Bagamoyo itself – our true starting point for the expedition!

We arrived on 16 January 1984, ten days later in the new year than Stanley in 1871, and immediately entered Zanzibar's oppressive heat-cloud, more sultry and clinging than the mainland coast. The colour and energy which so characterised Zanzibar had gone, replaced by mouldering buildings, vast expanses of rusted corrugated-iron roofs, empty shops and streets.

The few tourist hotels were abysmal. Unlike Stanley's residence – he had been sheltered by the American Consul – our hotel was a microcosm of Zanzibar: ancient and decrepit. Outside were impressive thick double wood doors studded with gleaming brass spikes to keep off attacking elephants, and just inside past a morose caretaker were carved wooden chests overlaid with patterned brass. Any further, however, and the illusion of grandeur faded. The grubby walls and tipsy floors became apparent, dusty threadbare carpets and multiple flimsily partitioned rooms. Frequency of water supply and friendliness of staff were never certain. And although extortionately priced there was rarely fresh food, cold beer or soft drinks, but the rats that nibbled our clothes and nightly stamped hysterical paso dobles in corners of our room were in plentiful supply.

The hotel staff sulked unpleasantly. Guests were not allowed to telephone after 9pm for no good reason, deliberately misinformed as often as possible, and locked out of the dining room when two minutes late for breakfast. The food was *repulsive*. Potatoes were uncooked, all meat was bleeding and served cold. The soup, in whatever variety of flavour, was always comprised of flour and water plus raw onion or particles of green. The chef's fervid imagination once created 'coconut soup'. Just plain flour and water!

We spent days plodding determinedly through alleyways, past dilapidated Arab-built buildings with rotting carved doors and tarnished elephant studs, hiding away from the battering sun amongst our own short shadows. *Madafu* (coconut milk) bought from street carts fuelled our energies.

All sailing vessels formerly had their anchorage at what was once known as 'Oswald's Corner' at the bottom of the main road, opposite what was then the British Consulate. Stanley's American whaling boat would have anchored a distance of possibly 700 yards offshore, and Stanley would have been rowed into the sandy shore to be greeted by Captain Webb and led to the American Consulate and residence, from where he called on Dr John Kirk, the acting British Consul and Political Officer. It was here where Livingstone's body was eventually brought from Zambia for identification.

Of his visits Stanley wrote, 'Dr Kirk very kindly promised to give all the assistance in his power, and whatever experience he possessed he was willing, he said, to give me its full benefit. But I cannot recollect, neither do I find a trace of it in my journal, that he assisted me in any way.' In conversation Stanley found that Kirk was not very forthcoming about Livingstone and his whereabouts and seemed to treat the subject casually, almost flippantly. 'He may be dead… nobody has heard anything definite for over two years. I should fancy, though, he must be alive. We are continually sending something up for him. There is a small expedition even now at Bagamoyo (on the mainland) about starting shortly. I really think the old man should come home now...'

Zanzibar appeared to us as a small ramshackle town pressing claustrophobically in on itself. In Stone Town, the shops were empty, lacking even the most essential goods. The overall flavour was neither Arab, Indian nor African – merely sordid. In vain we searched for a romantic, adventurous, mysterious past and attempted to sniff cloves and cinnamon on the air only to be assailed by the insanitary smells of sewage. The neglect was obvious, and it was deliberate policy to allow historical buildings to collapse into oblivion. They were relics of a slave and colonial past.

We were glad when it was time to leave this isle. Like Kenya it was making us extremely irritable, intolerant and even, horrifyingly, a mite racist. We eventually clambered onto our dhow, which sat surprisingly low in the water, and lay back on *makuti* (coconut leaves) in the shade of a large patched sail as the sailors scrambled to load much unexpected baggage and flour and to hoist the sails. We pushed off using a recently sunken dhow as leverage. A few punts with poles and we were out of the shallows. We passed another small sunken dhow and another and another.

As we moved further away I was relieved to feel the oppression lower.

We quickly skimmed out of the small harbour past the breakwater and were facing the small white beach on the far right where Stanley docked offshore when he first arrived on 6 January 1871. Zanzibar had shrunk to a clean horizontal line.

I asked our captain why there were so many sunken dhows. 'Heavy loads,' he said. 'Greed!' Then he opened the hanging makuti covering hiding the hold for twenty more paying passengers to emerge. Among them a leper woman missing both hands, a sobbing child clinging to her back. '*Lala salaama* (Peaceful sleep),' he whispered to distract us as gentle waves raised and lowered our small dhow like a creaking seesaw.

Stanley needed not one but four large dhows to transport all his goods to mainland Bagamoyo: 'Into one were lifted the two horses, into two others the donkeys, into the fourth the largest, the black escort, and bulky moneys of the Expedition.' Having already arranged to split his caravan into five, they anchored at Bagamoyo: '… on the top of the coral reef plainly visible a few feet above the surface of the water, within a hundred yards of the beach'.

Six hours later, still safe but suffering cramps from sitting rigidly among so many bodies, we were in good sight of the African mainland and closing fast. Just as we approached and the buildings of Bagamoyo became clear, visibility was suddenly lost. The African sun dropped like a heavy coin at 7pm. We balanced the waves unable to approach closer in darkness and at high tide. The dhow could smash aground.

No other boats were available, so the captain said there was no other option but to swim ashore. We refused, suspicious. How deep was it? The captain grabbed one of his crew and slung him over the side. The water fortunately was only neck deep. The crewman laughing with relief offered to carry Christine over on his shoulders. She went first to stand guard over our rucksacks when we could get them off in relays. Giggles and shouts of encouragement arose from unseen people on land. Andy and I stripped to underpants and plunged into the soupy water. We carried our gear over our heads to Christine and piled it up on the slipway, on which long ago slaves were led into dhows bound for sale in Zanzibar. A further mile south was the present Old Arab fort and police station in which the slaves were kept in the depths of the fort and led through a dark underground passage directly onto the beach and into dhows at low tide, to prevent panic from their seeing the vast waters for the first time. As we were now totally wet, we decided to assist the crew in unloading the dhow. I carried the leper's child holding it above my head while it looked down at my just visible white face not sure how to react.

The slipway became crowded with dark figures as Andy and I shared a towel on the sand. Suddenly a dark-blue-suited figure stepped forward looming out of the black:, 'Are you Graham?' Andy peered up. The spotlight was blinding. Then a barrage of Kiswahili which we managed to follow: 'I am Mr Ndonde, the District Commissioner. We have come to welcome you to Bagamoyo.' We blanched even whiter. My underpants were black, but Andy's were now a soggy see-through white. I quickly whipped on my sandy trousers and handed Andy the protective towel. We stepped barefoot onto the slipway. Immediately disembodied hand after hand was thrust out of the darkness for us to shake. 'The CCM Party Head . . . Head of CID . . . the District Development Officer . . . etc., etc.'

Father Frits then stepped forward. He had been the only Holy Ghost missionary in Bagamoyo for thirty-five years. A down-to-earth, straight-speaking person, born in Holland, he was unassuming and dedicated, daily preached in the church and single-handedly ran the mission and excellent Bagamoyo Museum he had created. He had arranged for us to stay at the mission.

He nodded his head and grinned broadly. 'I told them… I told them you would not be expecting this…'

We were in the empty Sisters' House next door to the Bagamoyo Museum. We dumped our rucksacks in our rooms and thanked our escorts. Inspector Katuga of the CID, before leaving, smilingly commented, 'Don't be surprised if you see men around the place. They are protecting you and your things.'

Father Frits waved us over to his small house and supper. Rolls, butter, homemade jam, salami, homemade yoghurt, real coffee and cream. To us these were luxuries. We in turn presented him with a gift of vodka.

'Wonderful!' he said. 'People usually bring me rosaries.'

The father found the whole enterprise enormously amusing, especially the fact that we had four armed militia guarding us at night. 'I told them when you leave they should stay on to protect me.' A refreshing shower and a cold beer sent us to bed with a final comment from Father Frits: 'It is not yet over. There are celebrations being planned…'

We were happy to be back on the mainland. It was true what the Zanzibaris claimed: 'Zanzibar is *not* Tanzania.'

We arrived in Bagamoyo on 6 February 1984, the same day and month as Stanley, only we were 113 years later. In his account Stanley definitely notes that he left Zanzibar just before noon on 5 February and that his dhow crossing took ten hours (we beat him by four hours). Probably it was well past midnight by the time Stanley's group strode over the reef at low tide and unloaded all his staff and goods. The following morning Stanley returned to his camp to find that two donkeys and a coil of thick wire were missing.

Originally, Bagamoyo was joyfully named *Bwagamoyo* (Lift up your heart). But when the slave trade was underway, the trafficked people – after an arduous and sometimes mortal journey, approaching for the very first time the terrifying vast expanse of waving water on which they were to travel – exclaimed in distress, 'Here I lay down my heart.'

The name was retained as Bagamoyo (Lay down your heart; or, Crush your heart).

Though entailing a much longer journey, Bagamoyo rather than Mombasa was the preferred entry route into the interior for Europeans, for directly behind Mombasa lay a waterless 2,500 square miles of impenetrable scrub and thorn bush with lions, mosquito and tsetse fly. The most formidable obstacles then were the warlike marauding Maasai tribe who decimated caravans. Few Arab/Swahili traders braved the journey.

In Stanley's time, during a good season in a single week, seven, eight, ten thousand strangers arrived in Bagamoyo with caravans. Apart from slaves, sometimes a caravan of 2,000 porters would proudly bring in 70,000 pounds of elephant tusks.

*

PART TWO – GOING DOWN: FROM CAIRO TO BAGAMOYO

Kiswahili song of the caravan porters (travelling from Ujiji, Lake Tanganyika, to Bagamoyo):

Be happy, my soul, let go all worries
Soon the place of your yearnings is reached
The town of palms – Bagamoyo.

Far away, how was my heart aching
When I was thinking of you, you pearl,
You place of happiness, Bagamoyo...

Oh, what delight to see the ngomas
Where the lovely girls are swaying in dance
At night in Bagamoyo.

Be quiet, my hearts, all worries are gone
The drum beats and with rejoicing
We are reaching Bagamoyo.

*

Bagamoyo was riddled with countless spacious rectangular, mud-built huts, small lanes criss-crossing between them created with absolute contempt for straight lines and right angles. As a bustling Zanzibar must long ago have been, there were artistic ironwork window screens and brass-studded carved doors and door frames – all extremely exotic. Senses were assailed by drying fish from the fish market, straw mats strewn outside houses, burning incense, essence of cloves, rancid butter and coconut oil, rose water.

We woke in the Sisters' House, externally well protected,

although our *askaris* (guards) were in danger of killing us off from lack of sleep as they sat under our open window and talked incessantly all night. Also, on rising from a damp sheet-twisted bed I was hit by a fist of nausea. I spent the whole night sweating. The room staggered drunkenly, bending like plastic. I stumbled a few steps like a geriatric. My vision wouldn't hold still. I collapsed back onto the bed. I knew what this was – malaria! I had been bitten severely in Zanzibar by mosquitoes and the bites had been irritating me for over a week. I prayed that my system would fight off the illness as this was not the time for a malaria attack. I spent another two hours sleeping, then awoke feeling better and was able with Christine and Andy's support to walk to Mantep College, a teacher training institute just beside the mission where the principal had kindly arranged for us to have our meals.

In the afternoon, surrounded by the shade of huge green mango trees, frangipani, baobab, orange and lemon, custard apple and palm, we relaxed among peaceful bird sounds and distant wood chopping, with a faint buzz of schoolchildren rhythmically chanting today's rote lesson – '*Leo – tutakula – ugali – na – dagaa*' ('Today – we will eat – *ugali* – and small dried fish'). The church bells' lazy clamour lifted the sleepy air… Abruptly a great commotion broke out at nearby Mantep College, alarm bells jangling, people shouting. A mass search was in progress. There had been a burglary. The burglars were not found, but someone was discovered with a sack of coconuts stolen from the trees in the mission grounds.

Father Frits reported: 'Before, Bagamoyo was peaceful and beautiful. The houses were whitewashed once a year, the roads kept clean and repaired. The grounds in front of the Government Administration building were one vast garden of flowers. There was a tennis court. One Goan ran the post office; now there are four people and it doesn't work so well.'

The German Government, whose administrative centre Bagamoyo once was, had twice volunteered finance to build a proper modern road from Dar es Salaam to Bagamoyo. A fat report funded by UNESCO had also been compiled on Bagamoyo and its conservation as a historical town, but little had happened since 1980.

'Seven, eight years ago, there was absolutely no stealing,' Father Frits continued. 'Then it began and increased so fast… Now you cannot go down to the beach as you will most certainly be robbed. People blame many things – the shortages, the Ugandan war, the colonialists exploiting them – but it is none of these. Perhaps, people don't care anymore.'

The Uganda–Tanzania War (usually referred to in Uganda as the 'Liberation War') was fought between these two countries in 1978–79 and led to the overthrow of Idi Amin's regime. Tanzanian forces captured Kampala, and Idi Amin fled first to Libya and later to Saudi Arabia.

I have no religious beliefs, but Father Frits stood out for me as a truly honourable man. He harboured no illusions about Africa, however. 'I dare not put out many other objects I have locked away in the museum. They will be stolen. Like the slave certificates and coins that are being openly sold to tourists in the marketplace.'

Idi of the yellow teeth and crossed eyes claimed to be a freed slave. And readily displayed his deed of freedom – of which he possessed a never-ending supply! These were an exorbitantly priced but unique souvenir for tourists, who were desperate to discover the slave trade's darker excesses. Ignoring the informative museum at the mission, they sounded from their feverish and predictable questions to be searching for instruments of torture:

'The chains, the chains. Where can I find the chains?'

'In the museum there are neck chains,' Father Frits softly answered.

'No, no, the place where the slaves were chained?'

'There is no place where they were chained.'

'But we were told in town . . .'

By the seashore tourists are shown triangular stone blocks with vertical metal protuberances to which the slaves are said to have been chained, which if it were true would mean the time-travelling slaves would have been affixed to the foundations of a German warehouse. In the Customs House they are guided to the exact spot where slaves are supposed to have been herded together to be auctioned, though there was never a slave market in Bagamoyo and the original Arab Custom House was long ago moved to Saadani. The present building through which tourists sleepwalked with the fanatic gleam of ancient discovery was built in 1895 by the German Administration.

The truth is that Bagamoyo, apart from having been the gateway into the interior, only has a few existing slave sites: the caravanserai – a quadrangular inn; its simple port – the most accessible sea route to the island of Zanzibar; the slipway from where slaves were shipped to Zanzibar by dhows; a shrine to freed slaves at the mission; and outside the environs of Bagamoyo, allegedly all the way to Ujiji and Lake Tanganyika, clumps of mango trees where slaves supposedly dropped mango pips on their forced march toward Bagamoyo.

Father Frits visited Holland every four years relieving parish priests who took leave. 'I tell the congregation there about Africa. How hospital patients lie in unprotected beds with mosquitoes biting them so they contract malaria. The congregations donate generously. But when I arrive here with bundles of second-hand clothes and excellent mosquito nets I realise once again how deluded I have become back in Holland. In the hospital here in Bagamoyo they readily steal the drugs, even the wash basins. So the second-hand clothes would be sold down the road for a large profit, the mosquito nets would be taken home by the doctors. You know, here the health service is meant to be free, but if you require an operation or hospital attention, the doctor holds out his hand and says, "Pay me", the anaesthetist asks for beer money, and so on . . . Ah, you have to do what you think works best.'

'But Father Frits, you said you've had these mosquito nets for five years. What are you waiting for?' asked Christine.

'I'm waiting for one good man, Christine. One good man . . .'

The Holy Ghost Fathers were the first missionaries in Tanzania. With a nucleus of freed slaves they founded the first mission station in Bagamoyo in 1868 (the first in East Africa). Staffed by ten fathers and ten sisters, they purchased slaves from the Arab traders. Setting them free, as well as clothing and housing them, the missionaries trained them to be gardeners, tailors, bricklayers, farmers, printers, carpenters and metalworkers.

Stanley had been impressed: 'They not only endeavour to instil . . . the principles of religion, but also to educate them in the business of life.'

By this time of course the slaves had also been heavily indoctrinated with Catholicism. All should have been well. But as Father Frits related, they very soon after reverted to their own culture and wanted more than one wife. So they became Muslims.

Germany had been a dominant presence in this part of Africa for some years. In 1884 Karl Peters founded the Society for German Colonisation (*Gesellschaft für Deutsche Kolonisation*) and later in the same year marched inland and made twelve treaties with local chiefs who conceded their land to the society. The following year Germany declared the areas that the treaties covered to be under German control. More treaties followed and by 1888 Sultan Khalifa of Zanzibar, who controlled and administered the mainland, leased this ten-mile-deep coastal strip to the Germans, and in Bagamoyo the Germans felled the Sultan's flagstaff. From the outset the locals – particularly the Arabs – began to revolt, but any resistance was fiercely put down within the year, their leader hanged.

With such a strong German interest in East Africa it was inevitable the area should be drawn into World War I, later inspiring such Hollywood films as the classic *The African Queen*. The Germans in Bagamoyo had fortified the town against a British attack, while the mission – harbouring over 2,000 townspeople – flew a flag of neutrality. But British troops did eventually land, and the administration of the conquered areas was taken over by Britain in 1916.

PART TWO – GOING DOWN: FROM CAIRO TO BAGAMOYO

*

The Cultural Officer of Bagamoyo arrived on a motor scooter and handed us a typed programme of events to be performed in our honour commencing in one hour! Why did he not tell us well in advance so we could have time to get ready? He said, 'I was absent and my assistants prepared this… Tanzania… Tanzania…'

We embarked on a feverish rush to find an antique solid-cast iron heated with charcoal to press our shirts, trousers and Christine's blouse.

'Do you have these in England?' Father Frits's cook asked in Kiswahili.

'Perhaps in a museum,' he chortled.

Father Frits was bustling about, tongue in cheek asking, 'Have you got your tie on? What! You don't have a tie? Stanley had a tie. You must do it the same way.'

The father stated we would set the historical records straight. Then he winked, already tickled by the local newspaper accounts he had been diligently following which one day stated we were following the footsteps of Stanley and the next the footsteps of Livingstone. That we were historians, Stanley was a missionary and that we would discover the truth about how these two figures had exploited Africa.

A young plain-clothes police officer armed with a tightly folded newspaper insisted on escorting us to the old German *boma* set up as administrative quarters when Bagamoyo was the capital of German East Africa. This was where the entertainments would take place. 'There are many thieves,' he said. Groggy from illness and tetracycline capsules (not the cure for malaria, but all I had been given at the hospital), I explained that we were embarrassed at being given more protection than the Queen of England. We didn't think it necessary. We could look after ourselves…

'No, no, you must be escorted. We have had notification from the PM's Office and we want to look after you in the best way we can. We want you to feel completely safe and welcome.' He had an automatic pistol hidden away in the newspaper.

Under the shade of a huge mango tree a seated delegation of district officials awaited us. Musicians and strange instruments were grouped at the side with palm trees and frangipani bushes curving behind them down to the sea. A small dhow sat stock still on the surface. An audience of locals dressed in their best looked on as we shook hands with the officials. The local MP spoke and kept calling our proposed donkeys 'camels'. The District Commissioner, sweating in a tight suit and waistcoat, gave a long and dramatic speech describing our journey and the importance of it to Tanzania.

The audience turned to study us when they heard we were to walk all the way; to encounter wild animals; cook in the bush and eat *ugali*.

We sat stiffly not really knowing how we should respond. A young girl approached and sang a poem she had written welcoming us to Bagamoyo. The girl handed the poem to me and withdrew. The entertainments began: traditional dancing and music by the National Institute of Bagamoyo created to preserve and foster these African arts. Singers trooped on to sway and sing rhythmically before us. The instruments were ones I had not seen before:

wooden glockenspiels, crude mandolin-shaped one-string instruments with curved wooden bows, soundboards whose metal tongues were flicked, flat shakers and a harp-looking instrument which provided plucked bass notes. There were no drums! The repetitive ebb and flow of music had a tranquilising effect and the wailing vocal laments made the hair stand on end. An original sound, which I'm sure would be well received in Europe. If only I could have recorded it… A young acrobatic team, the youngest being seven years of age, created pyramids and various spectacles of engineering – human fulcrums and balances. They had only been practising a year! Their trainer had spent time in China and Korea on a scholarship.

Afterwards, the father on our behalf had arranged that Abudu, a donkey seller, would have four donkeys ready and waiting for us. We walked to his rectangular, corrugated-roof house. Abudu was reclining on straw matting sewing donkey cushions, dressed in a white smock and wearing a crochet Muslim cap. He grinned, revealing prominent rabbit teeth. After the customary handshake, extended greetings and enquiries after health, house and family (Abudu had a stomach problem), he picked up his donkey stick and brought out from a nearby shed three males and one female donkey.

'You want to buy donkeys?' he began repeating.
'Yes,' we dutifully replied.
'And you don't want to ride them?'
'No, we don't want to ride them.'
'But you want to buy donkeys?'
We nodded wearily.
A reflective pause. A time to think of a price. A

scratching of figures in the dust, and tapping his donkey stick in time to, 'You want to buy...'

We stopped him and emphatically declared, 'We don't want the female. She will be in heat every twenty-one days for twenty-four hours, and we will have to struggle with the males to get them off her. But we do want four donkeys. Just all males.'

He glimmered, opened his mouth, snapped it shut and smiled at our knowledge (from donkey manuals). He told us to return in two days. The donkeys were to be paid for in Tanzanian shillings. Five thousand each. An extortionate price, as he well knew, but he said he would throw in some lads to instruct us in giving the donkeys correct orders (making the right sounds etc.). In addition, he would make us four kapok-filled donkey cushions to rest the panniers on, four donkey muzzles made from sacking and for us three wide-brimmed palm-leaf sun hats. We had no option but to agree. Abudu seemed to be a craftsman of straw.

Feeling less wobbly – it couldn't have been malaria (but what?) – and sipping glasses of chilled vodka with Father Frits reclining in an armchair, his feet resting on a cushioned stool, he revealed that he also thought the donkeys too expensive.

'But the local Tanzanian veterinarian was also present,' I explained.

Father Frits wisely nodded his head. 'I'm wondering if the vet is also involved,' he said. 'You never know. You can never trust anyone.'

He had the first editions of all explorers' accounts in his library, annotated with comments from missionaries at the time. He was a mine of information: 'The fathers were greatly annoyed with Stanley's account of his dinner here. He called them Jesuits and he made it seem as if every day the fathers wined and dined in great style. Yet they had painstakingly prepared a special meal for him and together drank a bottle of champagne given to them by the French Consul which they'd saved for a special occasion.'

Volunteering to assist Father Frits with some maintenance, Andy and I climbed the precipitous sixty-foot-tall bosun's ladder up to 'Livingstone's Tower' (originally part of the mission's church) and onto a small roof, squelching through black mud and rotting mangoes in order to clean out muck from the water storage tank and repair its cover. The tower was so called because Livingstone's mummified body was placed temporarily inside by his loyal servants, who had carried him all the way from Zambia. He was later transported to Zanzibar and finally to Westminster Abbey where he is buried.

We finished the work just in time as bees began to attack. Climbing down the rickety bosun's ladder I suddenly experienced illogical panic and froze to the rungs, gripping hard. I could not move. Andy, realising what was happening, guided me very carefully by being below me and positioning my feet one by one onto the metal rungs – 'Slowly, mate, slowly…'

I was so very grateful. My nerve for heights had completely vanished. And I could only put this down to an abortive parachute jump in the Lake District. Andy and I had been flown up into the skies by a small aircraft. When I jumped, my main parachute failed to properly open: it had released but had flowed out like a Roman candle, its strings twisted and bunched behind my neck. Finally, with a sudden jerk, it had fully opened. 'Oh, thank you, God. Thank you,' I cried out.

We woke Abudu from off the straw matting outside his house, having come to collect our four paid-for and promised donkeys. Abudu wiped his bleary eyes and collected his wits. He brought out the donkeys, but one appeared very old, fluid oozing from its ears. It was clear this was not one of the ones we had originally seen. Abudu insisted it was. We explained to him in Kiswahili that we would possibly have to report this to CCM – *Chama Cha Mapinduzi* (the Party of the Revolution, the political arm of Tanzania, local offices in every village). A local bystander said, 'This is like a dinner with everything ready. The guests arrive and at that moment a cockroach runs through the food.'

Abudu grudgingly walked the old donkey back into the shed and brought out another. This one seemed absolutely wild. He butted, bucked and reared, kicking at anything that moved, Abudu weaving successfully but only just out of its way. We confessed we didn't think we could handle this donkey. Either he was going to kill one of us or inadvertently himself. We could not even approach him; how would we tether his leg at night? Then as if a kerosene lamp had lit up in his brain Abudu told us he had another donkey but wanted an extra 1,000 shillings. No way! Grim and worn into unfriendliness, Abudu produced a broad, strong and quiet donkey. I jumped onto his back and he unconcernedly chewed on. Perfect.

Having chosen, we very slowly walked the four donkeys to the mission. Father Frits met us in the gardens and immediately proceeded to name the donkeys, muttering in Latin and sprinkling holy water over them. 'Shhh... I am baptising them,' he said. 'This old serious-looking split-eared one with a dent in its back where it has most probably been beaten in the past shall be Livingstone. This stocky, faithful-looking one with chunks out of its ears, standing beside him head to tail and flicking flies off Livingstone's face is Stanley. This placid, confident donkey (the last, stocky one Abudu had brought out of his shed) will be Burton, and the youngest one, of course, is Speke.'

We were joined by the local MP, curious to discover more about our trek: 'Ah... You ride?'

'No, we will walk. The donkeys will carry the bags.'

'And how will you feed your camels?'

I looked for help from a giggling Father Frits, who had dropped his water container and slipped away.

'And how much will your camels carry?'

Abudu, true to his word, had boys accompany us to teach how to handle the donkeys, though it's more accurate to relate that the donkeys taught us how to handle ourselves. These African donkeys were half wild and highly sensitive, unlike the docile, well-behaved Mediterranean types. Apart from the one named Burton it was impossible to get on their backs. They bucked and reared. We learnt how to load them, tether their hooves, and to make tutting, tongue-clucking sounds to call them and 'Ooosh...' to stop them. We began to see their personalities emerge. Whereas Livingstone originally led the line of donkeys, Burton had now barged himself forward and taken the lead role, bullying anyone who approached the front. Livingstone with good grace had fallen to the rear. We felt the other donkeys disliked Burton. Speke hated him, never losing an opportunity to tease, bite or kick at him.

Livingstone point blank refused to drink from a red bucket, staying aloof. We realised he was wary of anything new and strange. It was either the red he disapproved of or our strange smell on the bucket. When putting on his cushion Andy had looped the slim tie around his belly at the rear and inadvertently whipped his genitals. Livingstone bit the nearest thing – leaving toothmarks on my thigh. From now on the rope would instead be tied behind the buttocks.

Andy seemed to get unduly affected by the sun and became dopey and careless; he was doing everything in slow motion. Here in Bagamoyo one of Stanley's men apparently blew out his right eye after receiving an advance on his wages, so as not to continue the journey.

At the mission I wrote our notes and diary, oiled guns, and Andy sharpened and de-rusted our *pangas* (machetes), sheath knives and axe. If unused, metal rusted within a week on the coast. Christine had been busy assembling goods and medicines we were to take, especially the basics we would need for food: beans, rice, flour, macaroni (there was no spaghetti), mixed herbs, tomato purée, garlic, and some okra we had been given. She was convinced we could purchase plenty of vegetables on the way and was presently experimenting in making bush bread – cooking dough in a saucepan over an open fire.

As we were leaving soon Father Frits informed us there was cholera at Chalinze and Kibaha. They were both quarantine areas and we could possibly need permits to walk through them.

Our personal bodyguard (with his folded newspaper now days old) was intent before we left on showing us the location in the gardens of the mission where Stanley tied his donkey to a chain embedded into a baobab tree.

Father Frits corrected this misconception: 'This was where in the distant past a sister had tied her pet donkey.'

I suffered thoroughly confused visions of Stanley in a nun's habit tethering a pampered donkey to a baobab tree.

PART THREE –

DEPARTURE

In which we discover how unprepared we are for a trek in the African bush

5

Uzaramo: Land of the Tree that Gives Salt

'The *kirangozi* (caravan leader and guide) unrolled the American flag and put himself at the head of the caravan, and the *pagazis* (porters), animals, soldiers and idlers were lined for the March, we bade a long farewell to… the blue ocean, and its open road to home, to the hundreds of dusky spectators who were there to celebrate our departure with repeated salvoes of musketry.'
Henry Morton Stanley, *How I Found Livingstone in Central Africa*, 1872

Time to leave – 21 March 1984

In 1871, within some days of each other, Stanley's five caravans departed Bagamoyo: the first with twenty-four porters and three soldiers; the second with twenty-eight porters, two chiefs and two soldiers; the third with twenty-two porters, ten donkeys, one cook and three soldiers, and a white man – Farquhar – in charge. (Stanley had decided to separate the dependable Farquhar from his other support, Shaw, who to Stanley was humourless and irritating, and '…fully showed the uneducated Anglo-Saxon's inaptitude for travel and intercourse with other races'.) The fourth caravan had fifty-five porters, two chiefs and three soldiers; the fifth and last caravan to depart – with Stanley and Shaw in charge – contained twenty-eight porters, twelve soldiers, one tailor, one cook, one interpreter, one gun-bearer, seventeen donkeys, two horses, one dog and two dismantled boats to carry twenty-six people. Shaw rode on a donkey, Stanley on a horse.

Lacking Stanley's advantages and heavy-laden with trepidation, we could not fire joyful salvoes into a cloudless sky. We moved silently, only concerned with last-minute preparations, for once the trek began we knew it would be impossible to recoup goods that had been forgotten. It was crucial that everything had to be right before we left.

The four donkeys had all been injected against sleeping sickness the day before, but already their panniers looked unwieldy, too heavy, and the donkeys themselves – Livingstone, Stanley, Burton and Speke – were not looking or feeling their best: we thought they were suffering ill effects from the sleeping sickness drug.

Officials in their best suits had decided to escort us for two miles to Daraja ya Kofia (the Bridge of Hats – named because of its stone hat-like crenellations) where Abudu of the rabbit teeth and the vet would be waiting. After a group photo taken in dripping sun with twenty besuited officials at Livingstone's Tower, we set off 10.45am at a good speed toward the old stone-built German blockhouse, a defensive structure erected by the German rulers to guard the dusty crossroads during the uprisings against their rule by Bushiri bin Salim; Bushiri had displayed his contempt for this by cutting off the hands of the African mason, Fundi Dundir, who had worked on the construction of the blockhouse. Inside, there was room for only two snipers. From here, our perspiring procession was drawn hypnotically into the long road leading to the interior.

We finally felt light-hearted that we were properly undertaking our expedition!

*

The first part of our journey led us through the lands of the Wazaramo – the people of the tree that gives salt. Long ago people from the Nguru Mountains journeyed to the coast to fish and, more importantly, to pan for sea salt with which they could then preserve their catch. Panning salt was a laborious task, however, involving the digging of a channel for seawater to enter shallow troughs. The water then evaporated in the sun and left behind crusted salt crystals. Another method was to boil and evaporate the water over a wood fire. But the salt retained impurities. Then they discovered that a certain tree – named *Zarama* – possessed leaves which when pounded and squeezed yielded a clear salt liquid. In the sun it would dry to pure crystals. This tree grew only near coastal areas, and so these people had decided to settle on the coast, close to these priceless trees, thus earning their name.

Father Frits miraculously appeared, having driven up in his car after church, and walked a hot hundred yards with us. 'Don't forget,' he giggled, 'Stanley could not speak Kiswahili and got things wrong. You are correcting history!'

The District Commissioner and Inspector Katuga took everything in their stride – not a drop of sweat. Abudu – regally barefoot at the head of the procession in yellow shorts, new flowered shirt and a gleaming white crochet *kofia* (hat) on his head – set a grand, flamboyant pace. We wondered whether we and the donkeys would be able to match it. And at the *Chemchem* bridge (the spring bridge), Speke fell weakly to the ground for a second time and the other donkeys wilted in sympathy. We struggled to help him up, having to bear the whole weight of the loaded panniers ourselves. Abudu told Andy they needed lots of water after the injection against sleeping sickness, though the vet said it was nothing to do with that. Half a mile further on Speke dropped yet again. We tried desperately to feed them water to flush everything out, but Livingstone, who was the least affected, balked at the new collapsible plastic orange bucket. We were helpless.

We headed on to Daraja ya Kofia, and the bridge over the Sanzale river. The land here was a lush cultivated rice-growing area with scattered thatched settlements squeezed between the two rivers. These rice paddies were what had initially attracted Arab traders to Bagamoyo with their backdrop of palm, mango, orange and lime trees.

At the bridge we stumbled down the bank to collect water and finally (except for Livingstone) got the donkeys to drink, which we hoped would counteract the effects of the powerful drug they had absorbed. We didn't yet realise the effect it would have. Abudu rebalanced the panniers, Mr Ndonde made a speech, also the MP who insisted on referring to our donkeys as camels. I returned a speech of thanks and then they all turned back.

Now we continued alone, thank God, but with two armed game scouts: Issa Amani, a solid-as-a-whetstone, independent fifty-three-year-old who hardly spoke unless directly questioned; and Francis Kaengwa, a younger, mousy, apologetic type. They both had strong instructions not to help, advise or lead us, unless we asked. This was exactly as we wanted it, but the situation didn't last – after all, this was Africa.

It was a relief to have properly begun the journey. We felt free and optimistic, reassured by the fact that the donkeys had not escaped and run back home as we had been warned. The simple act of placing one foot in front of the other clearly meant widening the distance between us and the place we had left, and the simplicity of it now thrilled us. Like all journeys the 'doing', whatever the subsequent problems, always proved to be easier than any planning.

I was later to eat these words…

A line of trees and thick greenery ahead indicated the muddy Ruvu River and ferry crossing; Stanley had called it the 'Kingani River'. Our dusty road led past a ferry shack selling sugar cane, some of which we bought, then straight onto the waiting ferry-boat (a series of logs tied tightly together). We struggled vigorously to push the reluctant donkeys aboard. The twenty-yard water crossing was propelled by Tanzanian figures reclining on their backs on the log floor, their upside-down horny feet pedal-pushing on a steel cable.

It was 3.15pm. We'd only covered six and three-quarter

miles, but the weak state of the donkeys meant we decided to bush-camp under a small shady tree.

A bush camp is an impromptu camp in the bush, away from a village. We collected firewood, unloaded the donkeys and led them back to the river. Temperamental Livingstone refused to drink and backed away from the brown water. We were sure it was unfamiliar colours that Livingstone found fearful.

Or perhaps, in addition, he sensed other wildlife nearby? Many hippos still frequented this river, strolling two to three miles at night to raid the neighbouring cornfields. Last month, we were told at the ferry, a local farmer had been bitten in half. Stanley, apparently, whilst waiting on the banks for his canoe ferryman, had amused himself by peppering the thick hide and foreheads of hippos with, I assume, birdshot. What a different era! We made an unsuccessful attempt to shoot crafty guinea fowl for dinner, but they constantly kept flying away to distant trees.

Christine cooked rice over the wood fire, but attempts to purify the brown water through a Millbank bag produced, it seemed, one drop per hour before it could be boiled to kill off further bacteria and then cooled for drinking. Andy and I sat chewing the sugar cane, which definitely did not quench our thirst! The sweet gloop merely gummed our lips together. We sat in the oven-hot darkness with our late supper of boiled rice, *bamia* (okra) and gallons of muddy tea tasting of fibreglass.

Our first night camping in the African bush!

In the early hours we were woken by much stamping of hooves and loud snorting. Stanley was crawling with biting *siafu* – safari ants – the most formidable insects in Africa. Most of them are blind and led by guides – *kiongozi*. They have no permanent nests because they always devour everything in sight and so are forced to relocate. Every thirty days they pause only to raise their young. The queen lays eggs. The rest forage locally and tend the newborn larvae until they are grown and together they then travel to fresh territory. They sometimes exit temporary nests when it rains, searching for dew, succulent grass shoots or disturbed ground (banging in of donkey stakes, trampled grass) which arouses their curiosity so they will investigate for spilt water, food, or living bodies they can eat. They can completely devour a tethered horse in twenty-four hours, leaving only white bones behind!

We moved Stanley, and Issa burnt several patches of dry grass to drive the ants away from our tents, and we saw their thick black trail finally change direction. 'They can smell you,' he explained, 'and will feed off your flesh.'

We fell into an aching sleep, to be woken again by loud snuffling sounds and a snapping of twigs around the tents. We heard Issa stamp off toward the donkeys, calling in Kiswahili to Francis, 'It's OK. It ran away.' Possibly a serval cat. I unzipped the tent door, but the animal had scampered away before I had a chance to see.

Impossible to sleep. Francis had explained that although we were still close to human habitation there were also lion and hyena present, particularly in Kikoka Forest.

We were woken by Issa talking loudly at 5am and a cackling African saying in showing-off English, 'They must still be in the sleeping. That is the why they have not gone on yet.' This was a new environment, the smell of warmed vegetation and woodsmoke. There was a feeling of languorous freedom, of new beginnings. Andy found his shirt, which he had hung on a tree the night before, had been almost eaten away by minute tree ants. Many prints of buck and the much smaller *dik-dik* (a type of antelope) around our tents. We had to mark time until the first suitable light at 6.15am to pack and load the donkeys.

Andy went for water, I wrote our diary, Christine sorted through the beans; our five kilos, we had discovered, were riddled with maggots. As cook, Christine was ultimately responsible for weight in the double panniers – a general task I did not in the least envy. Whatever was taken out of them or put back in, the weights had to be meticulously equal on either side to prevent them being unbalanced when placed on the donkeys. We only possessed an imprecise, difficult-to-manipulate hand scale and I really didn't know how Christine did it! We were extremely stiff and weak. I felt nauseous and thought it was the Ruvu water. We still had to refer to our maps, work out mileages and water sources and repack the donkeys' panniers.

The ferryman had told Andy we would recognise the turning at Kikoka where we would enter the wilderness – two coconut trees and mango trees growing there, very old cultivation. 'There is nothing more to guide you. The old track is badly overgrown. There are wild animals in the forest. You should not go that way.'

But Issa said he knew the paths and that there would be water at Rosako.

Francis added, 'There's a well, plenty of rice and *bamia*.'

Not again! In the heat, we drank lots more tea. Speke

threw a fit in anger at again having to carry weight and nearly hanged himself on his own halter which was attached to a tree. I shouted ineffectually. Andy, who was closer to Speke, eventually cut through the rope. His reactions were extremely slow though and I wondered whether this would prove a future problem. Big Burton bellowed; we could not ascertain whether in sympathy for Speke's condition, or joyful triumph. We always tethered them far apart from each other.

Speke's recovery and proper repacking of his panniers would force us, however, to stay another night.

A military Land Rover transported Sergeant Robert Ole Mako to the ferry and thereafter to our camp. Robert was a young, slim, attractive Maasai from the Ngorongoro anti-poaching unit, armed with an up-to-date rifle. It had been arranged that he would accompany us all the way to Ujiji, representing Tanzania. Andy was happy to see Robert. He was another pair of hands, and his age, closer to Andy's, meant he would be good company.

Through acacia and *miombo* woodland to the Kikoka Forest, where it was as the ferryman had described – a disused narrow track leading into the thick darkness.

In Stanley's time the entrance to the forest and the interior was via a small settlement he described as: 'a collection of straw huts… a sluice and some wells provide water, which though sweet is not particularly wholesome or appetising owing to the large quantities of decayed matter which is washed into it by the rains, and is then left to corrupt in it'. He had camped at Kikoka before decisively taking the route on which, according to him, 'no white man had previously travelled'.

This point marked the extent of the coastal Wazaramo tribe's territory.

As we took compass bearings Stanley crumpled, then Burton, eventually even Livingstone. No sooner did Andy and I lift one donkey up than the next one dropped to the ground. We needed to get to water. There was a river clearly marked in the forest, but it could be dry. The nearest other water was at Rosako – seven and a half miles away, according to our map calculations. We had no alternative but to get them moving and into the thickets before they had a chance of collapsing again. The sleeping sickness drug was clearly badly affecting them.

Francis repeated there was water at Rosako. Issa said that as a boy he had walked goats to Rosako and thought he would remember the way. He had been more definite earlier…

6

Ukwere: Land of the Millet Stalks

File silently through narrow pannier-splitting openings between trees during the morning, hacking at grasping one-inch- long 'wait a bit' acacia thorns which tear cotton trousers to ribbons and threaten to rip tough canvas panniers. Follow Issa, balancing kitbag on head native-style... Above it all the possibly imagined sizzling sound of multitudinous insects and sticky layers of heat making us and the donkeys desire to lean toward the thick undergrowth and cool dark shadow filled with unknown dangers. Bitten mercilessly by insects. Constantly walk into tightly woven spider's webs, hand-sized yellow spiders patiently waiting near centres...[1]

*

---

[1] Here and throughout passages in italics are from the author's expedition diary.

Thickets forced us to retrace our steps. The slow clopping of donkey hooves, the crackling sound of dried grass crushed under their delicate feet, the swing and clank of our own clunking boots stumbling against roots, rocks and our low panting. The donkeys were visibly groggy, and Burton collapsed, wheezing, then Stanley, followed rapidly by Speke. Continuing without water could kill them.

It was shattering. Even Sergeant Robert, who had spent a year fighting in Uganda, was now completely exhausted. '*Karibu kufa, karibu kufa...*' ('Nearly dead, nearly dead...') he kept muttering.

Hours later dense woodland opened into a glorious vast green parkland teeming with buck, *ngiri* (warthog), *ngurumwitu* (wild pig) and, according to Francis, some *simba* (lion) obviously hiding away. Our clothes were soaked in sweat. Despite wearing Abudu's wide-brimmed straw hats, our faces were beetroot red. But we felt elated to be walking in this untouched land. We arrived at a crossing of tracks, one of which eventually led to a tiny hamlet. It was 6.50pm. A villager, dusty black cloth wrapped around his waist and carrying a *panga*, appeared like an apparition. We shook his large calloused hand, which was crusty and scaly from constantly handling *panga* (machete), *jembe* (hoe) and unsuccessfully washed-away *ugali* (there was no soap).

Both men and women in the African bush, I noticed generally, had thick, rough hands from handling flaming firewood and heated pots – particularly the women, who did most of the work, collecting and carrying wood and buckets of water, and thumping dried corn kernels to powder with tall heavy pestle poles. We wondered whether it was because their hands were so desensitised that they could handle boiling pots straight off the fire, or if their ethnicity led to the development of some different nerve impulses to ourselves. The texture of our skins was certainly different. They were naturally hairless. And if a Tanzanian was cut with a *panga*, they recovered with incredible speed, whereas the same injury could kill us.

In our most fluent Kiswahili we hailed the unkempt villager: 'Greetings, old man. Is that Rosako?' We pointed into the distance.

'No.'

'What, then?'

'Karabaka Kwere, a village of the Wakwere tribe.'

The Wakwere tribe, I knew, were once known as the Mindu, a clan of the Waluguru tribe of Morogoro. Wars between the clans forced the Mindu people to retreat across the Ngerengere River to a fertile area where they grew millet. It became known as Ukwere – Land of the Millet Stalks. A man in their language is still known as *mindu*, and a woman as *mamindu* to remind them of their origins.

I was puzzled though. On my map of the area, the Karabaka area was marked as being a half-mile north of Rosako.

'Where then is Rosako?'

He held his arm out like a sundial, pointing to a sun of his memory, thinking we could interpret his imagined hours. He gave up at our ignorance: 'Very far.' This did not bode well.

'How many miles?'

He paused to think and visualise the route, but mileage,

we later realised, was impossible to gauge. Distance was marked by smokers in cigarettes and for non-smokers in natural landmarks and corrugations of the land, or with the sundial arm. No one, it seemed, travelled further than six miles from their village.

'Three or four,' he guessed.

'South of here?' I tested.

'West...!'

My brain buckled at his erroneous answer. In increasing darkness, racked with confusion and mental exhaustion, I gave up, except to ask if there was water in Karabaka.

'Yes, yes, much water.'

Francis let us know for the first time that no one now lived at Rosako and that there was no water there at all. Nor at Karabaka. But there *was* water at Fukayosi, which according to my map was three miles north of non-existent Rosako. I didn't want to trek an extra hour to Fukayosi, especially when I was no longer sure of the maps and their mileages. Issa said we should head for Karabaka Kwere, which was close to an Ujamaa village with a well (Fukayosi?). Was it far from Rosako? It *was* Rosako! But Rosako had no water? Ah, the name was taken to Karabaka when the inhabitants were moved from Rosako. It was called Karabaka Kwere because the tribe of the area were Wakwere and this distinguished it from the Northern Karabaka Doe where the Wadoe resided. (I didn't know this, but I did know the Wadoe tribe were long reputed to be cannibals as well as rainmakers.) So how far was it from Rosako? Very far! But according to our calculations this was impossible. Issa shrugged. I was completely confused.

In the dark we followed our scouts and the old man

towards the first mud house lit by the glow of an outside wood fire. Locals appeared in various tattered garments and guided us to a suitable place to erect our tents. We painfully unloaded our gear. We could hardly see to light a fire. Francis made clear, with much nodded agreement from locals, that there was definitely no water here in the village or anywhere near. Much heated argument.

The old man volunteered to lead us and the 'muzzled' donkeys to the nearest well, but instead of a straight ten-minute route he illogically took us in a large half-hour circle. We couldn't see them in the dark, but later we found out there were cassava plants all around us. So Andy and I both lost our temper. I should mention here that I was not particularly kind to the Tanzanians at this point. I do understand that they were guarding their scarce water and food – essential for their own survival – from us, and they simply did not know how to time distance as we did, except by describing it in their own way. Tanzanians as far as I am concerned are true *bin adamou* (human beings). I shall always be grateful to them for their guidance and generous hospitality. We were always successfully guided to some sort of water, though we usually had to pay.

At the well (a cave-like gash in the ground), however, there was no water! Francis and Issa, taking two buckets each, now guiltily rushed off to Fukayosi three miles distant. Meantime villagers attempted with a long pole, an old baked bean can attached at the end, to scrape at the gritty well bottom. Slowly trickles of water seeped through at a snail's pace and were scooped up in the can (together with grit) and dropped into our bucket. One bucket took almost half an hour to fill. And it went to the long-suffering donkeys – a bucketful each. With shame, we realised that the village inhabitants' vociferous denials had been an attempt to protect their precious water source.

We lay down at the edge of the gaping well, stickily staring at the swollen stars. Our bodies throbbed painfully. We had been up since 5am and it was now 10pm. Our mouths were gummed and jaws heavy, our bodies were burnt and bitten, almost fevered. We were too tired to speak. The stars vibrated. We could feel their heat inside us. Francis and Issa arrived with full buckets of water having 'run all the way there and back', just as all the donkeys had finished drinking. The buckets would suffice for tea.

On return Christine had tea ready. She had managed to borrow enough precious water from locals. We revived long enough to tether the donkeys, carry the heavy panniers into tents, eat a dish of rice (the only edible food left), drink pots more tea each and fall at 2am into a heavy sleep.

The donkeys dominated our journey. We could not always follow the most direct and simple route. We automatically began to think like donkeys, to imagine ourselves in their place, to detour even if for only three to five yards at two miles per hour. We speedily learnt to choose the most suitable way: no deep holes or crevices that could trap delicate hooves and break bones, no over-steep inclines or declines that would unbalance heavy loads when a flatter way lay nearby. No rapid flowing rivers or noisy energetic streams when a calm ford could be sought for, no gapped narrow planks or holed tree trunks bridging rivers. It was always essential to aim for rivers or villages with plentiful supplies of water.

We also not so quickly unfortunately learnt to depend solely upon ourselves, on our maps and our compass. Asking directions had of necessity to be a rigorous cross-examination. To an African, *karibu* (it is near) can mean a place is anything up to six miles away and *mbali* (it is far) upwards of that.

Stanley had men to lead and care for the donkeys, to put up his tent, find water, cook his food, do the washing. He even had a tailor to repair his clothes. He relied on his interpreters and this, as we were to see, led to much wrong information being obtained. Each travelling day left us drained of energy purely because we had to do everything ourselves. We found we and the donkeys needed sufficient time to rest, which slowed us down.

It was now 24 March. After only three days of fraught travel, giving us a good idea of what we could now expect, the sun boiled us awake in Karabaka. Out of our dome tents we were surprised to find ourselves in the middle of an extensive but sunken cassava patch surrounded by acacia woodland. At three corners of this cultivated patch, spaced 500 yards from each other and our tents, were three squat, grass-thatched mud houses. This was Karabaka! Families dressed in stained and ragged clothes arrived throughout the day from Fukayosi to greet us and sit and stare emptily into space for hours and then suddenly get up and leave. Dusty children wrapped in holed black *merikani* cloth (the same type of American cotton cloth that Stanley traded) with red-tinged hair and swollen stomachs brought *mihogo* (cassava) to sell. The small group living in Karabaka, because they had no water except the 'scrape and wait' well and what they could carry from Fukayosi, could only grow sparse cassava – a long starchy, knobbly, brown-skinned root, creamy-white inside, which could be boiled, fried or grated into powder when thoroughly dried to make a flour for *ugali*. How different from the lines of tall, proud stalks of maize (their preferred diet) with drooping elongated ovals wrapped in green leaf. A yellow head of young corrugated corn oozing milk when pressed, and from its narrowed end a hanging thick silken tassel of golden hairs. We definitely all sought young corn for the sweet-tasting rush it gave us and the convenience of only having to roast it on an open fire or bring it to a simmer. Here the villagers' diet comprised boiled cassava root and cassava leaves, sometimes supplemented with the occasional egg from a chicken.

Andy and the donkeys, after having rested, travelled to the larger village of Fukayosi to collect water. I suspended tarps from tree branches for the little shade available while I attempted to make sense of our route – I was not even sure where we were exactly – and consumed great quantities of liquid. It was essential that the donkeys regained their strength; we were feeding them the scarce maize kernels and oats we carried.

We intended to end up in the large town of Chalinze, and Francis also stated that in Chalinze there were water shortages. They were selling water at ten shillings per large can. But was this true?

After a day on mushy boiled cassava, Andy and I were led by a settler (almost at the trot) through a vast uninhabited region reminiscent of Hampstead Heath, criss-crossed by wide bush paths, to shoot warthog. They were plentiful and a large target, and it was easy for me to shoot. We cut off the head and disembowelled it to reduce weight and carried it, dripping with blood, back to camp to be greeted with relieved cheers. We thought about poachers killing animals for their tusks – which fetched huge prices – and big game hunters killing just for trophies and leaving the rest of the meat to rot in the bush. We could understand and have sympathy with why poachers functioned in ever-hungry Tanzania, but paying-hunters we could not fathom, especially as ordinary locals were legally forbidden to kill the abundant animals for food, risking jail and large fines they could ill afford. *Nyama* was the Kiswahili name for animals and it also meant 'meat'. The attitude to animals was therefore cold, verging on cruel. A minister had once told us, 'These are *our* animals – we can do with them as we wish. We are not *your* zoo!'

Warthog and wild pig in the Karabaka area were plentiful and could easily be trapped, but the locals, despite their obvious malnutrition, refused to eat this meat. Being Muslim they were forbidden to eat pork.

Two days later, the *masika* (monsoon rains) began with a vengeance. Great drops smashing into the ground, speedily turning it to mud. We rushed around collecting the bouncing rainwater in saucepans. A soaked Athamani Kobo, the chairman of Fukayosi, brought us a gift of coconuts in a small shopping bag. He was dressed in a loose shirt and drenched *kikoi* (a patterned cotton cloth swathed around his waist), wearing an embroidered Muslim cap on his head, holding his shopping bag in one hand and a *panga* in the other. I offered him sugared tea and crude biscuits that Christine had made. We sat and sweated together in friendly silence.

'The English before,' he finally uttered, 'did not sit and eat with the people, nor did they walk unaided. They wanted Africans to carry heavy packs over long distances.' He remembered as a young man helping to carry a government official and his wife on litters. And having to stand to attention when the official descended and imperially ordered, 'My wife and I want our tea now.'

He laughed and then inadvertently told us what we were desperately eager to learn: 'When the English were here the crossroads at the bottom of this track were known as Rosako. There were few houses then.'

Phew! This finally made sense of our modern maps and mileages. We had been correct throughout. He then explained what we already knew: that this acted as the frontier outpost of the Wakwere tribal region.

Kikoka Forest was a buffer zone, a no-man's-land.

Athamani, now armed with an ancient flintlock he had made himself modelled on old Arab firearms, walked with us to ensure we did not miss the spot. The densely wooded hummock that was once Rosako was to the left of our narrow track. Old mango trees marked the site. This was where Stanley had camped and been given the gift of a local bed by the chief! Here from his well-supplied medicine chest, his account tells how he doctored three ill porters and temporarily lost his dog Omar in a rainstorm.

From here on, we began to fall into a routine. We never stopped for lunch but chewed dried warthog chunks while continuing to walk. A full water bottle for each was clipped onto our belts. Having learnt our lesson in Karabaka, we never drank our water until the end of the day. And even then it was poured into a large blackened kettle and boiled up for tea or coffee. We walked in single file, Andy at the back, the donkeys with Christine in the middle, and myself at the front to check the route and its suitability for the donkeys – a loaded revolver in my hand. Burton was always the lead donkey following my backside. He wouldn't move if I was not there first, providing protection. As we walked I shouted out directions and warnings: 'Snake on right... safari ants... thorns, watch the thorns... stop the donkeys, we'll hack a way through... No, no, can't go this way... bog on the left... Hole! Hole! Take the donkeys around... Oh, no, shit, a river...'

The landscape dramatically altered from the boring flatness of scruffy woodland and thickets to green rolling hills, lush grass and thick inviting glades, natural and unspoilt. The bushes and trees crowded with singing birds and twig-snapping unseen animals evoked memories of the animal-less hearts of Devon and Cornwall. For a distance of thirteen miles, this wilderness was deserted of humans with no traces of cultivation, except in the neighbourhood of villages which we passed.

'This really is beautiful,' sighed Christine.

We found a huge day-old print from an elderly lion, probably a male forced to hunt alone for anything it could stalk to stay alive. Such animals have often turned man-eaters. The encountered pungent smells of putrefaction and rotting corpses caused us to gag. On the path wildly scattered feathers, indeterminate fur and porcupine quills. Our thin cotton walking-trousers became ragged; from now on we would have to wear the heavy Italian Army trousers.

At Usigwa River we had to cross a holed wooden bridge

– a series of halved tree trunks laid along struts. Burton tripped and fell before he even got near. Then Stanley rolled and Speke began to gallop away in fear. Andy and I had to drag all of them over the precarious bridge with ropes stretched across their buttocks. I could understand their uncertainty, but this was the nature of African bridges, and by now I would have thought they'd have got used to them.

We carried the panniers over ourselves. These double panniers, closed with buckled straps, were made of strong canvas in Dar es Salaam and displayed the name of the expedition 'Stanley's Footsteps' and beside it the British and Tanzanian flags. Andy and I had to lift one of these hefty double bags between us, hug it tight to our chests and stagger in tandem across rivers and over bridges, unable to clearly see the uneven stumbling ground. It happened so often that I became sick of this process and years after suffered from slipped disc problems. Christine, thirty years after the expedition, still has amoebae in her blood and liver.

Tangy *ngongo* fruits (like sour plum), on which elephants loved to get drunk, revived us until we reached the *Ujamaa* Mkenge, which did not exist in Stanley's time. Many prosperous-looking banana-leaf thatched houses were sitting on a rolling hill, surrounded by rich cultivated fields of banana, maize, lime, pineapple, papaya, tamarind, rice and of course the ubiquitous cassava. This surprised us after the scarcity of Karabaka, but all was explained by a large man-made lake half a mile away where clean water was available all year round. Aid projects, I felt, would do well to concentrate on creating bore holes and unbreakable pumps in every village; at this time, it would have entirely changed this region of Africa.

Throughout our expedition, in every village where we camped we always asked to speak to the elders of the tribe – the *wazees* – since they were of an age to remember the distant past, and their parents or grandparents might even have met Stanley. Elders and Tanzanians in high position were always treated with respect and we too offered a firm handgrip and uttered '*Shikamoo mzee*' ('I grip your foot and place it on my head, old man') as a sign of subservience and they would reply with the ritualistic '*Merhaba kijana*' ('Blessings on you, young man').

After our arrival, a large procession followed us to our campsite on the outskirts of Mkenge. We tried, in most cases, to erect our tents away from villages for reasons of privacy and to ensure the safety of our goods, especially when packing or unpacking. There was always the odd opportunistic thief, and we naturally became paranoid since we couldn't afford to have any one thing go missing. We put up our tents under a tamarind tree, with mourning doves trembling the air in descending scale. Long curling grass and gentle woodland spread away on all sides.

We gazed into miles and miles of thick green. Into its very heart, stretching to the far horizon, melting in heat haze. We felt it drawing us in and however tired always experienced a glowing euphoria. At such moments I felt an irresistible urge to hurtle forward howling soundlessly, wishing to be overwhelmed in green, to vanish into growths so that my sojourn in the world would become nothing more than a ripple in the pool of time.

A crowd sat on the grass, silently watching. Two Wabaraguyu warriors dressed in purple robes and coloured beads, wearing ochre on their hair, led their cattle past us to the lake. They were on the way to the Chalinze market and asked for soap.

I said, 'No, it is expensive, why don't you buy it?' They laughed at my cheek and invited us to visit them at Chalinze.

The Wabaraguyu tribe (in the Kimaasai language *barawui*–people who bow down to till the land) are a clan of the Maasai, referred to by the explorers Burton and Stanley as Wahumba, who were long ago defeated and driven out of the mainstream Maasai tribe.

Night fell, a sudden closing down of the conscious world. The whisper of leaves; the creaking of branches attempting to kiss; sometimes water caressing and fondling smooth stones in the river; the friendly crackling fire and our lazy human voices sitting around it deeply wary of shadows. A thick overpowering darkness blanketing what was known, unpierced by artificial lights until the civilised glow of scattered kerosene lamps or man-made wood fires breaks the dark. Electricity and its conveniences were too far away in distance, time and concept to bother contemplating. In this blackness a multitude of fireflies turned our campsite into a fairyland, sitting on our clothes and hair, winking their lights on and off as though on Christmas trees.

Sharp griping stomach aches woke us. The *ngongo* fruits had fermented in our guts much as they do with elephants – only they leave elephants staggering drunkenly. Not us. The morning exploded for us with racing into bushes and piercing rain. Unfortunately, tsetse appeared after the rain, plaguing our environment with painful bites (just like being injected with a thick needle), curses and killer slaps. The donkeys bucked and kicked through the pain. Tsetse can be fatal to cattle, domestic animals and humans and have inadvertently been responsible for the formation of large African game areas where only wild animals remain immune.

Dr John Kirk in Zanzibar had foretold the certain death from tsetse of Stanley's horses and donkeys. And European so-called experts such as Alan Rodgers (zoologist at the University of Dar es Salaam) had also fatally condemned our donkeys. 'They will never reach Morogoro,' he insisted. We were determined to prove him wrong. But we were all beginning to suffer African side-effects. Christine occasionally felt nauseous without cause, and her gums and mine had receded and were bleeding from vitamin B deficiency.

Andy was getting dottier by the day. 'I'm doing my best,' he kept repeating. But he was perpetually feeling weak, kept accidentally cutting himself and losing things and never completing a job. He would leave water containers behind, drop his *panga* somewhere, lose tent pegs and all-important pieces of rope. And, importantly, he was responsible for mending the donkeys' panniers, but he regularly forgot, so that day by day they fell apart. Unfortunately, loss affected us all; we had no replacements. I had to keep encouraging him. 'Well done, Andy,' I'd say at a task completed.

On our way toward Tarawanda (Stanley's 'Kingaru'), just outside the village of Mkenge, we found a local chopping trees down for firewood. I wondered if one day despite the man-made lake, those in Mkenge would have to move away because of lack of wood for fuel and building. We began to climb slowly. Tarawanda was on top of a steep hill with expansive views. We kept a lookout for the Udoe

Cones and Dilima Peak that Stanley had mentioned, but although the day was clear, neither was visible. I wasn't sure if Stanley hadn't misspelt the name of the peak. 'Dilima' had no meaning. *Milima* on the other hand meant a hill, and so was much more likely.

In Tarawanda we were greeted and asked to sign the visitors' book in the wooden-shacked CCM Office. An uneven beaten-earth floor, a leaking corrugated-iron roof, cobwebs and lizard droppings and locals peeping through dusty windows. In the corner a thrown-together pile of rickety school desks, a dog-eared ledger scribbled over with ancient comments, dust blowing from its curled pages, was brought out of its drawer and everyone gathered over its indecipherable signatures as if over a holy relic. An *mzee* pointed down the hill denoting where Chief Kingaru's house used to be. 'What is your name?' he asked. 'One day your grandchildren will also arrive and ask if this was the way you passed.'

Outside, Speke was attempting to roll in the dust, squashing the panniers, so we had to rush to his aid. As we were leaving the school band marched out, sadly too late to show us their paces.

Explorer Stanley found the village gloomy: a swampy stagnant area with dense grey clouds glowering overhead. I'm amazed that with his reported weather he could see any peaks and cones at all! Rain pelted down before he could set up camp. Imbiki and Msuwa, Stanley's next two named camps, we had pinpointed on our maps as rivers correctly spelt as *Mbiki* and *Msua*.

Lost in dense woodland, stumbling over roots and ducking barbed branches, we realised that this was so vastly different from our own culture and birthplace that we could never really learn to adjust. From nature there was no indifference to humans and their affairs. In fact, there was an active hostility. This is the way we genuinely felt until stopped by a repetitive hypnotic whistling and a jingling of cow bells. The whistling changed tone, each phrase ending on a shrill extended note like pan pipes. A small Wabaraguyu boy, naked under his flapping purple robe, holding a home-made flute and loping in and out of light and shadow, approached to show us the way. Interspersed between trees and bushes were women balancing jars of water on their heads. We called out a greeting:

'*Hamjambo?*' ('Problems?') to alert them to our presence.

But instead of ritually answering '*Hatujambo!*' ('No problems!') they dropped their water jars screaming '*Wamumiani! Wamumiani!*' (bloodsuckers) and raced away from us like terrified rabbits.

Tanzanians living in the bush were naturally suspicious of all strangers, but this was an extreme reaction.

'What's wrong with them?' Andy asked.

A quarter of a mile further on we came to crossed paths and a man who was shaking with fear but holding out his hoe like a weapon. We calmed him with our Kiswahili greeting: '*Hujambo? Tunapita tu.*' ('Problems? We are only passing.') Feeling it necessary we took pains to explain why we were in the bush and he called the women out of their hiding places. He told us they were afraid we were after their blood!

'*Kweli* (Truly)?' we said, amazed at their behaviour. There were many reasons, but it was widely believed that ghoul-coloured whites in the bush, like vampires, required blood to thrive and to provide colour to their bodies. They were referred to as *wamumiani* and *chinja-chinja*: the first word literally means mummifiers though it has come to be accepted as bloodsuckers; and to *chinja* is to slaughter. Many bodies were found in the bush, we had been informed, drained of blood and with vital organs missing.

For African children the bogeyman is an *mzungu* (white man), damply frequenting the bush like a leech, his moon pallor peering yearningly through the trees at the glow of warm-blooded settlements. In many villages we had visited, even though it was still early on in our expedition, children had broken into tears and screams of terror as we passed. Francis theorised that Greek plantation owners a long time ago had captured locals and taken blood from them with a needle, which seemed to us like a very accurate description of taking blood samples in order to investigate local illnesses.

Descending steeply to the valley of Chalinze through thick woodland and lush greenery, the path was completely overgrown. Villagers no longer used the ancient track for fear of the elephants who drank at the Mbiki River. I had always imagined our journey would be through plains of burnt savannah grass, dried rocks and dustbowls, but instead we were walking through a perpetual rich green curtain. Paths multiplied, criss-crossed, disappeared entirely and reappeared again in completely unexpected places. We came across a wood-gatherer walking towards us with an enormous weight of branches balanced on his head that bent him almost to the ground. He turned his back and, swaying with the load, voluntarily danced directions for us in the dust. His arms stretched to the sides like a scarecrow to keep his balance, his bare darting feet scratching indecipherable hieroglyphics and crossroads with labyrinthine turns in the path, all accompanied by machine-gun Kiswahili. Having performed his dance to his own satisfaction and without having once bothered to look at us he waltzed off without further comment.

As our overall journey was approximately 1,200 miles calculated day by day from our numerous 1:50,000 maps, we surmised we had so far completed just sixty miles. Phew! Going by what we had encountered so far, would we and the donkeys manage the entire journey? Highly unlikely! What unexpected problems would we face in the future? 'I don't think I can go on for ever,' Andy muttered.

*

Early April. Keep passing miniature thatched shelters like houses children make for dolls. Inside, offerings of ugali, beer, broken crockery containing herbs and incense. According to Issa they are 'rain shrines'. Incense is burnt by witch doctors who chant spells, pray for rain. Disturbed duiker *(small deer) hopped into woods – a rounded bent spine, pathetic wilting backside. Walk by compass-bearing only, much to Francis's amazement...*

Eventually we hear the 'whoosh' of occasional fast traffic and come across a main road that runs from Dar es Salaam through Chalinze to Morogoro. Wading through swampy ground, we arrive in the middle of Chalinze Mzee – a small, semi-abandoned settlement consisting of little more than a few crumbling mud houses around a large open square. Other than a stall selling sugar cane, there was nothing more.

A friendly drunk reeking of *gongo* (local raw spirit) directed us to the nearest water a quarter of a mile away: a minute lake-like swamp.

'Is this the only water?'

'Yes.'

'Is there a tap?'

'No.'

'Not even in Chalinze town itself?'

'No.'

Finally the information dribbled from the drunkard's lips. There was a dam outside town to which people, if they could, travelled for water. In the town itself you bought water at a shilling a gallon. It was understandable. In Africa, water was a precious commodity.

The swamp water was very likely contaminated with bilharzia and we boiled it to death before drinking any. But as for washing after a sweaty day's walk… well, it would take too long to boil sufficient and wait for it to cool. We had been instructed by Europeans to let the water stand for forty-eight hours in the sun, but this was ridiculous. In practice, unless we remained unwashed and took unrealistic precautions such as wearing plastic washing-up gloves when collecting water, there was no way we were going to prevent suspect water touching our skin. It took all our determination on some baking days not to jump into still rivers and swamps.

We headed to Chalize town itself, then investigated our surroundings, leaving Christine with the donkeys.

The main road was a shock. In soaking rain, Chalinze was nothing more than a sordid, bustling crossroads. Corrugated-roof shacks had sprung up calling themselves bars and lodging houses. The open scruffy market sold overpriced goods while Wabaraguyu and Maasai sat miserably and waited for the roar of lorries or cars to beg lifts for a price. Three young girls with matted hair sold boiled potatoes, intestines, lungs and spleen.

At night Chalinze came alive and the beer, girls and bare electric lights dispelled the mud, filth and man-made sordidness of the day. The bars insisted they didn't have beer, but if you wanted a girl you'd get a beer. Whilst we sheltered from the rain and chatted to one of the prostitutes, a chief inspector of police, out of uniform, walked warily toward us through a narrow passageway. 'You don't recognise me?' He insisted we have a beer with him – more than one – and we got gloriously drunk, the girls all around us giggling at our inane comments.

On our return Christine was visibly annoyed. During our absence, drunks had bothered her, asking for things, and she complained that she didn't want to be left guarding the donkeys each time we decided to go off exploring. But somebody had to stay behind! Anyway, she hadn't missed anything. I gave her a detailed rundown on what had happened – all the raving drunks! She didn't look entertained by my descriptions.

Under huge shade trees we hacked a camp space out of thickets and poured swamp water all over ourselves. Issa was elsewhere getting secretly drunk on *gongo* and had taken it upon himself to become our spokesman. We often heard him under the stars spinning tall yarns of our trek and intentions, always getting names and history completely wrong. Locals interspersed his exciting stories with exclamations and gasps of breath. He enthralled them with tales of hardship, narrow escapes, lions stalking the camp.

Francis topped this by describing in detail his wrestle with a leopard. Locals always looked forward to visitors bringing them news. Francis told me that to wrestle a leopard you had to firmly grip its forelegs, not realising we already knew that it's the sharp back claws that are lethal. Once a leopard sank its front claws into the chest, it scrabbled away with the back legs, quickly disembowelling its victim. Unlike a lion whom you stare fixedly in the eyes, you were supposed to keep your eyes down and pretend you hadn't seen the leopard while carefully backtracking out of its safety zone. Very confusing!

At night Francis slept on his back, legs held far apart with a piece of wood tied between the ankles, a cloth tied around his mouth and nose (we actually witnessed him sleeping in this way). This was to make it difficult, he said, for a python to swallow him, while the cloth was to prevent lizards sucking up blood from his mouth and nose. Unusual bushcraft!

The next day – 3 April 1984 – was my fortieth birthday! Time had become suspended. I discovered our badly dried warthog had given me worms. Oh, wonderful. I could see them joyfully wriggling in my stool and causing intolerable itching at the anus.

Stool analysis at a handy missionary clinic showed that, apart from the warthog worms, I also had a high infestation of roundworm and hookworm. But we couldn't wait around for treatment. Roundworm and hookworm are passed from faeces to mouth, it seems, through lack of cleanliness. Once roundworm eggs are swallowed, young worms hatch in the small intestine and enter the bloodstream, then travel through the lungs to your vocal chords. The young worms are coughed up, swallowed for the second time and reach the intestines where they grow to full size. This second invasion can cause serious problems. Hookworm larvae, commonly found in inhabited muddy, swampy areas, enter via a person's bare feet or hands, reach the lungs and as in the case of roundworm are coughed up and swallowed. They then attach themselves to the walls of the gut and can cause weakness, severe anaemia, chest pains, fever, asthma…

Andy and Robert immediately dosed themselves with worm protection.

The rain had swollen and tightened the tethering ropes making them dangerously cut into the donkeys' fetlocks and difficult for us to untie every morning. In Morogoro (a large dusty town yet to be reached) we decided we would have to find a leather craftsman to make simple leather straps and buckles to be attached to the soggy ropes, as well as leather reinforcement for the bottoms of the ripped and constantly tossed-off panniers.

In the darkest early hours of the morning, rain beating down, we attempted to routinely pack and load the donkeys, absolutely filthy with rain, mud and donkey shit. Andy was doing the opposite of what he should, dropping stakes and ropes in the drenched deep grass. Even at this unearthly time a crowd gathered to watch. Much inevitable frustration and irritation. I spotted a bulge in one pannier which threatened to rip through. It was the axe. Contrary to what we'd agreed, Andy had pushed it deep down in the bag without its leather guard over the blade.

It seemed we would definitely need our waterproofs. Christine and I rushed about throwing tarps over the donkeys to keep them and, more importantly, the panniers dry. Then Andy handed us only Christine's waterproof; he had packed the others at the bottom of the bag. We had to unload this bag in the soaking rain. Andy then dropped his side of the heavy pannier while I was holding the other side and the bent metal buckle, which Andy should have straightened a day ago, ripped a great gash into my waist. I hollered in pain. I wanted to scream, to clobber Andy repeatedly. What was he doing? 'Pull yourself together. Concentrate!' I snarled, resisting the urge to grab him by the neck. I really could not understand his behaviour. After all, he had worked as a survival instructor.

'OK, OK,' he said, 'I'm doing my best.'

There was no path! Grass was head-high, soaking our clothes. We depended on our compass, wading through shallow bogs, our boots coated with thick mud. Our way was then blocked by tall thickets. We hacked for what seemed hours, thorns ripping our clothes and panniers, sharp-biting ants falling down our necks from high bushes and trees. Our hands were blistered from handling our *pangas*. The gash in my waist was smarting, the bandage spongy with sweat. Christine had applied iodine which stung fiercely, but it usually worked like magic.

We realised it was impossible to escape African seasons – drenching rains or brain-broiling sun. You inevitably met climate at some stage of an extended foot journey in the bush. The only thing you could do was hide away, waiting for uncomfortable weather to pass. Tanzania was a land of paradox. After rain the landscape rushed into growth, smoothing brown earth in varieties of green. Land that seemed so changeless slowly changed. Roots grew, splitting rocks, shoots spread, binding earth tighter. Green shrubs wriggled to the surface and wildflowers no one knew existed disclosed themselves.

Sustained effort in the sun affected us each in different ways. Andy slowed and came to a stop; he gave way, deteriorated in physical appearance and in spirit. Christine's concentration lapsed, while the glare drove her mad, and she became intensely irritated by flies and insects but nevertheless kept up with her tasks. She was patient and capable with far quicker reflexes than Andy or myself. I just became irrationally impatient, could flare up into killer moods, but also had the ability to become extremely single-minded and stubborn. However much I exploded though, Andy would give me a sidelong look and we would both collapse in fits of giggles.

We arrived at a slippery steep decline leading down to a coating of thick black oil in the Kideka River. Francis said this was leakage from the pipeline that travelled all the way to Zambia. The donkeys were reluctant to move, afraid of the sharp downward angle and the smell of oil. Andy and I readied Speke and drew him down the decline first, stretching a rope behind his buttocks – curses and clattering hooves. Suddenly Speke vaulted across the river, bucking his panniers into the dense oil. We forgot Speke and struggled and heaved at the panniers frantically to get them out of the oil fast. We were covered in the lumpy muck as well as being splattered with mud in the scorching heat. Now we knew we would have to unload the other donkeys and carry their panniers over the river ourselves to safeguard them, before pulling the donkeys across one after the other.

'Now I'm really knackered,' I admitted as we regrouped on the other side.

We heard cattle bells and knew that Wabaraguyu were close. On the opposite bank where Christine was battling to hold the donkeys by their halters, Livingstone's panniers slid off his rearing back, while Stanley sat down and goods began falling out of his badly packed panniers.

'Andy!' I admonished.

Christine scrambled to gather up everything, now covered in glutinous oil. 'Unbelievable!' she screamed.

Hacking a way through began again and we could hardly hold our *pangas*. A tall lanky Wabaraguyu *moran* (warrior) accompanied by a small boy, leaping, whistling and walloping his long-horned humpbacked cattle like a busy imp, chose to lead us. Evading most thickets and thorns he followed cattle paths to the waterless Msua River.

We didn't seem to have got very far during these early days.

The author's inspiration for the expedition acoss Tanzania

The expedition team on Zanzibar before crossing to Bagamoyo

Reception in front of the Livingstone Tower, Bagamoyo, to mark the start of our expedition

The expedition is seen off by people of Bagamoyo

Helping Burton over a wooden bridge

George and Andy have to carry panniers across the Usigara

We're equipped for all seasons

George with villagers reviews our camp area at Masimbu ravaged by a bush fire

George prepares to inject a blood-stained Stanley with antibiotics after an assault by hyenas

7

Uluguru: Land of the Withered Leg

Mjawanu, past Arch-Chief of the Waluguru, whose name means 'man-eater', used to sell children from his own tribe to the Arabs. For this reason his people speared him in the leg so he limped thereafter. The leg became deformed and he mockingly became known as Lugulu (Withered Leg).

*

Past Wabaraguyu, men and particularly the women slapped their thighs and let out whoops of laughter, arm bangles jingling, at seeing whites leading donkeys in the wilderness. Some young boys ran away when they saw us. Others hid and shadowed us through the bush.

The effects of my worms – roundworms as long as a pencil, and hookworm which had latched onto the lining of my stomach – had become noticeable, sickeningly attempting to escape via my mouth and nose. Gagging, I had to stop and drink water from my container to mindlessly swallow them down.

Apparently Kisemo had a *bwawa* (a ready pool of water or spring) where we hoped to camp. Issa, Francis and Robert raced ahead. Up and down steep muddy banks for twenty minutes – the spring should only have been ten minutes away – only to encounter a flyblown swamp. Again!

'Where's the clean water?'

'Near.'

'Then what is this?'

'For the donkeys,' the scouts said.

'The donkeys need clean water,' we said, 'not this filth!' But they were wholly unsympathetic. Having made our point, Andy and I then ignored the scouts and Robert. We turned to our reliable compass.

We reached Kisemo on 6 April, and camped there in a beautiful, soulful leafy glade, our dome tents under the shade of straight-trunked ancient *mgude* trees (*sterculia* – a protected species) close to the bubbling crystal water from the spring. Stanley calls these trees '*mparamusi*'.

The slow-flowing river captivated us. We didn't want to leave, buried in pollen beneath the nestling care of *mgude* leaves, stifling in vegetation. The small village was situated well away from the river and us. You knew when you were in a good camp by the feeling. Always a stillness, a feeling of peace. Here we could safely cuddle down in Nature. In other camps it was as if anything could happen, making you peer over your shoulder at the jagged cry of a bird or shrilling insect. It sometimes took an hour of trudging about, testing out various places before I would choose a site. Streaming with sweat, covered with sticky dust and bark, I would march about, peering into the distance, almost going into a trance at each spot. I had to be sure. Lots of shade, guns loaded and lined up, brush cut down, fires lit and stock of wood piled ready. Time was spent at night pacing the distance of donkeys from each other, from the tents and fire. This was essential, guaranteeing a restful night.

*

The spring at Kisemo was reputed to be enchanted. The word *Sheitani* (Satan) was muttered many times under the locals' breath as if to ward off evil. And this related snugly to Stanley's account of how one of his Englishmen – Shaw – was stopped, when pegging out tents, from removing a small flat stone. '*Uganga* (Medicine),' he was told. Stanley was later shown under the stone where an insect – 'the cause of a miscarriage to a young female of the village' – was pinned to the ground by a sharpened stick.

Two new game scouts arrived, Rajabou and Rashidi, and Francis and Issa shot off like bullets. Francis hated this unprofitable safari. On other jaunts together, Issa and he would kill hippos which plagued farmers' crops, and then sell the meat: they had earned 6,000 shillings from their last hippo. Not with us. We'd also realised that misdirections from them had often been so that they could end up in villages where they knew they would be fed and sexually pampered by women (married or not). Francis said he paid five shillings for a married woman's services and food. But being white I could get a better woman if I wanted for twenty shillings.

'But don't the husbands mind?'

'Why should they? They receive money. Andy should try,' he said. 'They like his red hair.'

Andy, terrified of getting HIV, since we believed AIDS was endemic in the area, diplomatically replied, 'I'm too young.'

Rajabou, bewhiskered, toothless and Arab-looking, immediately asked us for ammunition. He continued to ask for things and his nagging, whining voice which repeated everything twice wore away the nerves. Rashidi, a thin ferrety creature, merely looked on as Rajabou continued to talk about firearms.

*

Sudden silence descends at twilight. Nature gone into trance. Night begins: nocturnal insects; hyrax; yap of jackals; crackling bushes; crunch of trees; grasses stretching. Sky ablaze with sparking stars; large white crusted moon. Sit on rocks or donkey cushions beside the log fire. Glimmering Southern Cross, clear constellation of Scorpio which Andy points to, competing with multitudes of fireflies. 'This is why we're here,' whispers Christine. Hollow honking of giant ground hornbills, large ungainly, dirty-brown, turkey-like birds that cannot fly, a blazing red pouch under their throats sounding out ancient signals in hollow drum beats. Always something crawling over ankles, naked arms, tickling necks. Begin to tell difference between featherlight touch of mosquito, heavy dot of beetle, lengthy crawl of caterpillar…

Morning. A pale grey begins to tint the deep darkness. Stars faded and disappeared from the sky. A pale blush of blue slowly thickening in colour now made visible wisps of cloud, white smoky streaks which also disperse. From somewhere the sounding sizzle of hot oil joins the sound of waking insects.

In our tent I found Christine had a crab-like tick attached to her waist. Cattle were frequently herded through the area, and ticks dropped off them into the tall grass, then clung to passing humans. Christine was disgusted by it, dodging unhelpfully away as I applied the bush knowledge given us by various Europeans by trying to scare it out with a lit cigarette, choking it with paraffin wax, saturating it with kerosene. It didn't budge! The head was buried deep in Christine's flesh. I eventually burnt it to death and extracted its sharp jaws with tweezers in the half-light of a useless torch. We found another tick running around the tent and Andy discovered one attached to his thigh.

Rajabou had set off for Ngerengere, for the second time in just a few days, and we had given him money to buy us honey. According to Rajabou and Rashidi, they had waited for us in Chalinze for eight days, subsisting on meagre *ugali* and cassava. The Game Officer in Morogoro had only supplied them with three cartridges and ten bullets (more than they normally get), but no rucksacks, blankets, torch batteries or waterproofs. Very little food or money, so they expected goods from us. Rashidi, to prove his worth, agitatedly informed us there was a black mamba on the riverbank. He would shoot it and we could eat it stewed with onions and peppers. He rushed off.

I washed by the bubbling spring and when women arrived to collect water, they first cried '*Hodi, hodi* (Knock,

knock)' to let me know they were present. I could answer '*Subiri kidogo* (Wait a little)' or '*Karibu* (Welcome)'. A young girl unselfconsciously asked me to 'load her'. What she actually said in Kiluguru is '*Niishi* (I am ready)'. I could hardly lift the bucket which she so lightly carried on her head. A mother and her two daughters filed down to the spring for water. The mother had previously sold us *mchicha* (a cross between kale and spinach) and limes. She allowed me to take her photograph. I had to dissuade her from rushing off to change into her best clothes.

A deaf and dumb villager named Bubu, in tattered smock and oily-brimmed hat, *panga* carried under his arm, huge newspaper-rolled tobacco stuck to his lips, urgently signalled us to follow him. Stopping in a Vietnam-like forest of gnarled trees and creepers he pointed to distant trees and placing his forearm horizontally to his nose imitated a hornbill – *hondo hondo* – which were visibly nesting. Hornbills are similar to toucans with black bodies, a yellow band of feathers around the neck and huge yellow, downward-curving beaks.

Andy, Robert and I returned with our shotgun. They all flew away except for one up high, perched close to the trunk, necessitating a sharp vertical shot through branches. An impossible shot but I squeezed the trigger, hoped hard and the bird fell! From then on, Robert kept calling me 'My Brigadier.' Andy was merely 'The Private.'

Hornbill meat is red because of the fruit and berries they consume. I have to admit that I don't like to shoot any animal, but I am not vegetarian and we desperately needed the energy from some fresh meat. Christine had in the meantime discovered an efficient method to de-feather birds. She cut firmly along the length of the breast of fowl (hornbill, guinea fowl, duck or chicken), pulled the skin and feathers back over the legs and wings so de-skinning and de-feathering at the same time. 'Most bugs are found in the feathers and skin,' she explained. She had also finally got the hang of lifting hot, handle-less *sufurias* (saucepans) off the fire by using thick pieces of folded-over cardboard like makeshift oven gloves. Eureka!

The *sufurias* were usually balanced on three large rocks or rough logs and it was important for balance to have the rocks or logs of equal height. You could, though, only use one balanced *sufuria* at a time unless you possessed a wire grill to lay over the rocks and fire that could cope with multiple cooking containers. When making camp Christine first heated water in a large fire-blackened kettle for drinks as we were parched after a day walking, and put the rest aside to cool for later. The quickest meal was an all-in-one stew with ingredients of garlic, tomato purée and mixed herbs.

After supper that night Christine, Andy and I strolled down to the spring to wash our hands. Walking back to our tiny tents I suddenly found I was talking to myself.

Christine was no longer there! I could just make her out weaving and zigzagging in the distance. I had always told her that in the event of us being unarmed and meeting with wild animals in the bush she should run as fast as she could and leave me. I could function better without her. And to zigzag if the danger was from a gun.

'What is it?' I shouted into the dark, also asking Andy, 'Can you see...?' I felt him freeze, gasp 'Oh, shit!', and streak across my vision, loping after Christine.

I could hear a terrific tearing, crunching and mangling of trees and undergrowth. I turned in the dark to confront not a man with a gun, but, towering menacingly over me mere feet away, the granite face of a huge bull elephant, butterfly ears flapping madly, rubbery trunk loose and waving wildly, sniffing the air in my direction, practically touching me. It lumbered towards me, picking up speed on its log-like feet like a toppling four-storey house. It emitted a rasping screech which almost melted my spine.

I ran. The rush of adrenalin tossed me over fallen tree trunks, finding a way through tearing thorn bush and miraculously helping me out-stride Andy. All the rules when charged by an animal were never to run and panic as this would encourage it.

'Stop!' I shouted to Andy, gripping his sleeve. 'We shouldn't panic!'

'Fuck off, you bastard!' Andy swung mad punches at me as we ran alongside each other. 'Get off my fucking arm!'

'No, stop!'

'Fuck off! Fuck off! Get away!'

Mweka Wildlife College advice was to run uphill, so slowing the elephant down, to lie behind a wall or mound over which an elephant cannot leap, but under no circumstances to climb a tree. Tree trunks fifty inches in diameter could be easily uprooted. We should always stay upwind. None of these instructions was in our minds. We just sped as far away as we could, grunting with fear. After about half a mile away from our tents we were halted by Christine, who pointed behind us.

'It didn't follow you.' The pursuing elephant had stopped. We realised we were out of his danger zone. He had been just as frightened as we were. This was a mock charge.

And we recalled our lessons in Mweka: if his ears had been flat against his head, the trunk neatly rolled up, so leaving the tusks free to impale, the heavy feet to crush, we would have died.

Rajabou returned at 9pm whining about how difficult it was to buy anything, when we knew Ngerengere was meant to have everything. The honey was extortionately expensive. Andy was furious and Robert cross-examined Rajabou. It transpired that he was lying and inflating prices for the goods he bought us, then keeping the difference. Both Stanley and Livingstone had suffered similar problems, with their porters constantly stealing from the supplies. Livingstone's medicine chest had been drastically ransacked and he nearly died as a result.

Four Wabaraguyu warriors, easily identified by their purple cloaks over their shoulders, sniffing snuff which they carried in intricate containers hanging around their necks, strolled into camp to greet us. Seeing the jar of honey by the fire that Christine was to use to make *uji* (maize-meal porridge), one *moran* (warrior) picked it up. He studied it and then retorted, 'It is full of water. It has been sold to you by a thief.' Rajabou kept quiet.

The Wabaraguyu found their honey in the bush. 'It's free. You don't buy honey!' Rajabou chose this moment to ask for batteries. And promptly set off for Ngerengere.

We told Rajabou to stay behind as we left, as we no longer needed him. Climbing out through the actual hill village of Kisemo – a charming settlement scattered among luxuriant cultivation catching breezes – we passed women sprawled on shaded hard-beaten earth. Beside them children with scabies, malaria, TB open sores, skin peeling away on backs and thighs, lips and around the mouth. We really wanted to help them, but we only had chloroquine for malaria, which we gave. They would have to get lindane (a cattle dip) from the vet to treat scabies, but there was nothing we could do for TB. Other standing women were pounding *sim-sim* (sesame) seeds in giant wooden mortars, although we failed to witness what Stanley had recorded with such fascination: 'The belles of Kisemo, of gigantic posterioral proportions... swaying with the pestle as it rises and falls, the pectoral and posterioral exuberances alternate to her strokes in the very drollest rhythms; so strongly marked that I feared for the walls of the hut before which I saw the corn pounding going on.'

We had found their posteriors to be no larger than those of other Tanzanian women. Large posteriors are nationally in Africa considered a sign of great beauty. The women of the Giriama tribe in Kenya even wear cushions under their robes over already buoyant buttocks to further accentuate their charms.

We travelled for five hours, with straight ahead of us tempting views of the Uluguru Mountains forty-nine miles away, looking like cracked teeth so close and blue-hazed in the clear morning light. The countryside on either side flattened out into low and seemingly cropped green grass as if it had been mown. Trees and bushes seemed evenly distributed. The donkeys seemed to be speeding along doing two and a half rather than the normal two miles an hour. Such unexpected flat landscapes Stanley compared to

New York's Central Park 'with its refreshing lawns, gentle hollows, and grove-clad ridges.'

On the way Robert showed us Maasai medicinal plants easily recognisable:

1. Cactus (*euphorbia* species). To treat scabies. In Kimaasai, *Olsukuroi*. The leaves were cut and boiled and the water used to bathe the afflicted body parts.
2. *Ndulele* (Kiswahili). The roots were boiled and the liquid drunk to alleviate stomach cramps. To treat rotting teeth, the yellow, round, plum-like fruit of this plant could be cut and juice squeezed onto cotton wool which had already been soaked in spirit or kerosene and wrapped around a stick. This was then lit and the flame held close to an open mouth so smoke and fumes entered. The bad bacteria we were told would fall out of the mouth. He warned us though not to eat the yellow fruit; it contained high doses of strychnine.
3. The male pawpaw tree (it bore no fruit). To treat bloody diarrhoea, the roots should be boiled and the liquid drunk. Three to four teaspoons of milk from the green fruit or trunk of the tree mixed with an equal amount of honey in a cup of hot water also apparently killed roundworm. Swallowing the pips of the fruit generally killed all sorts of worms. Sadly, I tried it to no avail.
4. Bark of the mango tree. To treat bloody diarrhoea. The bark needed to be boiled and the liquid then drunk.
5. *Mbonokaburi* (Kiswahili). To disinfect wounds, the

sap from a broken stiff leaf or twig was rubbed onto wounds.
6. *Engauka* (Kimaasai). To treat wind and clean the breath. A noxious plant. The leaves were boiled and the liquid then drunk to act as a digestive, to clean the intestines and sweeten the breath.
7. *Mbaazi* (Kiswahili). To treat hoarseness and loss of voice. Again, the leaves were boiled; then chewed. The pap was then spat out and the water drunk.
8. Raw egg, or honey. To treat burns. Either egg or honey was smeared on the wound.
9. Zebra bones. To treat rheumatism. A soup of zebra bones, marrow and some meat was held to be a very powerful remedy.

I was always suffering stomach pain from what I ate and drank, particularly from fresh milk and raw honey, and I found that boiled *ndulele* roots was the only bush remedy that alleviated the pain. The roots, unlike the fruit, contained only a small proportion of strychnine and the bitter, woody tea tranquillised the intestines and possibly killed unhealthy bacteria. Christine boiled up four pieces of well-washed root (five inches long) to one cup of water for five minutes. This was drunk on an empty stomach or before food. Roots could be reused up to four times. If only it would kill my worms; pawpaw and its pips didn't seem to work.

13 April. The Catholic Mission at the large *Ujamaa* town of Ngerengere (population approximately 600), where we camped under huge shaded mango trees, was situated on

a rise just above the broad brown river of that name and seemed to be the only peaceful spot in the whole craziness of the place. The centrepoint of this town seemed to be the roof-less market building up a steep hill, with hardly any produce for sale. Around it were empty, winding, earthen streets, stone-built buildings with stone stoops; several Indian shops selling the same shirts, pens and knick-knacks, the owners and patrons sitting idly on their stoops curiously studying passers-by; wandering drunks obliterated on *gongo* – for there were a large number of bars.

Bwalo Club was a drinking, eating and lodging place for the *Jesh* (army) and so was immaculately clean – the toilets cleaner than tourist hotels in Dar es Salaam. We'd been invited there for drinks by the insincere but jolly *Katibu* (the CCM party secretary). There's one in every village, as well as a village-elected chairman (*mwenyekiti*). The *Katibu* arrived with the chairman and stuck to him like a fly. We bought them a beer; they didn't reciprocate, and we purchased our own *mushkaki* (cubes of meat on small wooden skewers).

8

Ukami: Land of Waste

The Wakami were originally a clan of the Waluguru who descended the mountains to live on the plain. They hunted and the game there was plentiful.

The land between the mountains and the Ngerengere River was uncultivated and there was little water. The plain became known as Ukami – 'the wasteland'.

We were heading now for Wakami territory, climbing steeply up into rolling, thick meadows with a few grazing cows. 'Devon beef country!' Andy exclaimed. He was not far wrong. This whole area had been previously cleared and beef-farmed by Europeans. No more. In one minute corner of land, the Tanzanian Government now had 200 milking cows and reared pigs, most of which were sold to the Kilimanjaro Hotel in Dar es Salaam. The rest of the vast fields were unused and the extensive farmland was beginning to revert to bush.

As we walked, we were plagued by innumerable stinging tsetse. They waited in shade, in shallows on dusty or sandy tracks, under leaves of bushes by the side of the path, alert to the vibrations of passing beings.

A sweet *mzee* with a long shirt hanging over his

trousers and Muslim cap on his head met up with us in the bush. Saidi Kimemile was born in 1900 and knew the area well as he had walked with the Germans all over the region. He had first seen the English, he said, during World War I. They came storming out of the bush asking, '*Wapi* (Where) fucking Germans?' The British Army, he related, was comprised of Punjabi troops – Sikhs – as well as Zulus and men from the Congo: cannibals who greeted everyone with '*Jambo, nyama* (Problems, meat)?' Saidi had a brain as corrugated with detail as the maps. He described carefully with much arm pointing and bending of wrists every ascent and curve, and it fitted exactly with contours on our map.

The mountains on the horizon were shrouded in cloud. With a compass bearing we isolated 'Kira Peak' which Stanley had described. We slowly descended to a dry stream-bed, *miombo* woodland and ten-foot-tall grasses which brushed against us, leaving itchy grass seeds stuck to our sweaty forearms. Tsetse biting more than ever, the donkeys snorting and stamping. Speke sulked every time he was badly bitten; we were familiar with the obvious look on his face.

Many elephant trails and the intoxicating smell of *ngongo* fruit crossed with the burnt-rubber stink of leopard. It must have just passed as after five minutes the smell disappeared, but we saw two deep day-old lion prints six inches from claw to heel and four inches wide.

The worms were causing me big problems now; – I had to get to a doctor or missionary hospital soon. Incapacitated, the left upper side of my body was now completely paralysed, my mouth lopsided and frozen in place – an allergic reaction to the huge infestation. Christine took my useless arm and pulled, guiding me through the woods for miles. She was being marvellous.

Andy hacked away a clearing, though it was a mistake to bush-camp as soon as we did and in such a poor place, but we were forced by illness (mine). We heard lions roaring as we fell asleep. 'They're far away,' said Christine, calming me.

That night we were woken by loud snuffling and scraping against the outer of our tent. An animal attempting to gain entry. No sound from the donkeys. A rasping out-breath close by my left ear sped my good hand under the pillow to the Ruger revolver. A musky, rancid smell pervaded the inner. Lion! This would have to happen at this present time. We held our breath. We didn't dare speak. The animal was on the darkest side of the tent away from the donkeys. What was it after? Christine nudged me. I would have to go outside; the donkeys were in danger.

I slowly unzipped the outer, then propelled myself out of the tent naked and terrified, the shaking revolver held in front of me, to observe a dark shape crunch into the bushes away from camp. I called Andy awake. He emerged groggy with sleep. Now that the animal seemed to have gone we bravely investigated the area. Nothing. The rush of adrenaline had knocked me out and speedily returned me to my seized-up self. I collapsed back into the tent. Next morning, inspecting the very large lion prints at the back of the tent, which must have come from an aged beast, we realised that the lion must have been a man-eater.

Gombero, where Stanley camped on a ridge near a *boma* (fort or protected building) with a few thatched huts and a pool of water, no longer existed. The pool had dried up and only a lone coconut tree on the left of the track marked the site of this settlement. But the view was stunning. We looked side on to the triangular Kira Peak where Stanley in 1871 saw rich growths.

We dropped steeply into the valley, our views marred now by rolling rain clouds which caused us to hurry, then a climb again through brimming, well-cared-for crops: rice, *mtama*, cucumber, cassava, banana, *bamia*, *papai*, beans, oranges, limes, maize, all waiting for rain to explode into maturity. We reached the large, flourishing Muhungamkola: on our map this village, a combination of Gombero and Nyamnhwambe, was only marked as Nyamnhwambe. I should make clear that our Canadian maps were somewhat problematic. Because they were based on aerial photographs many footpaths marked were actually elephant or hippo trails, clearly visible at close range. Some villages were not mentioned (as in this case) or had taken on the names of rivers. The unreliability of the maps forced us to depend more and more on common sense.

We asked about water and where we could camp, and the *Katibu* in his calypso-flowered shirt and sun hat unhelpfully directed us to a muddy patch. We pointed to shade trees further away and he reluctantly took us there.

We asked to buy food. He said he had not heard of us, had no notification and besides the village was poor. There was nothing available.

But it was rich in crops, we said. Ah, but the rain had not come.

But we had seen ripe produce such as *papai*. Ah, but the wild pigs and warthogs had been eating the crops so there was nothing left. In any case he was not even charging us a price to camp. We could buy everything from a village nearby, the *Katibu* added. But we knew there was no nearby village.

We insisted on meeting the chairman, who turned out to be a young, energetic man named Kondo Abdallah Semsa, who immediately resolved matters. Continual visitors brought us goods to buy – eggs and chickens, presents of sugar cane, oranges, bananas, maize – and an appropriate area was cleared for our camp. Looking askance at my twisted, paralysed position and grimacing smile, he said his brother was a vet in the village. Perhaps *he* could help me with my problems.

The Wakami possessed very pleasant attractive features. Fine aquiline noses and high cheekbones, small narrow faces and thin lips. The women all had their hair cropped short. We were forced to stop in this burstingly green village until my many worms were killed off in layers. To destroy them all at once with the pills the vet carefully prescribed could cause a worm bolus to form, perforating my guts. Christine was very worried that I was taking pills meant for animals, but I soon felt much better, and while recuperating, watched rain fall like an anvil, making the ground bubble and froth with orange mud.

Eating dark and cold suppers of raw cassava and tomatoes – initially it was too wet for a fire – under a hastily erected tarpaulin shelter, we waited for respite. We were trapped in Muhungamkola by heavy rain. When the downpour ceased Christine began to scratch and slap at her legs, then her body. '*siafu* (safari, or soldier ants)!' Robert exclaimed. The cool rain had brought out the ants.

At night they fed off sweet sap in the grasses and anything else they might find on the way. We began stamping up and down. In seconds we were covered from head to foot. Their bites were acid stings and my head felt on fire as if each of my hairs had come electrically alive. Andy was getting them in his ears while I was squeezing my nostrils tight together to kill those that had crawled into my nose and were biting. We felt besieged, aware that they could start to eat our tender flesh.

Then I remembered. There were sweet bananas which ants preferred, wrapped up in the tent. I entered, unwrapped the bananas and squeezed them into a mash. Climbing out again, becoming smothered in ants, I tossed the mushy bananas into the bush. They took the bait and in an hour had completely disappeared.

Rain began pouring down again.

It was interesting how village problems changed and differed. At the lowest level at Karabaka Kwere, the most important issue had been lack of water. Cassava was the sole diet there, and even this hardy plant was scarce, struggling to survive from insufficient watering. At the more affluent level such as here, where crystal-clear water was abundant, complaints shifted to the lack of medicine and a vehicle to transport people to town. In the village there were also many abandoned mud houses cracked in places and profusely leaking. This was because the villagers spent four months (February to May) sleeping rough in their outlying *shambas* (small cultivations) to keep the *wadudus* (insects) away from their crops. 'What problematic insects existed?' we asked. 'Monkeys, wild pigs, baboon, warthog!' Apparently, the word *wadudu* is also used to mean 'pests' and animals are considered nothing more than pests. Again, being Muslim, they don't eat the pigs they kill, and their houses are easily repaired with mud on their eventual return to the village.

With local advice we managed to keep a fire going under the sheltered thick branches of a large *mgude* tree, tall and flourishing with leaves. The fire blazed in the hollow formed by its roots. And we ate warm food. Food played an important role in our expedition. While we walked, we would often talk of delicious dainties we had eaten or drunk in the past to encourage us onward. Here in Muhungamkola, we could have sumptuous meals created by Christine of fire-grilled chicken or pork in garlic, *mchicha*, cow peas in oil and lemon dressing, pumpkin and *matoke* (plantains). *Papai* for dessert, washed down with copious instant Africafe sweetened with tins of condensed milk. Even the donkeys' condition was better. They were growing plumper and Burton was dangerously full of succulent wet grass which could cause excessive wind.

The rain finally stopped, and the rattle of palms and pelting din on corrugated roofs and our anorak hoods ceased dramatically. Our ears hummed with the sudden silence. The sun appeared, cooking us, hardening the mud and drying up the grasses. Birds which had been silent in the rain begin to chirp, at first tentatively and then louder and louder until their various songs and the hiss and sizzle of cicadas threatened to become a hysterical frenetic shriek. It was wonderful to have no interfering pestilential rain falling on us. Rashidi was again cleaning his rifle, shooting the bolt loudly in order to impress. He rehashed tales of lions seen and lions fought: 'When there is *simba*, I don't sleep. I keep watch with my gun and torch. I sleep in day.' Nights, we heard him gratingly snore with the tension of having possibly kept himself awake!

The journey to Mikese was only six and a half miles, but rain again poured down in solid sheets as we exited our tents, a clamour over which we had to shout. It was punching and slapping at us with venom. Donning our waterproofs we climbed the fertile spine of Kila Peak for a mile and a half. Long ago more people lived and farmed high on this peak than below. The paths were clear then and it is inevitable that Stanley would have travelled this way.

In drenching rain before we descended into the valley of Kiwirima, we faced seemingly impenetrable thickets and acacia thorns towering over our heads. We'd been told it was all downhill and we would be cutting through the massive vegetation for only an hour and a half. From the bottom of the narrow valley Stanley would have then followed the old established path direct to Mikese. This was now overlaid with a narrow single rail track.

On the way the sound of villagers; women and children shouting aloud in their *shambas* (allotments), creating bloodcurdling screams to scare away the wild pigs and baboons from their crops. We began hacking, hands soon covered in blisters, hair overlaid with twigs and insects, boots and feet saturated, condensation, as well as rain, dribbling down our backs. My second pair of trousers hung in tatters around my ankles because of thorns. As soon as flesh was exposed, grass seeds worked their way into skin, insects crept into crevices for shelter and to suck blood. Tsetse bites made our arms, necks and cheeks swell. Large

PART THREE – DEPARTURE

safari ants hung onto microscopic pieces of flesh on our bodies, the pincers on their heads furiously working from side to side to tear bits off and carry them to their nests.

Robert complained that he was extremely tired and thought he had malaria. I took his pack, Andy had his rifle, and we climbed trees emerging well above the thick vegetation to judge the direction of our journey. Robert was trailing half-heartedly. His malaria, he said, was getting worse. He had in actuality vomited a few times and to cap it all had been stung on the head by two bees! Tenaciously we carved an arched avenue through the vegetation – wide enough for donkeys and their panniers – like a fairground caterpillar which snaked all the way down the slope to the valley bottom. A hacking misery of a day. We chopped for four hours at half a mile an hour and the battering rain never ceased. It was cold. Our teeth were chattering.

At the narrow bottom we had no choice but to follow the rail line. There was no other space. The donkeys' stiletto-like hooves stuck in the narrow slippery mud track alongside the rail. The curtain of vicious rain cut down visibility like a thick fog. Slatted bridges over the many small rivers were uncrossable. Foot-wide gaps defeated the most willing donkey. 'This is too much,' I gasped. Each time we were forced to unload the donkeys, leave them in Christine's care, descend steep banks and wade through fast-flowing water carrying the panniers ourselves. Then coax the donkeys down after us, pulling them up the other side with ropes around their buttocks.

Struggling to heave the heavy panniers up muddy banks was a series of still poses from slapstick comedy films. Amidst the muck and curses, Andy and I had been rigidly stuck in deep mud with dropped panniers; had slipped and rolled into the river water; been crushed under panniers; and confused donkeys had meandered back onto the muddy banks and slid in on top of us so we were helplessly spreadeagled.

Further down the track a sudden sharp hoot and unexpectedly the 'once a week' train stormed toward us. We quickly pulled the donkeys off the narrow path and into the parallel of tighter bush. The whoosh of air and roaring carriages so close just missed my head and spooked the donkeys. They tried to break free. Robert was 200 yards further back and could not help us. Andy, shouting warnings, fell back into a ditch, pulling Stanley and Speke down with him. Livingstone, most frightened of all, was bucking and rearing, dragging me backwards and forwards. I looked behind and saw Christine five yards away wrestling with Burton. She was down in the mud but holding on. We were within distance of each other. I shouted above the roar and clatter and passed Livingstone's halter to Andy so as to turn and help Christine, but Livingstone's halter slipped through Andy's fingers and the donkey moved hypnotically towards the blur of passing carriages. I just managed to grasp his halter as one of the speeding carriages smacked him heavily on the snout. I pulled him back and we tumbled over in a heap.

The train passed. Silence. We felt shell-shocked, slowly climbing to our feet. The donkeys were calm now the train had gone. Livingstone was snorting blood through one nostril, his tongue lolling out the side of his mouth caught tight between his teeth. We could not tell how serious the injury was. Christine whispered soothing words into

Livingstone's ear and stroked his wispy cheek. Feeling helpless, I uttered useless curses into the gloom. We had to continue. There would possibly be a vet in Mikese, which was only a quarter mile away.

Another uncrossable broken bridge. We descended the bank, cutting our way through three-metre-tall *mtama* (millet) grass, and in a clumsy line we weaved through swampy banana plantations. There was no shallow incline to escape the bog and there was no path. In mud up to our ankles we lost count of the times the donkeys sat in muck, one after the other, as we rushed to lift them and their panniers and bullied them forward.

Unbelievably the light began to fade. We proceeded from one bog to another. In a rice paddy both Burton and I became stuck fast in the mud. Panicked, he bucked his bags into the filthy water. We were now up to our knees in water. There was no leverage to raise the bags. We dragged and pulled until we could get them to higher ground. In darkness an exhausted and panic-stricken Burton threw off his panniers and tiredly sat six times in fifteen yards of swamp crossing. Something stung me in the water and one hand became numb and useless. Facing us was a steep climb up a bank which I could hardly see. In the black everything became larger, longer and further. Donkeys were unloaded and led up singly. Then Andy and I dragged and punched and kicked the panniers up the muddy slope, both of us coated in mud. At the top we gasped for air. 'No more! No more!' uttered Andy under his breath. 'Keep concentrated!' I barked.

We were finished. Our arms didn't work any longer, our nerves perceptibly twitching. We felt numbed in mind and body, and Mikese was still ten minutes away. We had to find a vet! After another twenty yards of squelching, to our utter disbelief we were blocked by another steep bank rising almost vertically and disappearing in darkness.

Similar to the Ancient Greek paradox that to travel a mile you first had to travel a half mile and after that a quarter mile and after that an eighth of a mile and thus by subdividing your journey you could never reach its end, we also, because of our experiences, felt there was always something more to overcome, yet another interruption, another obstacle one after the other in unbelievable illogical rapidity.

We all stood and looked up at this impossible incline. I grabbed Burton's halter. If I could get him up alongside me, I knew the other spooked donkeys would follow. After a summoning of energies I didn't know I possessed, a loud war cry from me and a snort from Burton we rushed at it until we came to a natural halt, our bodies beginning to slant backwards and slipping, arms windmilling, hooves slithering. It felt like running up a tree. Groaning, we both rolled back to the bottom entwined with each other. A tangle of hooves, my splayed arms and legs and mud. We were unable to move. I was trapped under Burton. Burton was upside down lying on my stomach, hooves galloping in air. The panniers had slipped and twisted across *his* stomach, imprisoning him. Andy quickly grabbed Burton's tail and yanked him the right way up before he could choke, also releasing me. 'Thanks, Andy,' I managed. Burton stayed where he was, panting.

Enough! It was 8pm. We would camp in this rice quagmire and walk to Mikese tomorrow to enquire for a vet. Amazingly Livingstone seemed comfortable. The blood had clotted. He was munching away at rice shoots quite normally. We allowed him this well-deserved reward. As soon as we had erected the tents in a shallower part of the paddy field, and after swallowing the chloroquine I gave him for his suspected malaria, Robert immediately fell asleep.

At camp we put up the tarpaulin (tied to distant tree branches), sealed the tents with plastic bags and sticky tape and covered them with broad banana leaves. We begged the use of a *jiko* (charcoal brazier) from our solitary neighbour, a bedraggled *shamba*-watcher on a raised wooden platform, keeping an eye on his rice. On the dry platform we ate boiled plantains and cucumbers.

Back in our tents we began itching madly and spotted tiny dots leaping around the interior. Oh no, fleas! We were infested with the buggers and had obviously caught them from the *shamba*-watcher's platform where we had sat to cook and escape the wetness below. Fleas could give typhus or plague (yes, plague!) which was common in Tanzania.

The donkeys' characters were becoming more apparent, and their baptismal names by some magic seemed to fit them exactly. Livingstone, sensitive and intelligent, pushed the other donkeys away from obstacles he considered dangerous. Lean and sinewy in appearance with a dent in his spine where he'd once been heavily beaten, he remained extremely independent. After one month he still at times refused to drink out of the yellow collapsible buckets. He wouldn't drink any water unless he had first thoroughly tested the situation and would spend days without it (a dangerous habit) until he felt comfortable. Wouldn't be approached unless he first accepted the person or approved of the visit, otherwise he would turn his back in the defensive back-kick position.

When the vet arrived he stood in absolute trust while a finger was rammed up his nostril, his teeth examined and his jawbone put under pressure. I would never have been allowed to be so free.

He used to be the lead donkey, until Burton appeared and by force pushed his way forward. Livingstone voluntarily retreated to the rear. But when Burton tired, despite his large frame and bulky strength, Livingstone automatically took the lead at a steady, conscientious pace. He was absolutely reliable, taking the best route around an obstacle, even when I personally made a mistake. He waited patiently when I was hacking a way through thickets and was desperately wary of crossing bridges or water. The other donkeys trusted and depended on him.

His best friend was squat and large-bellied Stanley. They liked being together and worked well in tandem. Stanley too was independent, would not let anyone approach he didn't trust and would also turn his back. He hated being tampered with by us or by vets and would fight furiously. He was a conscientious, brave worker and would run up hills or cross bridges that other donkeys feared. He rarely took the lead but was very capable.

Burton was big and heavy-boned like a small bullock. We had realised he had impaired eyesight, which explained many of his clumsy actions; he would often catch himself on obstacles, for instance. From the first he forcefully took the front position. He was always eating, quick-tempered and a bit of a bully. When munching a particularly tasty dish he would kick out if approached from behind, thinking someone was about to steal his food. He greedily swelled himself up with wet grass which caused him to fart with every move. Burton hated anyone in front of him, except for Christine or myself, whom he followed religiously. His biggest hate was Speke. They were permanent enemies and we could not stake them near each other because of the fighting that would ensue.

Speke was small and dainty, the youngest donkey with a pretty, almost feminine face. Petulant and sulky Speke promptly sat if he was tired or when bitten. We always lifted him off the ground, took off his bags to alleviate weight and after a few steps he would sit again. This temperamental behaviour held us up and encouraged the other donkeys to copy him. The only way Speke proceeded was when prodded with a bamboo stick, and then he became bad tempered. He would rather die than move, though he eventually submitted.

*

26 April. Approximately 100.25 miles covered. Tiny Mikese – straggling uphill behind station. Two businesses thrive: Corn-Mill (toothless owner covered in flour like an albino) and Pombe House (alcohol). Local beer boiled up from maize-bran, billowing smoke issuing out of thatched roof, house seems on fire. Staggering brewer-family perpetually drunk on fumes. Two oil drums contain frothing grey sweet-smelling muck. Chunks of uneaten ugali, a rusty metal piece and old rag thrown in for luck guaranteeing diarrhoea for unseasoned stomachs. Taste? Lumpy acrid-acid plus slight touch of sweetness like roughest scrumpy. Even ducks are fed on beer waste, waddling dizzily, bouncing drunkenly off each other's fat feathers...

*

In Mikese, Livingstone was pronounced fit by the vet whom we eventually found stumbling about in a beer house.

'Thank God!' I exclaimed. Donkeys, like horses, breathe only through their nostrils, thus our worried state. On a stormy sea voyage where they could vomit, their nostrils would block and they would suffocate to death. Thanks to Livingstone's muscular shock-absorber of a neck his snout had possibly (and it's only a vague possibility) been fractured, but it would heal, we were assured by the vet. If Livingstone had been human the blow from the train would have taken off his head.

We needed Stockholm tar for the donkeys' many wounds, and chloramphenicol to add to a saline solution for their sore eyes. We would buy this from the vet, but he would obviously make a tremendous profit.

Robert hastily visited the unqualified local doctor who injected him with more chloroquine for his malaria and he collapsed in camp. We sent him off with a man on a bicycle who had offered him a lift to Morogoro hospital to have the excess chloroquine cleansed out of his system. He was relieved to go, whimpering his usual phrase, '*Karibu kufa. Karibu kufa...* (Nearly dead. Nearly dead...).'

Rashidi had been into the town and found nothing to buy. He explained that when he had passed through on a previous occasion there had been more villagers moving around and Indian shops stocked all goods.

'But they haven't been able to get enough goods as the government controls all produce. So having lost the profit motive the Indians have left or been arrested as racketeers.'

These shops had been taken over by Africans and now hoarding and black-marketeering were rife. The shops stocked hardly anything, as it was in the black-marketeers' interests to have fewer goods on show. The villagers were very reluctant to reveal any goods, though the surrounding area was extensively cultivated with fruit, vegetables and a valley chock full of cannabis plants (*bhangi*). In the village, a roofless market building had three squatting sellers on its vast empty floor beside dried, rotting fish, scant piled triangles of groundnuts and mouldy onions. One shilling for twenty shelled nuts.

Andy had been stalking villagers, desperate to buy us a chicken. He returned with the news: 'No chickens!' Yet I had heard numerous cockerels crowing merrily. Andy repeated like a fixed and clanging knell of doom, 'There's none!'

'How do you know?'

'Villagers said so.'

I stared sorrowfully into Andy's eyes. He eventually shrugged: 'Yeah, all right.' And trudged off to buy a chicken.

You learnt not to accept what you were insistently and originally told. Andy got his chicken, and the villagers did gradually appear with substantial produce, ready to haggle for hours; they always tried to overcharge. We had again entered a land of 'make scarce to make expensive to make profit'.

In grey drizzle the drunk with a damp cigarette stuck to his bottom lip guided us to the *Katibu* instead of to the chairman, and we left a message: telling him we were trapped in the rice paddy and needed help. And food.

Meanwhile, a group of young lads had come into our miserable camp and when they thought no one was concentrating – as we were cooking on the platform or occupied in washing mud off clothes in the rice paddy – they closed in and sat by boots and clothing we'd laid out to dry between rain stops. They were attempting quite openly to steal.

Christine sprang up and startled them with a brandished gas-gun and accusatory Kiswahili: '*Toka, shenzi, toka* (Go away, rubbish, go away)!' They struggled to escape into the undergrowth.

In the morning we overheard locals passing our tents on their way to their *shambas*: 'Walk fast, perhaps they are asleep still. Let us pass quickly. Why do they choose to stay here in the bush and not in town, ha? They have come to take blood. Pass quickly. Pass quickly.'

The efficient chairman at last arrived with five men and within two hours, using hoes, levelled the steep bank that enclosed and trapped us and our four donkeys. Gratefully we clambered out. Next stop, the Uluguru Mountains and the large town of Morogoro.

9

Uzigua: Land of the Diviners

The Wazigua tribe were traditional herbalists who believed that most illness, death and sterility in humans and livestock was caused by witchcraft. They traditionally used divination to diagnose the cause of illness and misfortune which to this day led to rigorous witch-hunts. Stanley wrote of them that they 'are about the most thorough believers in Witchcraft, yet the professors of this dark science fare badly at their hands. It is a very common sight to see cinerous piles on the roadside, and the waving garments suspended to the branches of trees above them, which mark the fate of the unfortunate Waganga or medicine man. So long as their predictions prove correct, and have a happy culmination, these professors of uchawi, magic arts, are regarded with favour by the people; but if an unusual calamity overtakes a family, and they can swear that it is the result of the magician's art, a quorum of relentless inquisitors is soon formed, and a like fate to that which overtook the "witches" in the dark days of New England surely awaits him. Enough dead wood is soon found in their African forests, and the unhappy one perishes by fire, and as a warning to all false professors of the art, his loin-cloth is hung up to a tree above the spot where he met his doom.'

Stanley's party followed the route of the present railway track from Mikese, passing through the area he names Ulagalla, to make camp at Muhalleh – then taken over by Arab and Wazigua invaders – but which now no longer existed. On arrival Stanley met a large caravan carrying 300 tusks to the coast and got his first real reports of Livingstone's whereabouts. The Arab caravan leader, Salim bin Rashid, reported that in Ujiji he had lived beside David Livingstone for two weeks and described him as, 'Looking old, with long grey moustaches and beard, just recovered from severe illness, looking very wan…'

The Wazigua tribespeople were not found by Stanley to be as civil as the Wakwere, Wakami and Wadoe. During barter they became angry and issued threats, not wanting to sell goods at any price but their own. Stanley compared them to hot-headed Greeks as opposed to cool and collected Germans. Here, Stanley contracted malaria, treating himself with fifteen grains of quinine taken over three days.

We were heading towards the dark sharp-toothed Uluguru Mountains after a seven-hour trek through forest packed with chattering vervet monkeys, barking baboons, warthog, buck and tree-crunching elephants. The rain had finally stopped. Our donkeys Burton and Stanley began to limp, obviously in great pain, edging away from hard-packed paths toward soft mud spots and grass verges. The Mikese bog where we had camped in the incessant rain had softened their feet and possibly caused an infection. It was 5.40pm and I discovered Christine was not wearing her gas-gun; her holster was empty.

Christine said, 'Oops! I must have dropped it when I walked off the path to go to the toilet!'

I was furious. This was irresponsible. She knew full well how every item was important and the gas-gun was invaluable for dealing with rogues we didn't want to injure. 'You can't leave it lying in the bush,' I said without thinking. 'You'll have to get it!' Aware that Andy was listening to any trace of favouritism, I emphasised, 'Now!'

'But it could be anywhere...' explained a startled Christine. Later she told me she was thinking, *George is furious and this is one of the most infuriating days of my life. It's very hard to pee and watch out for animals, so I dropped the gas-gun. So what!*

'I don't care. You'll have to find it.' I could not stop myself blathering now. 'You're just a member of this expedition...'

'But the animals — '

'I don't care!' I spat out.

Andy nodded in approval as Christine turned and stormed off almost in tears.

What had I done? I knew there were wild animals in the vicinity. Why did I have to be so self-righteous and stubborn? I wanted to go after her. I wanted to await her return. But that would be a bad example. We carried on. Each of my steps dragged. I despaired of myself. I was such a bastard! What if something terrible were to happen? My mind overflowed with possibilities. With great relief, looking back I suddenly saw Christine running toward us, waving her gun in the air. She'd found it! Instead of expressing my joy, catching Andy's eye, I turned forward as if taking her find for granted and said nothing.

Steep climbs and descents. Never-ending undulations of pain for the donkeys.

We reached Kingolwira Misongeni and it fitted our desires for a good campsite for the night. Unlike Stanley we found the chairman, Kingo, who was a Mzigua, hospitable and extremely generous. Seeing the state of our donkeys he quickly guided us to a grassy campsite under coconut palms. Darkness and rain descended. Flowing supplies of food (even chunks of meat) and firewood from the stocky, strong-bellied chairman and a plastic gallon container of *tembo* (palm wine) milked from his coconut palms. A milky dishwater in colour yet with a sweet rooty taste that sedated and became addictive. The longer you kept it, the more it continued to ferment and become very serious alcohol.

After a deep inebriated sleep, we were meant in the morning to visit the chairman at his home, and Rashidi stubbornly insisted on speaking a mix of English and Kiswahili in order to show off. He said, 'When finish blackface, *mwenyekiti* says *tutakwenda nyumbani*.'

I understood 'we will go to his house' but not the rest in English. He repeated, 'When eat blackface…'

I was completely lost. 'Is there blackface to eat?'

'Yes, *ika* (there is).'

Did he mean the *mwenyekiti* would bring us blackfaced monkey to eat? Or had Rashidi killed a blackfaced monkey and wanted us to taste it? I questioned further and Rashidi reciprocated, 'You eat blackface?'

'Well… yes.'

'Ah… then *halafu* (after) you go!' Why couldn't we speak in Kiswahili? My brain was scrambled!

'But where is the blackface?'
'Blackface is here!'
'Where?'
'Here!'

This continued for some time. And finally the penny dropped. He was saying 'breakfast'!

Villagers passed and greeted us, bending their right knee in a curtsy of respect and saying '*Shikamoo*' – 'I see you' – which is the customary Zulu habit of greeting. They also announced, 'I am passing': a polite acknowledgement that they were travelling through another's privacy.

Kingo, the chairman, was a direct descendant of Kisabengo, the savage past Chief of Morogoro, a name that everybody in Tanzania was familiar with and secretly admired. In Stanley's account, the town of Morogoro is referred to as 'Simbamwenni' and even the British sometimes mistakenly called it by this name.

Kingo told us that 'It is not true that Morogoro was renamed Simbamwenni. Stanley was wrong.' He showed us a British certificate of identity, signed and stamped with an official British seal: 'Sultan Kingo', followed surprisingly by the wrong place name, 'Simbamwenni'.

Kingo still passed judgement over villagers' affairs and invited us to sit with him at these proceedings. His four wives, so impressively blubbery they could hardly walk – a real sign of status for Kingo – lolled around us on the earth. He had ten children. Villagers stepped up to his specially created thatched shelter and raised seat and explained their problems. Despite the automatic positive answer to greetings there were always problems – usually to do with misappropriation of land. His judgements were fair and wise. We sat beside him nodding sagely. His swollen wives smiled indolently. He was accepted as a chiefly figure by villagers because he had many wives and showed by their size that he could feed them. He could afford to drink much *tembo* and had visibly and deliberately developed a pot belly to signify that he was not short of food and drink.

'It is true this was not the original country of the Wazigua as you have explained Stanley wrote,' said Kingo. 'We were originally from Handeni near Tanga. The Wazigua settled here acting as mercenary soldiers for the Arabs and as a ruling class. Even during British times this was known as Ukami territory not Uzigua.'

Kisabengo and his followers, armed by the Arabs, eventually conquered a large part of the Ngerengere Valley in the mid-nineteenth century, land which had belonged to the Wakami tribe. 'Kisabengo' was actually a nickname: this chief's actual name was Muhina, son of Kingo. A runaway slave under Arab rule, he gathered a force of other runaways and became known as Kisabengo, a formidable African presence in the south-east of the continent in the mid-nineteenth century. In the tribal language 'Kisabengo' means 'cutting into pieces', in short 'butcher'. A fearsome fighter, once this chief had shot his enemy he would drop his gun and dismember him with a *panga* knife. The fortified garrison he established around 1840 beside the River Mwele absorbed an earlier settlement, Bungo Dimwe (the name meaning 'fruit of the dwarf baobab tree'), standing on the Arab caravan trade trail linking the Great Lakes area with the Indian Ocean. When a tree fell into the water the usually placid water passing over the trunk made a glugging sound which the local people crossing it – who still have difficulty pronouncing 'r's – began to use to name the river 'Mlogolo'; the Arabs soon modified this to 'Morogoro', which came to be the accepted name of both the river and the town that sprang up on the spot. By the time of Kisabengo's death in 1870, Morogoro had become a thriving city. In the late 1880s it was made the headquarters of the East Province of German East Africa.

In old age Kisabengo proudly changed his name to 'Simba mwene' (The Lion Himself), bestowing this new title upon his daughter who succeeded him in 1870. We were very interested in this history as in Dar es Salaam (it seemed so long ago) we had discussed our route with the university and they had asked us if possible to delineate onto a detailed modern map Kisabengo's fortified town of Morogoro, a task they themselves had failed to achieve. In a fit of optimism, we had agreed to do this.

We spent some days in Kingolwira, washing the donkeys' hooves with potassium permanganate, scraping them clean with sheath knives (all we had), and spraying with tetracycline/gentian violet spray until they healed. Also squeezing antibiotic ointment twice a day into their sore eyes. We were beginning to feel comfortable in Kingolwira being looked after and indulged by much tasting of *tembo*.

And then we set off. It was now early May. We left the village of cool night breezes, peace and plenty, and trekked along a broad path. Scattered homes, plush fields and cultivation lined the route. Streams bubbled down from mountains. It felt like land rich beyond belief, and people and traffic increased as the road – potholed, worn-away tarmac – improved. The sides of the mountains were riddled with missions, seminaries of all denominations.

From the crest of the rise, we finally caught sight of the town sprawled flat on the plain. The walled city of Morogoro was no more.

10

Morogoro: Searching for the Old Walled City

I lead donkeys through unmade-up winding earthen side streets avoiding donkey-dangerous traffic on the main road towards railway station. Opposite is the New Savoy Hotel where the Tanzania Tourist Corporation (TTC) had arranged our stay. Unable to camp – no grassy areas – too large a town teeming with people, cars, crammed tight with two-storey stone buildings, shops. Bustling urban environment. Population of 110,097 as compared to Stanley's 3,000. Large areas of land around river now occupied by the Tanzanian army and members of the ANC (African National Congress) – an illegal 'anti-apartheid' political party of South Africa permitted to stay in Tanzania...

*

It was 7 May; we were twenty days behind Stanley Morogoro now was an untidy conglomeration of double-storey buildings bunched together under the watchful eye of the jagged Uluguru Mountains. To determine where the old city lay would be a difficult and time-consuming task. Covered in mud and dust, we tethered our donkeys to the stiff hedge in the New Savoy Hotel car park and approached Reception. There were no rooms! They insisted they had received no previous notification. There would not be a room free for another month.

Andy and I then spent four hours touring the town searching for accommodation, leaving Christine once more to guard the donkeys. Nothing! Finally, back at the hotel an unused staffroom that stank of DDT was found for us. Andy, however, had to camp on the hotel lawn for the night, the donkeys tethered tightly beside him on the postage-stamp patch of grass.

Before supper we rushed to see Robert in the hospital. We plodded into the ward and were allowed straight in, even in our insanitary boots and clothes. Robert, dopey on valium – and even more chloroquine! – looked as if he had just been prised out of a coffin, his feet slithering along the floor like a zombie, a fixed grimace of a smile on his pale face. There were three patients to a bed, head to toe, the beds covered in brown-stained sheets. Between the beds relatives were cooking on *jikos*. Robert's neighbour, sleeping on the ground, had died the previous night. We promised to have him discharged the following morning.

In Morogoro we met many Europeans and gained some valuable information, and equipment. From Bill Forsythe, a Canadian aid worker and knowledgeable hunter, we learned which particular shot was needed to down different animals and how to erect a fly-proof frame for making *biltong* (wind-dried meat): we first marinated the meat with garlic, vinegar and ginger. *Biltong* we made in Morogoro and elsewhere became our staple diet, chewed as it was for breakfast and boiled up with rice etc. for supper. Alternatively, while in Morogoro we could put the meat into an oven on a very low heat with the door open. The meat would dry in twenty-four hours and then keep for two weeks or more. *Biltong* proved essential; it was not that easy to shoot small game in Tanzania.

A bunch of Canadian railway advisers presented us with a Katadyne water-purifying hand pump. This was a wonderful gift, which though bulky and heavy could purify the scummiest water. Later we were eternally grateful for it; it kept us alive.

Someone thankfully gave us rare flea powder. We liberally dusted ourselves, clothes, bedding…

Other evenings we spent in middle-class superficial conversation that had no base in reality, while Tanzanians continued to bend our brains with irrationality. Mama Chuma, a government official who was meant to assist us, was always tired and hungry, wanting us to buy her lunch. She assaulted us with spatterings of Shakespeare and Old Testament sayings that we never understood.

'You can kill with kindness, eh, you know that? They can kill you with kindness and what and what… and when an outcast and what, like the dead son in King David, they put the sacks on. They kill with kindness and put on the ashes and sacks and what. Beware the Ides of March!' We could never really understand what she was trying to say.

Father Dranken, white-haired, pink jowls flapping, watery piggy eyes and lips flecked with spittle, exuded a musty odour of old sweat. Previously a Dutch missionary (though always married), past pedagogue to President Nyerere (Nyerere used to be a schoolteacher) and his present adviser, he honoured us with a book of Nyerere's sayings – 'I compiled it myself' – and more helpfully a missionaries' account of Morogoro in Kiswahili. Some days later we heard that the President had urgently called him to Dar where there had been a pitched battle over cattle rustling between villagers and *SunguSungu* vigilantes. Three thousand people were involved fighting with spears, bows and arrows. Forty-six bodies had so far been recovered and the fighting threatened to escalate.

We did though profitably learn from Dranken that long ago the caravan path had skirted just behind the conical Kigurunyembe Hill opposite the mission. We slowly retraced the old caravan route back to the hill, then followed clumps of old coconut and mango trees lining a path through an old settlement and entered Morogoro on the traditional caravan-way near to the present railway station. The route passed the former German camp commander's house and parade ground (now a football pitch and hostel for the nearby secondary school.

The walled town illustrated in Stanley's account of his expedition was badly damaged by a disastrous cyclone followed by a flood in 1872 and then disappeared without trace. If we were to find Kisabengo's grave we should be able to determine where the centre of old Morogoro had been and plot the approximately half-mile-square walled garrison onto our map.

*

Searching out and piecing together information on old Morogoro in the present year in order to track down and plot onto a modern map the original site of the fortified town, which for convenience we continued to call 'Simbamwene', proved to be a lengthy and laborious exercise in detection. We were frustrated at every turn by lack of information and the indifference of the present inhabitants. We knew though that, according to tradition, the graves of Kisabengo and his family had to be somewhere on the old city site. The Waluguru, who had now spread into the broad valley, had no knowledge of or interest in the Wazigua tribe and their founding of the town of Morogoro. After endless enquiries we discovered from Father Canute of the Holy Ghost Fathers, who ran the Catholic social centre, a useful description of the old town recorded in Kiswahili by visiting Holy Ghost Father missionaries from Bagamoyo in 1881.

'The town of Morogoro was built to a plan and specifications prepared by Kisabengo. It was surrounded by strong walls built of stone, almost 24 feet high and arranged in a square. In each wall was a huge carved wooden door. Within this enclosure lived Kisabengo and his family, his officers and favoured subjects. Around this royal area lived the majority of the population, protected by a second shorter wall built of mud bricks that had been baked in the sun. The top of this wall was covered with a roof of grass to preserve it from destruction by rain, and was strong enough to be used by look-outs. There were many projections or towers of different heights/lengths and numerous small windows (for muskets). After each level or length in the wall there were gates, which fastened from above by means of a rectangular piece of heavy wood. These small gates were always closed carefully at night to protect the stronghold from enemies. There were as many as 3,000 people in Morogoro and a large number of children, who behind the walls were safe from capture for slavery. A traveller through the territories of Uzigua and Udoe would rarely see children in the villages.

'Nearly every day in Morogoro it was usual to meet caravans coming from or journeying to the coast. Travellers buying food in Morogoro market – the market of Kingo – always paid higher prices than in their own regions or in rural areas. The town was clean in contrast to other parts of the country, and the men employed as cleaners were from the Wakuguru tribe [presumably slaves taken in battle]. Inhabitants of the town were forbidden to harm them in any way.'

The stronghold was beneath the Uluguru Mountains, and big open spaces well to the north and west were cultivated to produce corn, sugar cane, beans, bananas, etc. in plenty. In earlier times rice was also harvested.

In the Mission records of this time there is mention of a highly destructive flood, and Stanley, on his return through Morogoro on 29 April 1872 (after having found Dr Livingstone in Ujiji), gives a first-hand account of the destruction: 'What a change! The flooded river had swept the entire front wall of the strongly-walled city away, and about fifty houses had been destroyed by the torrent... The Sultana had fled and the stronghold of Kisabengo was no more!' The deep canal excavated by Kisabengo to bring the river flowing close to the walls 'proved the ruin of Simbamwene... masses of debris... piled everywhere great numbers of trees prostrate; and they all seemed to lie in the same direction, as if a strong wind had come from the South-West. The aspect of the Ungerengeri Valley was completely changed – from a paradise it was converted into a howling waste . . . a terrific destruction of human life and property had occurred, one hundred settlements had been swept away.'

Important news for us was that this undoubted cyclone (later extensively reported) had dramatically changed the course of the River Morogoro. The flood had served not only to ruin the walls of the city as it passed so close to them, but also to take the river back to its original position. We learned from Stanley that it 'had formed a new bed, about three hundred yards from the City'. As we interpreted this to mean *away* from the walls (taking into account what we supposed was the old centre of town) we concluded its position would have been about three hundred yards westward. This was invaluable in helping determine the western walls of the stronghold, and from this, all the other walls. We visited the Town Survey Department looking for town plans or sketches, but the oldest plans available dated from the 1950s. In these the grave of Kisabengo's successor Sultana Simba mwene was mentioned as existing near the railway station, but the exact location was unknown.

'The town has a badly preserved history,' we were told. 'Most plans and records were destroyed after independence in 1961 by over-zealous officials, who wanted to demolish remnants of their colonial past.'

Despairing of ever finding a link with Morogoro's past, we listened, crestfallen, as the Town Survey Director regretfully admitted he too knew nothing of the town's history, or the stone-walled stronghold. He was from Bukoba, and most other Government officials were from Moshi in the north. None was Waluguru or Wazigua. He referred us back to Father Canute. We left the Survey Department, and outside the building our eyes were frozen by a huge shield hanging over the entrance door. We exchanged unbelieving glances: the shield bore the coat of arms of Morogoro Town Council with a background representation of the Uluguru Mountains, and standing clearly in its centre was a depiction of the old walled town of Sultana Simba mwene, Kisabengo's daughter and successor. Despite the Missionary accounts, we were beginning to believe Stanley had imagined the place in a haze of malaria.

Tanzanian Father Canute was an enthusiast who had written a short history of the Waluguru tribe. He was interested in old Morogoro more from the Waluguru point of view, but he walked us about the town pointing out the older parts and places of interest dating from the German occupation. During our stroll he waved quite casually at a plot of wasteland and referred to Kisabengo's grave. We became stuck in the direction his finger was pointing. A little alarmed at our voracious attention, he led us off the road toward an ancient tree, under which the Muslim graves (of stone, low to the ground and uncelebrated) of Kisabengo and his oldest son, Kingo Mkubwa (Big Kingo), lay neglected at the back of a house hidden by overgrown weeds. As we had learnt that the grave of Kisabengo's daughter Sultana Simba was also close by we didn't linger to see it here. We were ecstatic at this find. People passed daily, unaware of their existence. These graves and clumps

PART THREE – DEPARTURE

of old coconut palms would have been within the western walls of the fortified town as was the custom.

Patiently investigating the area, we discovered a culvert draining a lengthy trough of swampy land running parallel to and situated fifty yards west of the graves. Three hundred yards west of this trough, which we conceived was the remnant of Kisabengo's tragic canal, was exactly where the River Morogoro flows today. Having determined the site of the old walls from Kisabengo's unattended grave and the past path of the Morogoro before it was moved three hundred yards by the cyclone of 1872, we were able to draw the approximately half-mile square fortress of old Morogoro exactly where it had been onto a modern map.

*

From the heights of the Ulugurus we looked down on present-day Morogoro: a sprawling, fast-growing industrial centre with canvas mill, shoe factory, textile and tobacco plant to its credit (built and overseen by foreign advisers); a large new dam and tourist hotel under construction and a plastics factory planned for the future. Right now, it was a neglected and dusty town which appeared to be crumbling for lack of care and organisation. The plentiful fruit and vegetable market was the best we had seen in Tanzania but as expensive now as Stanley found it in 1871. Old Morogoro was founded on butchery and evil, on the business of selling one's own people to the Arabs, and this spirit of oppression and greed seemed to prevail.

But we needed to keep on moving. Rashidi had gone, and Robert was on his way back to Arusha to recover. Two more scouts appointed by the Tanzanian Government turned up. Winston, armed with a straw shopping bag containing a waterproof tarpaulin sheet and a rifle, a bulky 'know it all' bully, disparagingly introduced his overladen and dishevelled partner Daniel – thin and silent – as his 'bag carrier'. Both were dressed in rags, and immediately asked for coffee and sugar. I had to show respect to the two of them because, like the previous game scouts, they were the personal representatives of the Prime Minister who had guaranteed our safety.

We were definitely not the scouts' employers. They were meant to be self-reliant, carrying sufficient food, equipment and ammunition to last their section of the journey, but they always turned up without maize flour or tent, and often only one bullet each for their rifles. Their brief was to accompany us and protect us if necessary. But we could do better on our own. And after a while we did.

A message arrived from Father Frits in Bagamoyo: our three rucksacks had been stolen from the Sisters' House. They had not contained much of monetary value, but my four daily-kept journals of our travels from Egypt downward to Tanzania, including Zanzibar, were invaluable. Despite notices placed in local newspapers, and with the police offering a reward far outweighing the value of the rucksacks, nothing happened. They were gone.

Since Egypt we had truly wrestled with our changing perception of people we met on a daily basis. There had been attempts to rob us at knife and spear point, and we felt not a second thought would be given to killing us if we resisted. We heard numerous instances of armed men murdering and robbing foreigners who of course often possessed very much more than we did. In London I had been an anti-apartheid protester. And once when a black lad was told by a racist bus conductor to leave the bus – for no reason other than the colour of his skin – and the delayed passengers had been shouting 'Get off the bus, you black bastard!' when the bus was halted, I had stood beside him and said, 'I'm with you, mate' until the defeated bus started off again. The Canadian aid worker Bill Forsythe had a term for it: we were definitely not 'prejudiced', as we were not pre-judging. But as we had experienced Africa for long enough and had come to a considered decision, so we were judging *after* the event/experience. We were therefore 'post-judiced'. It didn't make us feel any better.

According to African culture it was rigidly expected that a relative who was wealthy or in a position of power would readily pass 'goodies' and favours 'down the line'. It should be noted, however, that those Africans who were thieves would also rob each other, not just foreigners. Thieving, it appeared, was a spreading disease in Tanzania, and to combat it there had been a growing vigilante group, the *SunguSungu* (ItchItch – as *sungu* was the name of an ant-like insect that stings and provides unbearable itching) which did the work of the bribable police. These were from the Wasukuma tribe, nomadic cattle herders from around the Mwanza region who had originally formed themselves into a vigilante force (1983) to protect their cattle against rustlers. This had become so bad that the Prime Minister granted the Wasukuma elders permission to form the *SunguSungu*. Dressed only in ragged shorts, with shells around their necks, bells around their calves and ankles that jingled when they ran, they could travel for miles outdistancing any criminal. Armed with bows and arrows and clubs they would follow thieves for days. When they caught them the first time they beat them until they confessed, were made to return stolen goods and to pay a fine (possibly in cattle), otherwise they were ostracised from their tribe. The second time they were chased, they were covered in mud and beaten insensible, sometimes to death, and their bodies delivered to the police. In a large village we had clearly witnessed a team of four *SunguSungu* warriors jingling along at the run carrying between them the dead body of a criminal which they unceremoniously dumped at the door of a police station.

Within a surprisingly short time in Wasukuma *SunguSungu* areas, all rustling came to a standstill. Whenever they settled near an established village, all thieving stopped, and they became an unofficial police force that people turned to.

There was only one fordable crossing over the River Ngerengere at Mazimbu. And that is exactly where Tanzania had sited their South African ANC camp. Other than Zambia, Tanzania was the only other African country to allow political parties of South Africa refugee status. It was common knowledge that they received guerrilla and political training in order to become the next legitimate government of South Africa. And it was also widely believed that many of the refugees in the camp were not real ANC members but criminals who had escaped their jail sentences and fled to Tanzania, pretending to be members of the ANC.

Tanzanians described how these so-called refugees employed locals to do the dirty work and treated them with icy contempt. Bodies were often found floating in the river. Locals referred to them as *wakimbizi* (runaways). The British Volunteer Service was actively involved in sending selected volunteers to the camp, which received massive foreign aid from Scandinavian countries as well as Britain. We knew this was a sensitive area and so before leaving London I had sought and been given written permission from the ANC headquarters in Zambia to pass by. But at the river crossing, despite showing our permission we were refused entry by an officious resident, Comrade Arthur. It would have taken us no more than an hour and a half to walk through the camp and I told Arthur we were not interested in seeing what they did or in their political affiliations, so they could blindfold us. They could even blindfold the donkeys. No go! We left to ask for official Tanzanian assistance.

We waited for Lieutenant Chezi, the Tanzanian Security Officer, to hurriedly arrive, flustered and unable to meet our eyes: 'I'm afraid you've been too long. Your permission has run out.'

I smiled resignedly and commented, 'As you well know it doesn't include a termination period.'

'But it can't last forever —'

'We don't want it forever. We want to cross now!'

After a while, staring down at the fast-flowing water, he muttered, 'I suppose you could be admitted for just a short time. You will have to walk fast.'

Beneath the bridge – wooden but riddled with gaping holes and slippery metal plates to try and seal the gaps – Andy and I felt out an alternative route through the water for the donkeys. The shallowest point was hip-deep, the bottom layered with treacherous rocks. But we had no alternative. With Chezi watching we struggled to take Speke to the river and forced him in, hoping to guide him across by his halter. In panic he abruptly broke loose and leapt into the deepest part. Having had previous practice, he then bucked off his panniers and raced back to land leaving us floundering to save the panniers from soaking through. Plan B. We now carried the panniers over the worn metal plates, and then pulled the donkeys through the water one by one as we had done at other rivers. It took us an hour. Chezi was impressed.

As we sat to wring out soaked socks, empty our water-logged boots, wipe away blood from sharp strikes of donkey hooves and inspect wounds, I asked tiredly, 'Were you told not to let us in?'

Chezi shrugged. 'Yes, I should have stopped you, but you're having so many problems already...'

We walked through the camp in one hour fifteen minutes. Zulus dressed in slouch hats, cowboy boots and jeans, their strident voices standing out from the soft-spoken Tanzanians, possessively rested their hands on brand new motorbikes and gave us evil looks. It was a slick camp, with new buildings, modern machinery, smooth roads and pedestrian walkways, even an extensive agricultural nursery – all the result of European financial aid and expertise. There was no word of greeting from the aid workers, not even a wave, and they lowered their heads as we passed or moved quickly inside the buildings.

'I'm so glad that's over,' said Andy quietly.

'The whole place gives me the creeps,' agreed Christine.

Now we had to battle with the bogs of Stanley's dreaded Mkata Swamp.

11

Mkata Swamp – and Bush Fire!

The hundred-mile expanse of the Mkata Swamp is a dish-flat savannah with tall grass and scrubland interspersed with numerous bogs and very sparse settlements, meaning for us a lack of fresh vegetables and eggs, a profusion of wild animals and poachers providing new dangers, and a scarcity of drinking water, trees and firewood, which meant little fuel and shelter from the sun. The Mkata did still flood during the *masika* (monsoon). In places the rail line from Dar es Salaam to major towns became waterlogged as did local houses. People had to empty them out with saucepans.

This year we were told, 'The rains were not heavy.' Although records we had seen stated that this year had the same amount of rainfall and duration of time as in 1871 when Stanley described it as a 'catastrophe'.

The hardened, corrugated mud had been churned up by the rains. We continued into grass as high as our heads. Stanley accurately described the scene: 'When the *masika* season begins these grasses hardly ever appear above the knee; but towards the end, they have grown to their full height (fifteen feet). A month after the *masika*, when they present quite a bleached appearance, the natives set fire to them, and the country for days afterwards resounds with the roar of the fierce conflagrations, canopied by a thick curtain of black smoke which even lends its sombre colouring to the sky.'

Despite this forbidding description, Stanley later gave a truer picture, agreeing with our local information when he wrote: 'Water was on an average one foot in depth.' And it should be made quite clear this only occurred in certain places. Elsewhere it was shallower.

We considered that Stanley had over-dramatised this swamp crossing, for if this recognised, well-used caravan route had been as troublesome as he described, we felt sure that the Arabs who journeyed for quick profit and were certainly averse to hindrances and discomforts would have found alternative routes. On our clumsy modern maps the swamp areas – *mbuga* – were clearly marked so we could avoid them. We had, however, also been warned by white residents in Morogoro that we would never get through the wilderness, as there were no paths. We would get lost, wander aimlessly and be attacked by lions.

We followed labyrinthine tracks through a thorny wilderness, tearing our clothes, and emerged into expansive black areas of burnt grass and charcoal-buckled trees – the petrified look of nuclear desolation. We completely lost our way, worried that we were unable to make the compass needle behave; there must have been magnetic rock interference. I climbed an isolated tree to thankfully spot a rail line in the far distance.

Eventually we got to the tiny wooden station of Mazimbu, where the rotund stationmaster, Francis, greeted us enthusiastically. Contrary to the information we had been given he confirmed there was clean water there: station water kept in a large tank, regularly refilled by a train from Morogoro. We could use it.

We bush-camped three quarters of a mile after Mazimbu station, chopping away the seven-to-eight-foot-high dried grass and thorn bushes from around a lone tamarind tree, the only shade we could find. We were happy to fall into our usual routine in the bush and to make space for our tents and cooking fire away from villages and habitation, a break from lengthy local conversations and a welcome time to breathe. But the danger from wild animals and lack of water was always present. A mighty breeze rustled the grass stalks encircling us. The donkeys turned up their noses at their brittle food. 'How peaceful this is,' breathed Christine.

A local boy from Mazimbu climbed up the straggly tamarind tree and brought us down sour fruits to chew. Christine stitched torn clothes; Andy watered the donkeys, then sat placing iodine on his many cuts; I sat in shorts digging septic thorns from my hands and arms.

As locals sometimes deliberately watched us unpack to see if there was anything worth stealing, we had developed a routine to foil this and automatically repeated it like clockwork now each time we camped. First, we would decide on the best direction for rest-of-the-day shade and then we would clear an area, take out the tents kept in the top of the panniers, but erect only the outers of the tents before unloading the donkeys. Keeping them controlled, we lugged the panniers inside one of the outer tent structures for safety. Christine would already be inside by now, waiting to unpack in privacy. She would then hang up the inner of the tent and furnish the area with our light sleeping bags, sheets and rolled-up jumpers acting as pillows. The firearms would be slid inside the jumpers while the panniers would be left in the outer part of the tents which would be zipped closed, concealing them.

We could then comfortably go about our daily tasks and collect firewood. In the rains we had to chop logs apart to reach the dry wood in the centre, but we could use tree bark, dried maize leaves or anything under rocks and fallen branches as tinder. While Christine or I started a cooking fire downwind of the tents, Andy would take the donkeys to water.

The next part of our routine was straightforward. I would empty my water container into a collapsible canvas bucket, wash my face and hands, then use the same water to luxuriously soak my feet and replace heavy boots with relaxing plimsolls. Christine would spread any banana leaves we could find to create a flattened clean area, balance the battered and filled kettle over the fire on rocks for instant Africafe and begin preparing supper. I would write down the day's events, having purified the water, repaired torn or broken goods, prepared next day's route from maps and organised the weapons. Andy would tether the donkeys within easy reach of the fire – which seemed to deter lions and hyenas – while a kerosene lamp hung off the ground on a branch or piece of rope provided a larger area of light.

Once we were zipped up in our tents, we generally felt safe from wild animals. We were not a threat. They knew we were there, they could smell us. And they either

PART THREE – DEPARTURE

snuffled and rubbed against the tent outer or, as in the case of elephants, daintily tiptoed around the tents carefully lifting their heavy feet. When the moon was up we could see huge passing elephant shadows reflected on our tents and then in between them a baby shadow stumbling helplessly along. At night I would still tightly clutch the revolver at my makeshift pillow and try to stay awake as long as possible, expecting at any moment a spear, *panga*, lion's claw or elephant's tree-like leg to rip through the tent and kill us. The shotgun lay at our feet for Christine's use. Andy normally used the rifle.

Animals were just as afraid of us as we were of them. When we walked, snakes (*nyoka*), who are deaf, sensed our vibrations and fled in terror, swivelling and flattening the grass ahead of us. Exiting the tent one night I trod on what felt like a rubber hosepipe. I immediately backed off and the terrified and lethal grey spitting cobra rose up, swayed from side to side, then changing its mind abruptly threw itself into the dark. I was fortunate in that I had accidentally lowered my heavy foot on its head. They can spit at eyes from eight feet away and apart from damage to eyes will paralyse swallowing and breathing muscles leading to death.

Returning from watering the donkeys one day Andy turned at a thicket to practically crash into a sleeping lion. Shocked, they both backward-somersaulted away from each other. The lion scampered off, leaving athletic Andy in a stunned and trembling state.

Day after day we unknowingly passed numerous animals who, sensing our ignorance or innocence, breathed in our natural, unperfumed, tarry smell of woodsmoke

Mkata Swamp – and Bush Fire!

and simply continued about their business. Only when we became alert did our anxiety-vibrations disturb them. They smelled our fear. Our spirits cowered, expecting an approach. Our awareness called them closer and we invited our own fate. So far we had been lucky.

Animals increased the further into the interior we ventured. We had been told that lions and hyenas were as numerous at Koga River as herds of goats.

As darkness fell over the tall grasses, my eyes inevitably closed as the hyenas began their crooked wailing, whooping like crazed lechers waiting for an opportune moment to scamper in and take a mighty bite off the donkeys, tempted to madness by their smells. In the morning I would wake with my hand still cramped around my revolver, amazed we were still alive and, with my heart, thank the skies that we had been helped to survive another night.

*

Time slipped by beneath the sparse shade of the tamarind tree – it was now 6 September – and we reflected on how organised we now were and how confidently we should be able to cope with all future difficulties. We still had to confront the little-known villages of Ilonga, Kidete, Godegode, Mpwapwa, Handali, Mvumi – mostly in the deserted central plains – long before the large proposed capital of Dodoma would appear, but our journey to Ilonga would be straightforward.

Insistent crackling, however, kept disturbing our conversation. Though we could see nothing, it sounded like burning grass. 'I'm sure it's a fire,' I said. We wondered whether locals had begun burning nearby. But there were no locals living near us and no *shambas*. Up above we saw smoke rising over the tips of grass, blowing toward us with the strong wind. 'Oh no, we have to check this,' I insisted, getting up from a donkey cushion. 'I don't like this at all.'

Andy voluntarily set off to investigate, muttering, 'It's nothing, you're imagining problems.'

The sound like the crumpling of thin paper grew louder. I climbed the tamarind and from my high perch suddenly saw Andy emerge from huge flames and tall grass in the distance, shimmering in the smoking haze, his long legs hurdling over bushes, bounding toward us in great slow-motion leaps, his face a determined white, mouth open in soundless warning. His red hair looked like part of the conflagration as the chasing flames threatened to catch hold of him. The sound was in such a short time a magnificent roar so that even if Andy had called out we wouldn't have been able to hear.

I jumped down and untethered the donkeys. Christine attempted to gather some of our goods into plastic bags, but I urged her to get out fast and run with the donkeys who were wisely galloping diagonally across the fierce wind that was driving the flames speedily forward. There had to be an edge to the fire…

Christine staggered off with a firearm on either shoulder, dropping plastic bags on the way. The huge flames were twenty yards away by the time Andy, gasping helplessly, reached me. Christine had now vanished out of our sight, attempting to drag overloaded bags behind her. Together Andy and I tried to pick up a pannier. Too heavy! We dropped it. The fire was travelling faster than we could run.

Mkata Swamp – and Bush Fire!

It was impossible to attempt saving anything more. Our brains momentarily closed down. We stood frozen. Then, realising the grass we had cut was short around us, I shouted to Andy that we could beat the flames back away from our tents. We chopped desperately at our tamarind tree for branches to be used as beaters. In our panic and anxiety the axe and *panga* bounced off the tree as if it were made of rubber, and by the time we had carved out branches the flames were six yards away. Head-high yellow grass was catching like hair. We were too late. We could not beat or outrun the fire. We were going to burn.

I was terrified. 'Are you all right, Andy?' I asked, thinking of myself.

'I'm fine. I'm fine,' he answered, unable to move.

Could we jump through it as in films? I contemplated rushing through the wailing flames to the safety of burnt grass, but the thought of melting flesh and sizzling hair deterred me. It was stinging heat. I knew if the wall of fire was to reach and engulf us we would be charred to cinders.

Then we saw the fire imperceptibly slow and lessen three yards from our paralysed figures. The grass we had cut short around the tree was delaying the flames as I had originally thought. 'Beat the fire!' I almost screamed. 'Beat it!' Thrashing and coughing, I felt the soles of my plimsolls melting as the fire approached, albeit now low over the short grass. Andy's hair had somehow caught fire and he was slapping at his head. His eyebrows were singed.

The wind pushed the flames forward and we found ourselves encircled on a tiny island of shorn grass. The low flames had raced around either side and built up again behind us. Something flashed on our left as a nylon tent flared up beside our bodies. Heat and smoke was intolerable. A tent inner, dragged and abandoned with a bundle of other goods, caught fire and began exploding. There was shotgun and rifle ammunition inside. We were enveloped in flying bullets and lead pellets. Andy and I took a chance stamping down the sparking embers ahead of us and beating at the ground. We pulled one of the donkey panniers through the smoking passage to the charred blackness on the other side. Success! We dragged everything we could through this narrow, flattened passageway and stayed behind the advance of the fire which continued sweeping on mercilessly scorching miles of land.

I was incredibly worried about poor Christine. I left Andy and followed the fire, jogging in the direction Christine had taken.

I met a running Mazimbu villager who called out '*Mama salaama!* (The mother – meaning Christine – is safe!), *Yeye ni karibu nyumba* (She is near a house).'

I stopped running with a feeling of great relief. '*Wapunda* (Donkeys)?' I asked.

'*Salaama! Si wasi wasi* (Safe! Don't worry).'

The flames raged in the distance.

I trotted back to our goods, passing a pile of sizzling debris. I could make out our melted camera, my half-burnt sheath knife, a scorched, unfinished novel and, further on, blackened and twisted alloy tent poles. My brain slowed down and almost stopped with the realisation that everything of real practical value for the expedition had been inside this tent – the one that had burnt. Amidst the darkened desolation, singed and ash-dusty hair standing on end, faces begrimed with sweat and soot, Andy and I just stood helplessly staring at each other in silent commiseration. He had blisters on the tops of his hands.

'It's OK, boss,' commented Andy, 'we'll get through it.'

A group of villagers arrived and helped carry our meagre goods three quarters of a mile to one of the mud houses near the station. Christine was there in tears, telling me that all our money, passports, clothes were gone. I only had left the trousers, T-shirt and socks I was standing in. Christine's boots and notes on the donkeys and bush cookery were burnt. Films, photographs, money, passports, jumpers, sleeping liners, compass... The list was endless.

I closed my mind. 'It's OK, Chris, we'll be fine,' I uttered hollowly.

We would camp outside the house where our surviving fire-encrusted goods were piled up. The hard-baked earth border which surrounds every African house would stop any further fires spreading to us. Francis, the Mazimbu station master, arrived to say that a goods train had randomly stopped for a while in direct line with our camp and possibly a person who had alighted to urinate or stretch their legs had tossed a cigarette butt into the grass. He had called the police on his radio. The local police, however, believed the fire was begun by the ANC. To stop *us*. We had seriously been considered spies in Morogoro and the rumour had circulated. With the wind direction it was as if someone had fired a sniper's bullet straight at us. The police attempted to persuade us to return to Morogoro.

In a state of shock we sat dazed, covered in ash, with our goods piled around us. We chewed on *biltong*, looking into the approaching darkness as if hypnotised, remembering little by little what had been lost: Christine's boots, my eyeglasses, one pistol, two passports, one tent, 191 pounds sterling, 886 US dollars, etc., etc. Burnt remnants swam around our brains, haunting us to distraction. 'If only... if only...'

Ever the optimist, Christine muttered, 'There go my luxuries, but at least we survived and got this far.' It was true: we and the donkeys were lucky to have escaped with our lives. A wind blew blackened grass stalks over us. Christine had survived by literally following the donkeys who cleverly galloped at a forty-five-degree angle to the fire – veering away from it, but in doing so gradually reaching its edge.

We would not turn back to Morogoro or give up. 'We've done too much work...'

Christine and Andy agreed. We unanimously decided this was a war and we were going to win.

'Bugger it!' I pronounced ineffectually.

After the rains and asked-for research had delayed us in Morogoro, we now had to give up the unrealistic aim of keeping up with Stanley's timing. Now we would complete the expedition in our own time, however long it took. Tomorrow we would take stock and see what we could recoup.

We had covered approximately 149.25 miles. A long way yet to go. The onus, I knew, was on me. Could I cope if anything happened to Christine or Andy? I cringed at Stanley's behaviour towards his two English assistants, Shaw and Farquhar.

The fire was mentioned on Tanzanian radio. The BBC Africa Service (World Service) picked it up from there. The

Mkata Swamp – and Bush Fire!

Sunday Telegraph heard it, contacted us through Tanzanian officials, and said they wanted regular reports. It was now obvious we could easily die in Africa. This was news!

Tanzanian runners supplied us with clothes and shoes donated by whites from Morogoro who'd obviously heard of our predicament. Our remaining maps and list of villages on our route were intact, thank goodness, as were the panniers, and the rifle and shotgun Christine had saved. A Dutchman acquaintance, Aat Van der Well, said he would try to get us new tents and we could get more ammunition from the army. The British High Commission's representative, Mr Tucker, had agreed to get us another compass (how he was to deliver it was beyond me – possibly in Dodoma?). In the meantime, we would judge direction by the setting sun. We were after all travelling westward. Always into the sun!

It would be more uncomfortable, but we would manage.

Our way to the tiny Mkata station, twelve and a half miles distance, was mostly through an endless flat landscape burnt black and baked into hard cracks holding tight carbonised giraffe bones and deep lion prints. Our boots and bottoms of our trousers were black with soot. Where we bush-camped was an isolated spot away from the station.

In the Mkata there was existing high ground, and swamps in any case could have been avoided by Stanley. But then he illogically ascended the Usagara Mountains, viewing the prospect without the foreboding we so chillingly felt. We were beset with horror stories as to the steepness of the ascents and descents, which we would be able to cope with but not our fully loaded donkeys.

PART THREE - DEPARTURE

There existed a perfectly good fourteen-mile ground-level caravan route tramped by Burton and Speke in 1857 circling around the base of the mountains to Kilosa, and up the Mkondoa Valley was the mission. Why then did Stanley insist on crossing the twelve-mile distance over the Usagaras? This was a needless struggle for a saving of two miles. According to him he killed two donkeys on this cruel climb.

After camping at Mbwade (Water Lilies) and Rudewa (originally an Arab caravan camp – much like Bagamoyo) we decided that we together with the donkeys would definitely take the flat route around the Usagaras. But first we needed to *confirm* our fears by actually attempting the climb without donkeys. Christine did not really fancy the strenuous steep climb. But as we left her and the four donkeys at the Ilonga mission camp, on the side of a steep hill, she was clearly terrified that we could end up being away for a couple of days and that she would be left all alone. I reassured her that we would return that evening.

And so we began clambering upward. We followed the Ilonga River up to a natural dip and a whole valley of waving cannabis. Andy giggled. Was this why the locals were attempting to discourage our climb? They sold it for 300 shillings a *debe* (a tin container of commonly ten to fifteen kilos). We were soon exhausted, our lips gummed together, twigs, leaves and insects stuck to the sweat on our faces, necks and backs. Our hair was matted with powdered bark and cobwebs; Andy's was still frizzy from the fire. Our arms were streaked with scratches and our hands full of 'wait-a-bit' thorns that had broken off deep in the skin and opened Andy's blisters.

Mkata Swamp – and Bush Fire!

'This is too much,' Andy panted. The chest-high dried grass and tangled weeds and creepers that held back our boots made it feel as if we were struggling through deep snow. I constantly stuck my tongue out, fast-panting like a dog to encourage cool moisture onto my tongue. We looked grotesque.

By the time we emerged into the Mkondoa Valley, tongues cloven to the roofs of our mouths, desperately dehydrated and gasping for liquid, we realised that the only way to successfully get the donkeys over the mountains would be to airlift them by helicopter.

Had Stanley's obsessive head-strong decision to plunge into the climb been because he wanted to pioneer a new route which did not touch on Burton and Speke's easy caravan trail? Remember he strongly emphasised at the very beginning of his account: 'I must state that the route traversed by me was never traversed by a white man previously. If they will also take the trouble of ascertaining the route undertaken by Burton and Speke, subsequently by Speke and Grant, there will be found to be a wide difference between mine and that of my predecessors.'

'Stanley must have been completely mad and irresponsible,' I concluded to Andy and Christine, when we saw her again. Locals laughed when we told them that Stanley with his donkeys had clambered over the Usagara Mountains. 'It is impossible. He wrote *wongo* (lies),' they said.

Referring to the climb, it's inexplicable Stanley's description of this mountain journey only covers one side of a page. No facts such as which river followed upward, how many times forded water, which river followed down on final descent. No detailed dramatic account of scaling steep slopes with roped, struggling donkeys, the torture of ascending and descending seemingly never-ending gulleys. Furthermore, he seems to have completely ignored the note of warning sent from Farquhar (and his advance caravan). Farquhar was lying sick of elephantiasis two days' journey further on in the Mkondoa Valley, and wrote: 'If you want any help, I shall send my pagazis to help you, for it is between where you are and this place that nine of my donkeys died, and I have only one left.'

On his return to Bagamoyo in 1872 Stanley did not again attempt to clamber over the Usagara Mountains. He used the straightforward caravan route utilised by Burton and Speke. I can only surmise from the little that he wrote on the subject that Farquhar also stupidly clambered over the Usagara Mountains. No wonder nine of his donkeys died.

PART FOUR –
FINALLY FREE FROM GAME SCOUTS

12

Usagara: Land that Spread

End of September. Approximately 188.75 miles covered. Areas of burnt desolation. Black soot and ash wiping off onto panniers. Twigs whipping black lines onto clothes and faces. Nguru Peak majestically showing itself above other mountains on right. Landscape beginning to become desert. Rise onto elevated ridge – old caravan road encircling mountains. River below following our footsteps. Brown ants feeding off honeysuckle, kingfisher hovering. Three ground hornbill flapping giant wings hop heavily away. Winston pretending to know the way...

*

When we returned to our Ilonga mission camp, the African father told us we had to leave immediately. He explained that the donkeys were making too much noise (they hadn't brayed once during our stay) and rudely turned away without bidding us goodbye. Locals later explained that the donkeys had offended him by leaving their mess all over the grass. But donkeys and horses are known to be meticulous in choosing a small select place to defecate and we had in any event daily cleared the area. After we left, however, the father arranged for a group of children to scrape up the last donkey shit, take it off in a wheelbarrow and dump it in the bushes. I wondered what this Christian father would have done if Mary and Joseph had turned up on his doorstep!

The friendly chairman of Ilonga offered us a camping spot further down the hill – for as long as we liked. Then he invited us to his sister's house – a grass-thatched hobbit house clumped on the forest edge. An idyllic spot. We immediately felt at home, sitting on small wooden stools and drinking frothing bottles of milky palm wine drawn from her coconut trees.

Winston and Daniel, the game scouts, had spent most of their time in Kilasa, seven and a half miles away, which we ourselves reached at 1pm, an hour later than we had expected as the donkeys were playing up. Kilasa was a pleasant spreadeagled town which had been considerably influenced by Arabs in the past. British traces could be found in the public gardens, the clock tower in the middle of the roundabout and the general plan of the town.

Christine mistakenly greeted two old men with '*Chafu?*' (meaning 'Dirty') instead of '*Safi*' (meaning 'Clean' or 'Fine' – a recognised colloquialism). Startled by a white woman speaking Kiswahili, they automatically responded with '*Chafu sana* (Very dirty)' – a new and appropriate greeting!

We crossed the bridge over the River Mkondoa and immediately trod the old footpath that the explorers Burton and Speke had followed in 1857, all the way to Stanley's

'Goma Pass'. It was a scenic route through forests with the winding river to the right, towering mountains to the left. On the path a curious old man in rags asked if we'd been sent by Kingi Georgie of England to take photographs of Tanganyika, while girls respectfully uttered '*Shikamoo*' and bent their knees in a curtsy, goat bells jangled in the bush and distant people ran and hid in fear as we approached their houses. We were in the land of the Wasagara – a tribe who, once settled, had so many children that their population expanded and they scattered all over this area of land, so it became known in poetical and typical African style as 'The Land that Spread'.

At the translucent waters of the River Mdukwi, four and a half miles from Kilasa, there was a friendly family settlement where everyone seemed to be drunk and brave on *mtama* beer. Winston was elated. We camped under an old shady mango tree, and Andy and I (without Christine) splashed into the clean river. We hoped it was clear of bilharzia. Christine unfortunately couldn't join us as it wasn't private enough: for a full wash in camp, she first had to find a convenient isolated spot and take her water-filled canvas bucket as well as revolver with her; closer to camp Andy and I had to build her a hide with one of our tarpaulins. Her fingers and nails were permanently grimy from cooking on open wood fires and handling pans covered in black soot, and as she was always wearing trousers, she told me she felt unattractive and mannish, especially after I had accidentally hacked off most of her long hair whilst giving her an amateur haircut! When menstruating she also had to make do with tightly rolled toilet paper or leaves.

Mostly ignored, it was as though she was just a functioning ghost. I was aware that she and Andy had little time to think for themselves – the nature of this expedition – and that Christine yearned for the companionship of women. But at the end of a long day's trek, being swamped with Kiswahili questions by local women while very obviously trying to set up camp and cook before dark (so we could see what insects jumped into our food) bedevilled Christine.

On the morning we left, Winston repeatedly reassured us that he and Daniel knew the route well. Unfortunately, nothing they told us proved true, and the six and a half miles to sprawling *Ujamaa* Munisagara proved to be the most exhausting and nerve-wracking miles we had so far experienced.

The first crossing of the river was done in record time. Before we could unload the panniers, Livingstone voluntarily waded into the water and simply strolled through the river. But the route grew tougher. We were hacking at brittle yellow grass stalks reaching way over our heads, crushing them right down to enable the donkeys to see. Grass seeds caught in our clothes and on sweaty arms, and any path had disappeared.

We began to climb, and Burton balked at the sharp inclines and the thick stalks, continually stopping and bucking off his panniers. We were all exhausted; Winston had not prepared us for encountering vertical slopes. I was furious and repeatedly asked Winston for the promised paths. Then – an accident! In a narrow rockway with a sheer drop down to the river, Burton stumbled sideways, his rear end skidding through the stones, mooning at the water below. He was desperately scrabbling for hoof-holds. I flung myself onto a firm rock and with both hands tried to hold him up, but I couldn't bear Burton's weight. Slowly he slipped, then rolled onto me as we fell fifteen feet together to the bottom of a hollow ravine.

We were stuck between vertical boulders, and Burton was unmoving, lying painfully across my body. I didn't dare move a muscle in case I had broken any bones. Andy, Winston and Daniel climbed down and carefully lifted and pulled Burton off me. I was helped to struggle out from between the boulders and tangle of battered panniers. With my palms I felt tentatively over my body. I was miraculously uninjured. I was almost sure Burton had broken a leg, but after a little mollycoddling, he staggered to his feet and began nibbling at dry vegetation. We had been lucky. All we had to do then was get back up to the 'path'.

Winston continued to say the terrain would improve. Game scouts? He and Daniel didn't know what they were doing and wouldn't admit they didn't know. It was obvious neither of them had been on this track previously. After a pause I asked them, and it was true. They had made up the trail…

At my insistence we backtracked and forded the river again to flat ground. On the other side we wrung out socks, reloaded donkeys and prepared for a straight path which turned out to be anything but.

Fallen trees forced us to circumvent up a six-foot, muddy slope. Panniers off!

Thick banana palms and a broken bridge over water. Panniers off!

Donkeys pulled and pushed.

PART FOUR – FINALLY FREE FROM GAME SCOUTS

Andy and I were drained, our arm muscles twitching, mouths dry, madness shining from our eyes. And then darkness fell like a coin. Predator time! Warily clenching my revolver, Andy the shotgun, we descended in darkness to largish Munisagara at 8pm and headed for a hazily looming mango tree. In the process of putting up the outer tent and organising ourselves as quickly as possible, a group of local officials arrived for endless introductions. In Tanzania it's obligatory to shake hands.

Our torch refused to work.

Ants everywhere.

Tent zip teeth had not been binding since the fire.

Andy slumped against a tree, mumbling 'If I have another day like today, I swear I'm finished.' I began gradually to suspect that, despite taking the preventative medicine, he was suffering from suppressed malaria. Even though we were taking prophylactics, we had discovered we still suffered mildly suppressed symptoms.

We got to sleep at 1.45am. It had taken us twelve hours to cover six and a half miles!

Barely four hours later, we awoke, bleary-eyed, to find ourselves camped on a low hill, Ganga Peak before us and down below the river a quarter mile distant. In the heat there was a scent of musk that arose from the earth, from the very soil and undergrowth itself. A nearby bushfire wafted an unwashed, thick gagging miasma that attached itself permanently to locals, particularly noticeable when they perspired – the clinging unifying burnt breath of Africa. We too had begun to become African. Our skins slowly shed the English in us and took on the new in our surrounding environment: an exchange of bacteria.

We set out again the following morning on steep ascents and descents, sliding over slippery grass, tackling massively tall overhead thickets growing in great clumps. We had to cut away stumps and thorn branches that would otherwise impede the panniers. The donkeys scrabbled for hoof-holds, catching bags on branches, treading on our boots, barging us out of the way. Panniers fell off and rolled down the hill, cushions askew. Andy slipped in the loose earth and fell heavily, getting a twig up his nostril.

It was extremely late – 5.30pm on 1 October – when I decided to bush-camp by the river. Winston wanted to walk into Mzaganza, fifteen minutes away, and I overruled him. Winston repeated that he should go into Mzaganza to alert the chairman and get some food for himself. We gave in and said he could go, but according to the instructions from his Game Department he had to be back by dark.

We cooked, ate and waited in the overgrown valley. And waited. Winston and Daniel finally appeared at 10pm – and Winston admitted going to Mangaladasi where his wife lived. He said he'd had to go because his wife was ill.

How did he hear she was ill? *Someone told him on our way from Munisagara.* Why did he not tell me then? Why lie and say he was going to Mzaganza and would be returning before night fell? Winston hung his head and giggled nervously. I wanted to wring his neck. I was furious and made it absolutely clear that from now on they would follow the strict orders from their Game Department:

1. During the day, one scout had to be in the camp.
2. After 5.30pm until morning, two scouts should be in the camp.

PART FOUR – FINALLY FREE FROM GAME SCOUTS

I'd had enough!

I was woken by scorching heat after three hours' sleep and found Andy already up stitching ripped donkey cushions. I found a shady spot below the riverbank to write and eat breakfast in peace and was interrupted by Andy shouting 'Where are you going?' Winston and Daniel were slinking across the river. They sheepishly returned to tell Andy they were going to bathe. They didn't ever bathe! Back to breakfast, after which I climbed the bank to speak to Winston and found quivering air. They had both of them run off across the water like rabbits. Back to breakfast. As I was finishing, a *balozi* living nearby came to tell us that Winston and Daniel had crashed into his house covered in mud and grass. They said they'd run terrified all the way because I had picked up my gun to shoot them!

We left at 9am. The landscape began to undergo a gradual change without our noticing. The thick green had faded, becoming bare and dusty scattered with bushes. The soil changed colour from rich brown to grey shale and now a browny-red dust.

Lake Gombo (and in the distance the prominent peak of Gombo Mountain sloping down to the water) was a large circular lake which swelled during the rains, flooding for five miles. When completely full it almost reached as far as GodeGode thirteen miles away. This was clearly marked on our maps. Stanley described the lake as 'a map of England without Wales'.

Kidete nestled under Nyatikwanga Hill a half mile from the lake and spread over flat brown scrubland. We camped under three huge trees in the deserted centre of the village and learnt from curious people who arrived to greet us that Kidete was known as *Madete*, as Stanley had correctly named it. *Madete* is the Kisagara word for bamboo.

There was no clear path from here for thirty-three miles to Mpwapwa, and people preferred to walk along a portion of the old German railway track, which we didn't want to do. Once many animals had lived in or near the lake: hippo, buffalo, zebra, boar, kudu, hyrax, antelope. The surface swarmed with black swan, duck, ibis, cranes, pelicans and fish eagles. And in the vicinity were guinea fowl, pigeon, hornbill, owl, francolin and sandgrouse. Now there were no hippo, zebra or giraffe. The lake, however, was teeming with cormorants – all absolutely tame, having never been shot at. So with our blasting shotgun we guiltily bagged cormorants galore and ate them with *ugali* made from very yellow maize flour. It was so easy to shoot the cormorants just sitting there waiting: I definitely felt sorry for the helpless birds, but we had to eat!

Just before reaching Kidete, Stanley had camped on the 'Mukondokwa' river, sent back two donkeys and a cart and waited patiently for four hours for a sick Shaw to arrive. Shaw eventually appeared riding on a donkey and with a porter carrying the donkey cart on his head. Stanley simply wrote, 'We arrived at Madete at 4 p.m., minus two donkeys which had stretched their weary limbs in death.'

In Stanley's at times meticulous account, the donkey numbers and deaths he describes are so vague that it is extremely difficult to know how many donkeys he had at any one time. He began with seventeen donkeys in his personal caravan. After the Mkata 'only 5 remained'. At Madete/Kidete above, two more died, meaning he only had three donkeys remaining! Yet at his river camp he tells of Shaw and Farquhar miraculously resurrecting the animals: 'seven of my own have died.' In Mpwapwa attempting to buy new beasts he writes again, 'I had but 10 donkeys left...' Strangely, the usually so precise Stanley is completely imprecise about donkeys throughout.

He spent two days at Kidete and because the lake water was high, he was forced to traverse Nyakitwanga 750 feet above the water. But the rough path that we actually saw was only 400 feet high. Before reaching Kidete/Madete, Stanley wrote that he marched a distance of seven miles before sighting 'the Lake of Ugombo'. However, he would have sighted the 1,000-foot peak of Gombo Mountain whilst walking towards Kidete after four miles, not seven. I felt very confused. He continued trekking along the lake's north-western extremity and was obliged to camp there two days as his Indian cooper, Jako, had deserted with one of Stanley's best carbines.

Morning. Andy was raring to go. A farmer, the brother of the previous *balozi*, came from his home on the hill to say that he had witnessed the whole 'incident with the gun' – and he had seen no gun wielded! He also told us that yesterday people had seen our two scouts hurrying elsewhere. Winston's false accusations could have blocked our progress, so we were relieved. Amazing! Where had all this information come from? People talked about a bush telegraph in Africa, and this was an example. You were never alone in Africa.

The weather had perceptibly cooled, a strong breeze blowing.

*

Usagara: Land that Spread

Stanley made a big decision at Usagara. The donkeys were dying, so: 'Farquhar would destroy them all one after another. To save the expedition from ruin...'

At a grand breakfast of roast quarter of goat, stewed liver, sweet potatoes, hot pancakes and coffee, held to announce Stanley's decision, the two white men made it clear they too had endured enough. Shaw said, 'It is a downright shame the way you treat us... you are working me too hard.'

Annoyed at Shaw's criticism Stanley replied, 'Have you considered well your positions? Do you know that you are my servant, sir, and not my companion?'

'Servant be —' Shaw began to retort.

'But before Mr Shaw could finish his sentence,' Stanley wrote, 'he had measured his length on the ground.'

Raising himself up, Shaw replied, 'I tell you what it is, sir, I think I had better go back. I have had enough and I do not mean to go any further with you... I ask my discharge from you.' Stanley immediately gave orders for Shaw's tent to be struck, gun and pistol to be confiscated and Shaw and his baggage escorted 200 yards outside the camp. In the Africa of that time this was in effect to sentence someone to a lonely death.

In the meantime, Stanley explained to Farquhar that he intended leaving him with the village chief of Mpwapwa until he recovered his health, together with a six-month supply of cloth and beads. Farquhar apparently agreed.

Remember this was Stanley's own written account.

Inevitably, and quite naturally, the unarmed solitary and helpless Shaw returned to beg pardon.

That night a bullet tore through Stanley's tent a few inches above his body. Stanley rushed into the night, asking his men who had fired the gun? They replied 'Shaw.' But Stanley found Shaw asleep. On testing his gun, he found it warm – evidence that it had just been discharged. Shaw, when woken, explained, 'I dreamed I saw a thief pass my door and I fired. Ah – yes – I forgot. I did fire. Why, what is the matter?'

13

Mpwapwa: How Stanley's Man Farquhar Met His End

Our next major goal was Mpwapwa, where Stanley's man Farquhar was last heard of going to the village chief to recover his health. It was now a town with a population of 100,000.

We set off early, heading into the lands known as Ugogo, the land of dead wood. A long time ago an old and huge tree had collapsed across the caravan path, blocking part of the way, and travellers took to resting/camping there. The Kinyamwezi word for dead tree is *gogo*, so the area became known as Ugogo (the place or land of dead wood). The original settlers, from Wahehe stock, eventually intermixed with other tribes and became known as the *Wagogo*.

They had a distinctive look of flat faces and high cheekbones, with large wooden plugs in pierced ears. The true Wagogo of both sexes are by the age of two marked on the forehead with a small round scar called *nindi* by one of two methods: either the last leaf from a baobab branch is placed in the fire and while burning is stuck to the child's forehead, or a stick is spun between the palms of the hands against a hard block of wood until the tip of the stick begins to glow and is then pressed against the child's forehead until the child cries and the parents are happy. When a child is eight, the two lower front teeth are knocked out using the blade of an axe – this done so that if the child were ever to contract tetanus and the jaw become locked, milk and porridge could still be fed through the gap in the teeth. At the age of twelve to thirteen, the males had their earlobes burnt through and a large circular piece of wood inserted to increase the size of the hole. Eventually, they wore hanging metal weights to stretch the lobes. The bigger the hole the better.

The land of Ugogo was an orange-coloured, dusty plain riddled with deep cracks in the earth – *korongos.* In places there were dry, dense thickets, and dominating everywhere were thick-girthed baobab with grasping short branches like roots attempting to claw into the sky, crowded with flower-feeding bats and large-eyed bush babies. The straggly bare branches led to a belief that it grew upside down. We heard stories of how God had originally sited the baobab in the Congo basin, but the tree complained of heat and humidity. So God removed it to the Ruwenzori's. There it was dissatisfied with the intense cold. Losing patience, God tossed it into hot, dry, lowland regions. It landed upside down, and made no further comment! Homemade hollowed log honey-hives were suspended in baobab trees. Man-made holes in their trunks had sticks inserted, up which to climb to the hives.

At the almost dry Matamondo River where Stanley camped and which he named 'Matamombo' he commented that it was 'celebrated for its pool of bitter water of the colour of ochre'. This bitterness was the harsh saltiness that tainted all the water hereabouts, brought in from Dodoma by the Kinyasungwi River. Here Stanley's dog Omar died of 'inflammation of the bowels'.

Plentiful sharp-pointed wild sisal, which elephants loved to chew for its juice, the knocking sound of guinea fowl, cruel-looking hyena prints and the barking of baboons signalling to each other surrounded us. Baboons travel in troops, have sharp teeth and incredibly strong arms and when hungry successfully attack humans carrying food…

Sucking and chewing off the sour white tartar lining from the smooth pebbly seeds of hard-shelled dangling baobab fruit to alleviate our raging thirst, we continued past the salty river as darkness began and hyenas started to howl, to enter nearby GodeGode. It was a sprawling dust heap of stumbling drunks where I asked for the leftovers after beer had been made and fed this to the ravenous donkeys. Great donkey-farts in the night!

We reached Mpwapwa on 10 October (the Kigogo name is *Mhamvwa*) and camped in this medium-sized town, population 100,000, on the side of a humpbacked hill in the shade of a new church still being built. It was the only shade we could find, and we were immediately surrounded by onlookers and noisy children who threatened to fall onto our tent.

*

Explore Mpwapwa. Centre of town, blue flowering jacaranda trees (planted by the British) line earthen, dusty, myriad broad streets providing welcome colour to sad, dishevelled low buildings. *Further on huge mango trees – plentiful shade (planted by Germans). Numerous pombe shops. Dukas (shops) sell vegetables, cigarettes and Coca-Cola. Huge stone granaries (constructed by British) storing emergency grain in case of drought. Stand beneath giant Muganhi tree! Speculate whether this where Stanley first met Sheikh Thani resting under immense shade. Deep dried riverbed fifty yards to left. Under Muganhi tree, six resting donkeys, traders with wares – tomatoes, mchicha, cassava and nuts spread on cloths on ground. Beside them, market building where can purchase meat in morning when freshly slaughtered, spices and dried fish rest of time.*

*

An elderly man speaking immaculate English said, 'You must greet me "*Shikamoo*", as I am your elder.' He introduced himself as Joshua Reuben Mgoli, sixty-two years old, trained by the Church Missionary Society at Mpwapwa, and a typical villager, dependent on food from his own piece of land and father of eighteen children; he kept their names written on the back of his kitchen door in order to remember them!

He pointed out a rock thirty yards away on which Stanley was supposed to have carved '27th May' (the date of Farquhar's death), 'WL Farquhar' and 'Livingstone'. 'I will take you to see this tomorrow,' he announced.

We climbed to the top of our brown scrub-covered hill. The view was of the barren, forbidding plains of Marenga Mkali dominated by dusty thorn scrub. It was gradually turning to desert as the locals had cut down the trees for building supports and for fuel, grasses and plants had been burned and cows and goats had overgrazed the land. With minimal rain, the red sand soil failed to retain any crops, while strong winds blew with a vengeance, stirring up dust.

'People don't care,' said Joshua. 'They have made new paths into the hills and persist in collecting firewood and cutting trees to make charcoal, though the Government has made this illegal. If they are caught they pay a small bribe, say five shillings or ten shillings, and they are left free. Twenty years ago in Mpwapwa there were many trees and many animals – hyena, lion, leopard and baboon...'

Our evening was spent listening to hymns sung by the children, joyful and enthusiastic but like no hymns I had heard before with their improvisation and harmony totally African. Holding his head heavenward, Burton insisted on joining the singing, braying in a guttural tenor! The choir collapsed in nervous giggles.

'A singing donkey,' Andy commented wryly. 'Horses definitely don't sing!'

We fell asleep with our ears ringing rhythms, then woke early to find Joshua had called at 6.30am and left a note:

Dear George,
A short history of the place:
　The village now is called Vinghawe.
　Mr Henry Morton Stanley passed here. See (a) the stone which was written by him; and (b) the tree called Mlumbulumbu.
　The grave of Bwana Mwalimu ('Mr Teacher'). This referred to the first English missionary, John

> Richard Price, who stayed here preaching the Gospel of God from 1880–1895.
>
> The old church, which was built 1876 with mud and roofed with poles and grass, was burnt by an Arab called Abushir who was head of the Arabs dealing in the slave trade in 1884.
>
> The grave of the former famous Chief Chipanjilo.
>
> The grave of Mr Farquhar who was killed by order of the Chief.

I was dumbstruck by his statement that Farquhar had been killed by order of the chief, for the British authorities had unsuccessfully spent years attempting to find out the truth. Although Stanley only wrote a page on Farquhar's death, I was sure he must have had his suspicions as he was never shown a proper grave, nor could he find a trace of Farquhar's bones. Stanley inscribed words on a rock and built a stone mound to commemorate the spot where he believed Farquhar had died.

When Stanley departed, Farquhar had been left behind in a tent from which he moved to the chief's *boma*. According to Mapuga Chipanjilo (son of Chief Chipanjilo Lusito – more commonly known as Lukole), who would have been six to ten years old in 1871, Farquhar was buried in a hole or culvert in a gulley and the body covered in grass – contrary to Stanley's account in which he stated his belief that Farquhar's body was 'taken out, left naked, and not buried'.

Stanley was in Tabora when he received news of Farquhar's death. But as Farquhar had died only a week after Stanley left Mpwapwa, there had been more than ample time for a runner to inform Stanley earlier. Why was this not done?

'It is correct to say,' admitted Joshua adamantly, 'he was roughly buried and the location of the body kept secret. That is, until British times. Bear in mind the people in this village then and now were always of the opinion that the chief ordered Farquhar killed. Perhaps he had become too much of a hindrance. Sometime after Chief Lukole's death, there was some argument over who should succeed him. The British resolved the situation by announcing that whoever could point out Farquhar's grave would then be recognised as Chief. Ishmael Mapuga did so (grandson of Lukole) and was pronounced Paramount Chief. But I've found out more about this for you, there is an old man...'

Joshua weaved us down to Chief Lukole's grave, and where his house would have been. Great-grandchildren were still alive and lived nearby. His grave was a rubbish dump, but across the broad path and to the right, to the centre of a large maize field, almost flat on the ground was a simple stone plaque.

We picked away dried yellow maize stalks to read:

W.L. Farquhar
On Stanley's Expedition
Died May 1871

'This was where Mr Farquhar was buried,' said Joshua. 'The British laid this stone and also constructed a small path leading to it from the main road, but as you can see the path is gone. One day soon a tractor will tear the stone away. People don't care for history...'

On our guided walk we took the opportunity to visit the Land Survey Office, always seeking more detailed maps to provide further clues to the route Stanley had taken. There was a shout from the Game Office across the road; the officials wanted Joshua. He finally emerged in a quiet mood and I realised something unexpected had occurred.

'Joshua, were you being interrogated?' I asked him.

'Yes,' he replied, 'I will tell you. They called me in to ask who had given me authority to escort you around town. The officer told me there was a *mzungu* once who pretended to be a priest. But when he went up the mountain, he had a camera hidden in a pen. He was photographing army bases. "We must be careful," the DNR Officer – the District Natural Resources Officer – said, "these *wazungu* are very clever".'

Shades of Morogoro – we were seen as spies once again!

At the Land Office, the female secretary said the maps were all locked up – although, as Andy pointed out, the drawers in the next room were gaping open. She announced that in any event we were forbidden to look. Anyway, there were no town maps, no regional maps, no district maps – no maps!

The *fundi* (craftsman) found by Joshua and meant to carve our names on a rock to prove we were present (for money of course, had stopped working and got sozzled on *mtama* beer. The carving, like Stanley's original working of rock commemorating Farquhar, was almost illegible. Joshua asked us what we would pay the drunken rock carver.

I answered, 'Nothing! The job is not done.'

'But you took a photograph of the rock,' said Joshua, 'so

you must pay him something...' He tailed off at my look. It was obvious he was in on the 420-shilling deal.

I cut him short. 'We're leaving in five minutes!'

Three miles out of town the supposed stone mason caught up with us on his cycle.

'I have come!' he announced, forcing his cycle alongside the donkeys, panting and sweating off his beer with the effort.

'What for?'

'The work —'

He was cut off by our reply: 'The work is incomplete.'

'But the money? Joshua and I — '

'The work is unfinished. *Hamna maneno* (No more words).'

We walked on and he fell back, not knowing what more to say.

This constant being on guard, together with insistent and aggressive begging, and children attempting to steal from our tent, wore us down. Here it was not the kind of curiosity that we had previously witnessed. No, this was pure envy – a desire for our goods, our clothes, what we were – sucking us up greedily with their eyes. And this was not because they had nothing, not because they were poor. They were well off by African standards.

Well, it seemed we'd finally done it. We had to admit that if we felt this way – and we all confessed that this was the case – we were now well on the way to becoming racists. If this Wagogo burning stare, constant suspicion and declared enmity was what we were now to expect, I sincerely hoped that we could clear out of their area as fast as possible. We were all different, had different cultures, traditions and habits (I know whereof I speak as I can think in both Cypriot and English and the two attitudes are miles apart), but I wouldn't have wanted these Africans living next door to me. I didn't want to exploit them or their country – after this expedition I would be leaving – but I in turn didn't want them to exploit me.

Oh dear, this *was* a malaise. Long term? Or would we recover?

*

Approximately 238.25 miles covered by late October 1984. We're now trekking through the desert plains of Ugogo (not even a quarter of the way across Tanzania) and Stanley's account reckons it will take three days to traverse waterless desert of Marenga Mkali (Bitter or Fierce Water). Despite drumming dust-pelting wind gusting from south, constantly blowing hats off, the temperature is humid, short rains close. We meet dishevelled young Lazaro, wandering aimlessly in deserted land. Says will walk with us to Dodoma. For no pay. Has nothing else to do. Come across many waterholes...

*

Stanley noted that the Arabs and natives drank the water without ill results but were careful to keep their thirsty baggage animals away. Now no villagers drank this water. They only gave it to their cows. 'The people would have serious problems of the stomach,' Lazaro said.

Our new companion kept us entertained during

this monotonous flat landscape by pointing out useful medicinal plants and trees. Here are some he told us about:

Miswaki (toothbrush bush – *Commiphora myrrha*), whose slim branches are hacked off and the bark at one end trimmed until the green core is revealed. This, Lazaro showed us, is chewed until bristly and then used to rub at and clean the teeth. Lazaro kept a twig in his mouth all day.

Manzirani tree. When the skin of one of its yellow branches is pricked, a clear sap oozes. This can be used to wipe onto a wound and acts as an antiseptic. It also repels flies and insects, and can be used to cure a cough or sore throat by placing some of the sap on a finger and sucking it throughout the day, or to rub onto skin or through hair to get rid of ticks and lice.

The baobab tree produces a dry powdery fruit encased in a hard gourd-like shell containing vitamins and minerals. This fruit can be used to treat fevers and dysentery. Gum and juice from the bark are also used to clean sores, neutralise the effects of poison arrows and as a mouthwash for toothache. When a branch is cut and the bark stripped, the white pithy inner lining of bark is peeled off and can be used as very strong rope to secure goods or animals or to quench the thirst by chewing.

The bean tree, known in Zambia as *Akalunguti*, is used to treat AIDS. The same tree is found in Australia and South America.

Mchunga – very like *mchicha* – is boiled and strained and the bitter juice drunk to cure *surua* (measles). Babies too young to drink can instead be bathed in the liquid. They absorb the medication through their pores.

Mia Arobaini (Four hundred) – so called because it has myriad uses. This is the neem tree also found in India where it is known as the 'village dispensary'. Various parts of it can be used to protect crops from insects, as well as medicine to purify blood, treat rheumatism, eye, skin, kidney and bladder diseases. It can also produce soap, gum, solvents, toothpaste, and acts as a contraceptive.

We and the poor donkeys plodded over eroded, cracked gulleys. Then we spied the village of Mgunga from higher ground, only three miles away: many squeezed-together *tembes* – houses – spreadeagled onto flat red earth with nothing but aged yellow stalks, dried weeds and baobab trees.

Stanley wrote that the profusion of baobab trees was probably because it would prove a task to fell these giants and in addition, 'during a famine the fruit of the baobab furnished a flour, which in the absence of anything better, was said to be eatable and nourishing'.

We spent the whole day attempting to escape the frying sun and whirling dust. When we found a narrow shadow to sit in, the dust pelted into our faces in fierce gusts, and it was impossible to write, or even think. In late afternoon a dust storm raged across the plain. In seconds we were completely covered in red dust, eyes burning, our tent almost flat to the ground. This gale continued until 8pm.

'What's worse, the sun or dust?' I asked, my whipped body turned away from facing the fierce wind.

Andy and Christine both agreed on dust.

We ate stewed *matoke* (plantains) in tomato and onion peppered with wind-blown dirt. Christine, whose eyes were red with grit, then immediately entered the protection of the tent and refused to come out again. In the midst of these dancing winds a blanketed, flapping figure arrived with fifty eggs to sell. We had asked for half a dozen eggs the day before and none had appeared! We cleaned the donkeys' clogged eyes and our own with saline solution and purchased bran and dried groundnut (peanut) leaves from villagers for the donkeys. Unfortunately, this was all there was for them.

We left at 8am on a clear path between Chadhumba village and Kigwana Mountains. Approximately 275.25 miles had been covered. Slow progress! To the right of tiny Chadhumba we came to where Stanley had a rest stop. Then Handali, a sprawling conglomeration of numerous huts, corrugated-iron roofs glinting, which we reached by early afternoon after ten wind-battered miles.

The chairman offered us a room and we thankfully sheltered there from the wind and dust. An *askari* persuaded us to herd our donkeys into the main village hall, which was like a large warehouse. A smoothly dressed clinical assistant in Lee Cooper jeans, modern T-shirt and new European trainers – all presented by foreign aid – tried to sell me, illegally, a bottle of chloroquine, antibiotic ampoules and needles. Many hyena, he explained, approached the village seeking water. He had shot two the night before. They usually herded the *Ujamaa* goats and cows inside.

Handali seemed to be laid out somewhat like a showplace for aid visitors from abroad, assessing whether they would donate to Tanzania and how much. They flew into Dodoma (there's an airstrip) wanting to see a typical *Ujamaa* set-up in Ugogo. But Handali was a cardboard cut-out, a sham. There were vegetable-filled market stalls under a shade tree, the villagers frenetically pretending cultivation since the vegetables had been supplied from elsewhere. There was an *Ujamaa* lorry, which travelled into Dodoma daily, but it carried no goods for sale; an *Ujamaa* shop, but it had been robbed of everything the previous month; no one had any idea who by, though it was accepted the thieves would have needed a getaway car as cars could not arrive in Handali without being heard or seen. The shop had never reopened. Individual villagers brought in scarcity goods such as kerosene, but these were openly *gonga'd* (sold on the black market for high prices).

Before we left the following morning for East Mvumi, the chairman rudely told Lazaro we had to pay for water to clean stains from off the concrete floor. Andy, affected by his abrupt manner, told him to stuff it! And Lazaro agreed.

*

In East Mvumi, still in Ugogo, we were invited to dinner at the home of Dr Foster, an ophthalmic medical missionary. Here we scoffed food at a real table, drinking unboiled, clear water from a bore hole and watched the sitcom *Porridge* on video. Reeking of campfire smoke, we slumped in soft cuddly armchairs and tasted again the decadent and wonderful pleasures of the West; we were developing callouses on our buttocks from sitting on rocks and logs. Dr Foster's son was wearing track shoes fastened not with laces but by velcro strips and we marvelled at these, realising how our two-year sojourn had distanced us from developments in fashion, inventions, films, books...

In the evening we used a real toilet and had a hot shower and shave. We miraculously transformed into human beings. But after months of bush, back in a civilised house, this was the first time we'd really studied our faces in a mirror for a long time and we didn't recognise ourselves! We looked like startled wild strangers, with livid, burning eyes glaring out of featureless burnt faces, our hair unruly. Touching a careful finger to a peeling nose we noted the stranger in the mirror exactly imitated the action and began to laugh, a mouthful of dazzling white teeth shining at the self we'd just acknowledged.

It was Lazaro's first time in a proper bed; we were sleeping in bunks, and he took the top one and cuddled up like a babe gurgling to himself with pleasure. Personally I found it difficult to sleep on a spring mattress as I'd become used to the hard earth.

Alastair, the English pharmacist, invited us to lunch the next day. Andy was overjoyed. 'This is more like it. This is how it should be! Why did I agree to this stupidly difficult expedition? I should have come as an aid expert!' And lunch at Alastair's was a luxurious affair. I read the previous week's *Observer*! All the things I was trying to escape hit me in the face: VAT on most goods, political correctness, proliferation of writing competitions, writing courses... Depression never failed to creep over from England.

Before leaving, I took the opportunity to be tested for

new glasses at the eye hospital, and it seemed my terrible short sight had corrected itself! I theorised that my vision, unhampered by city blocks and buildings, was forced to stretch itself over plains and valleys necessarily checking for wild animals and so had improved. Dr Foster agreed, but warned that when I returned to London my short sight could return.

Stanley had continued on to camp with the Arab traders at Mvumi Makulu (the Compound of the Chief). Here Sheikh Thani and Stanley despatched two of their men to the sultan with lavish gifts (six bales of cloth) as a first instalment of their tribute or *hongo*, the omission of which would have been a signal for war. The sultan rejected the gifts as not being sufficient. He wanted ten times the amount offered since he was of the opinion that the white man (Stanley) was rich, a sultan in his own right. The Arabs schemed, then sent five times the first amount. Bearers were thus occupied for the rest of the day running backwards and forwards with gifts. A furious Stanley calculated that the sultan had finally received fifty-four bales of cloth – a total value of $49.25. But he knew he had to submit, for the truculent sultan, if irritated, could easily have demanded a double tribute.

Staying at Mvumi had raised my spirits. I was feeling optimistic as we approached Mvumi Makulu – only three or four miles distant. Scattered houses outside areas riddled with gulleys, riverbeds and dried *matama* stalks. Huge stone granaries built by the British now housed locals. In the scrubby market area, a few empty stalls hung stalks of green unripe dates for sale. It was amazing to see that this once-prosperous village had sunk into insignificance and

East Mvumi had expanded purely because *wazungu* had settled there and made it work with their eye hospital.

Baboons barked warning sounds from the trees. We came upon a dishevelled man, three mangy dogs and his son dragging by a skeletal leg the carcass of a baboon. The father explained that his dogs had killed it, and he would give them the meat and use the fur to make a hat for himself. We thought the man – who looked nearly starving – would probably eat the baboon himself.

No surprise: the water tap was again broken; water came from holes in a riverbed. We collected grey water there and refreshed it through our ultra-efficient water pump, and purchased firewood and a chicken. All the while, locals – particularly children – crowded around asking exorbitant sums for eggs, milk, and bran for the donkeys. We suffered great guilt in that we couldn't find anything more sufficient for our suffering animals. Speke often nudged me with his snout to show me he was hungry, but I was helpless.

Overnight, a short shower warningly spattered our tent. In the morning, we set off to Dodoma, the newly built capital town, past a local blacksmith's shelter where the blacksmith was pumping his bellows with one foot while hammering car springs into the shape of a *jembe* blade (hoe) with his hands. The path we were following was not on my map and was used by cattle herders as well as charcoal sellers, so flies plagued us. It was impossible to get lost, though, as we could just follow the charcoal droppings and flies and ignore the cow pats.

We had now covered 294.5 miles, and the expedition seemed interminable, especially in the face of illnesses which continued to plague us.

PART FOUR – FINALLY FREE FROM GAME SCOUTS

Two miles out of Matumbulu and 400 yards south-south-east of Misani Mountain we came upon old granite grinding stones at the side of the path: smooth hollowed lumps of rock which we would normally pass by without noticing, though Stanley mentioned stones like these in his account. Lazaro informed us that these here were from the 1917–20 hunger named *Mtunya* (Persistence) – all that were left as evidence of where people lived. The stones had a bowl-shaped indentation where sorghum or millet was placed and ground by hand with another stone. During hungers, people would secretly grind and cook at night so that their starving neighbours wouldn't know they had food, and as the stones were bowl-shaped, the sound of grinding was muffled so in the morning the nourished could also pretend to be starving and wouldn't be pestered.

The stone and method of grinding have existed since before the time of Christ; Lazaro told us they were developed at the same time as *mtama* (millet) was first grown in Africa.

14

Dodoma: Idodomera ('To be stuck')

Early November 1984. Have fierce stomach pains again. Thinking it malaria, took chloroquine. For amoebic dysentery, I took flagyl/metronidazole again and again – an excess can cause cancer.

Christine is keeping a humorous list of my illnesses. I can't seem to find it funny. She has lost weight; her asthma playing up. Andy accidentally chopped his hand with axe – blood sprayed everywhere! Poured iodine over and covered it tightly. Later tripped over rock, gashed knee; also bandaged. Now limping with useless hand. I'm bent over with abdominal cramps, Christine wheezing.

Really cannot think how we will manage lifting panniers. Christine can't do it!

*

We gradually ascended over rocky riverbeds to see Dodoma spreadeagled below us on the thirsty plain. On the right was the distinctive

Simba (Lion) Rock. It took a while to trail down past a new reservoir being built, and the Dodoma Winery to the Kilimani Club where we attempted to get directions from a group of drunken guys hanging around outside:

'Ah... you are the ones who have come to make fun of our people.'

And: 'You are also, I see, treating our people like slaves...' For they had seen Lazaro carrying his own bag on his head in traditional style! Soon after this Lazaro traipsed off quite casually, and I regretted not rewarding him somehow for his delightful companionship.

The Tanzanian Government had announced in 1973 that their capital would move from Dar es Salaam to a more central location to better serve the needs of the people, and Dodoma was chosen. Already an established town (caravan porters had always camped at this convenient halfway mark in the country now known as Tanzania), the town sat at a major crossroads with an agreeable climate, impressive landscape, and room for development. The town was meant by President Nyerere to be seen as the brave new official capital of Tanzania, but perversely, everyone still recognised Dar es Salaam as the unofficial capital and most government offices remained there.

Unfinished, unacknowledged, doomed to remain a half-finished crumbling façade, Dodoma stood in the middle of Tanzania on an arid 3,658-foot-high plateau surrounded by hills and massive granite outcrops. The centre was a showpiece of large imposing stone-built structures, but the rest of Dodoma was like all other Tanzanian townships – decaying, dusty and smelling of sewage – but very like Dar es Salaam in that *wazungu* aid workers ostentatiously

Dodoma: Idodomera ('To be stuck')

drove around in brand new four-wheel-drive TX-plate vehicles, these number plates leading to their getting the nickname of *ticks* (bloodsuckers), because it was felt that they were enriching themselves at the country's expense and continuing to bleed the country dry.

The market was badly stocked: mounds of rotting tomatoes and onions, expensive chickens and flyblown meat. In comparison, Morogoro had been a paradise.

Not such a far cry from the reality is the story of how Dodoma began on this site and received its name. Nearby there is a dry river, the *Kikuyu* ('fig tree'). Long ago this had been an uninhabited swamp, and an elephant attempting to drink got stuck in the mud – and died there. Locals (and caravan porters) observed the dying elephant day after day and began referring to the place as *Idodomera* (place to be stuck). This was later shortened to Dodoma. And Dodoma is still stuck! Without adequate infrastructure, still unfinished, ambitious plans dogged by a shortage of funds and lack of governmental political will, it was clear that the development of Dodoma would for the foreseeable future remain a pipe dream.

Worrying about the donkeys now. We de-wormed them, which helped with their breathing, but they were all suffering from mange, caused by mites feeding off the surface of the skin, and causing itching, scaly skin, with their hair falling out. The usual practice would be to shave the affected areas and apply insecticide all over, but Livingstone would be bald if we did this! Poor Livingstone was also wandering off, fording rivers unconcernedly, as he was suffering from sleeping sickness. At his advanced age, he may never recover from this.

PART FOUR – FINALLY FREE FROM GAME SCOUTS

We were offered an empty USAID house in Area D, the diplomatic area in town, where there were only two modern stone houses plonked in a spreading, dried, yellow thicket of stalks, builders' rubble and fierce wind. The donkeys could enjoy the grass on our small lawn there, but soon, despite continuous watering, there would be none, so we needed to track down a paddock for them. There were none! The best we could get was a school tennis court – they kept school cows on one of the courts – which was eminently safe, but we'd still need to find hay of some kind or cassava and papaya leaves for them.

We de-wormed ourselves too, and got on with repairs and cleaning of tent, boots, pistol, procuring and drying meat (*biltong*), stitching panniers… Christine and I both felt nauseous and groggy with sore throats.

That night I felt as if I was suffocating. I got out of bed and proceeded to the open window for air, but blacked out, my eyes rolled up in my head, my body convulsing. This was like malaria, I decided, and dosed both Christine and myself with chloroquine. We lay side by side in single beds holding hands just outside of our mosquito nets while Andy fed us rehydration drinks.

After tests the Italian doctor now decided that despite regularly taking a malaria preventative we had contracted dengue fever. Chloroquine was the correct treatment. But frighteningly it didn't work. We spent most of two weeks sleeping, barely able to open our eyes. With no electricity in the house, and only a little water trickling through after a mains pipe had burst, we had to rely on the water in our tanks, which locals from the town wanted to buy. But we needed it for the donkeys, and for us. Such a scarce but necessary resource.

A vet came to inject Livingstone with a powerful and risky drug to treat his sleeping sickness – but had no distilled water. He could not use the boiled local water as he was afraid of the minerals it contained.

'You see, the assistant with the key to the dispensary has gone out.' He'd have to go back and wait for him. Finally, late in the day, he injected Livingstone. Now our donkey had a chance of survival.

Whilst stuck in Dodoma, we received from England new boots, a new compass and better tents. We were eternally grateful for these small luxuries as we had missed them terribly.

After initial showers when we first arrived, the short rains had properly begun, but they seemed to have linked up with the long rains! They hit with a vengeance: thunder and lightning, torrents all day, overcast sky and cold evenings. Meat we had laid out to wind-dry in strips began to grow mouldy and smell gamey. We were forced to bring it indoors and dry it under a permanently whirring overhead fan. Locals commented they could not ever remember rain as continuous and heavy. It was the heaviest rainfall in Dodoma for twenty years.

The Bahi Swamp, where we were meant to go next, was now obviously flooded. Our only solution would be to take a path that skirted the edge of the swamp, with the Rift Escarpment on our left side.

We were told this path would be impassable. But we had to go and see for ourselves.

15

From Uyanzi to Unyambwa: Land of the Flies to Land of the Dog

Ready to set out again, first to Bihawna, in the 'Land of the Flies'. The legend has it that once Wanyatura warriors killed a giraffe and built a camp and stayed almost a month until they had consumed all the meat. Meat left over became fly-blown and began to rot, with numerous feeding flies buzzing around the carcass. Other natives passing by, seeing them living like this, began to refer to them as 'the people of the flies' – *Wayanzi*. As the Wanyatura decided to settle permanently, their area became known as the 'land of flies'.

A Japanese lad, Yoshikiro (Yoshi for short), who was studying to be a doctor in London and voluntarily helping the Flying Doctor Service in Dodoma, had been fascinated by our journey and asked to accompany us for a week. I warned him that he would have to help with the donkeys, especially up the Rift, and shouldn't carry anything heavy (he had a rucksack) as the donkeys would be fully laden so could not carry his goods. He would share a tent with Andy and eat what we ate.

He agreed. Then arrived with a gigantic rucksack.

'Yoshi, I told you —'

'I know, I know. I can manage.'

But after a few hours of walking, a dripping Yoshi was bent double by heat and biting insects, asking if the donkeys could take his rucksack...

There was a clear path all the way to Bihiwana with fresh hyena, lion, elephant and dik-dik prints and elephant dung looking like brittle broken birds' nests. We crossed several water courses and a wide river to arrive at Bihiwana Catholic Mission perched on a hill.

With the Tanzanian father-superior's agreement, we camped inside an unfinished seminary building sleeping on tarpaulins laid on the floor. There was grass and the donkeys munched happily despite the incessant rainfall. There was no dry wood and we needed to erect a tarpaulin rapidly so Christine could cook outside under shelter. Our visibility was impaired, boots and trousers soggy and clinging. Meanwhile Yoshi, who was absolutely knackered from the walk, was taking ready-soups and snacks out of his rucksack and then washing them in the clear water we'd pumped for cooking while we shaved and washed in the murky smoky-white water we had been collecting.

Because Stanley and his eight caravans had then camped at the village of Kididimo, Andy and I left Christine and Yoshi in the camp while we trekked over to Kididimo – which wasn't marked correctly on our map. Four and three-quarter miles north-west in keeping with Stanley's estimate, through muddy watercourses and across one river. Finally, we arrived in Kididimo where Stanley had commented: 'The water... in the neighbourhood had the flavour of warm horse-urine, and two donkeys sickened and died.' I was definitely intrigued by Stanley's mysterious donkey increase. How many *did* he have?

We were exhausted. We should have stayed in Bihiwana instead of attempting this trek. Andy almost blacked out, his head between his knees, while sitting listening to me talk to the villagers about Tanzania. They told us on that very morning a villager had met a huge lion on our path. *That* was encouraging news. On the wary way back, we were both limping, feet swollen and blistered.

Yoshi attempted unsuccessfully to chop some firewood for us. A passing old lady disgustedly grabbed the axe out of his feeble hands and proceeded to show him how to do it, chopping all our firewood. I asked her age. She said she had lived long enough now to be buried. I told Yoshi to give her ten shillings and she kissed his hand, his chest, his cheeks until Yoshi flung himself away.

*

Three days later, 3 April, I realised this was my second birthday now spent in the bush. There were serious warnings of lion as we set off on the twenty miles to Kipanga – our next goal – so we carried loaded guns, but saw none. Instead, a wandering group of marabou storks crossed our path, painstakingly moving like wizened old men. Reaching the top of a ridge, we could see on the far horizon a level blue line extending forever – the Rift Escarpment, 4,000 miles in length from Lebanon to

Mozambique: the biggest geological scar on the surface of the Earth. J.W. Gregory (1896), the first white man to identify it, said it would be visible from the Moon, and Neil Armstrong proved it!

Our tiny figures felt caught in time and place, as though stepping endlessly over the same ground, being drawn inexorably through waves of languorous heat until we finally reached the mountains. The Rift yawned above us.

'I really am not looking forward to this,' I muttered, even though we had already distantly searched out routes over which to struggle with our donkeys. It was late afternoon and we had yet to reach Kipanga which I guessed was still about eight miles away. Too far, and too dangerous to travel at night, so we decided to make a bush camp. Tricky, since we could not find any shade trees and where we eventually pitched our tents was infested with earwigs that got everywhere and gave us painful nips. We stuffed crunched-up toilet paper in our ears to prevent them crawling in. Hyenas whined hungrily nearby while Yoshi was wondering aloud why he had ever asked to join us, and Andy was simply staggering about. Malaria? I didn't have the time to investigate further.

We left next day at midday, earwigs still in our hair, hats and clothes, reaching Kipanga later that day.

Kipanga was a small place, flat and green but with a sizzling year-round humidity because of the close proximity of the hundred-square-mile Bahi Swamp. The Rift plateau was permanently visible across the plate-like plain. We bartered cartridges in return for maize and milk. Tattered travellers from bush villages who had already attended the *mnada* (open-air market) milked cows in an elongated mud shack near our camp. They then slaughtered the same cows and cooked them and goats on leaping wood fires. A medieval scene.

The immediate area was known as Unyambwa – Land of the Dog – as the Wanyambwa ('People of the Dog', who followed dogs to find water) were the tribe living here. Stanley wrongly named the chief as Pembera Pereh, when in fact the eighty-year-old man was called Mahomero Ihembe Lyampela, or *Pembe Lyampela* (Rhino Horn). He had been killed in a raid, but his grandson showed us his grave.

We woke the following morning at 5.30am to the sound of a clanging handbell and a croaking voice: 'Ehh… ehh… everyone should come and pick the grapes… and bring their donkeys to carry loads… Ehh… ehh… grapes need to be reduced…'

His voice and pealing bell circulated our tents. We were forced to get up. It had rained and we paid a quick visit as we had planned to leave our camp by nine. The market was in full flow as if it had continued throughout the night. Individuals were selling round cakes of tobacco; bloodied and hacked bodies of cows and goats hung from trees covered in flies while underneath were bundles of intestines, stomachs, bladders and lights (lungs); pots of mashed beans and *mihogo* (cassava); bottles of yellow *semli* (ghee); copper wire bundles; squawking chickens.

We were thrilled to see our very first tribesmen from the forest. They usually kept to themselves and were reputed to incorporate clicks in their language. They were perusing arrowheads and parts of rubber tyres scattered on a sheet on the ground, from which to carve out hard-wearing sandals.

These hunter-gatherers were the Wamangati, also referred to as Wabaibaig or Barabaig, a Maasai sect. They dressed in brown/black skins, falling like smocks, and wore dull beads and bangles on their arms and around their necks. They did not indulge in agriculture or breed animals and possessed much herbal lore and survival knowledge. The government had twice attempted to put them in contained villages in order to 'civilise' them but they simply escaped back to the forest. Apparently, the Wabaibaig had to kill a man and offer up a finger as evidence before being allowed to marry.

In the afternoon at Isanza village we encountered an old man, tall and bent, every now and then stopping to rest and lean on his stout staff, wearing his best red ladies' overcoat (a mission gift), a dirty pink sheet tightly wound over it. He was a typical Mgogo with craggy features and long hanging earlobes, one wrapped over the top of one ear to keep it in place, the other weighed down by a long pendulous earring. He had thick ankles and horny feet on which he wore thin, delicate sandals of cow skin given to him by his father. He introduced himself: '*Zamani ninaitwa Mdaaji. Lakini nina tupa hii. Sasa jina langu ni Daudi.*' ('Long ago I was called Mdaaji. But I threw this off. Now my name is Daudi.') He must have converted to Christianity. He said he was as high as his four-foot staff when the Germans first appeared in Kilimatinde (1890), where he was born. We calculated from the height of the staff he would have been ten years of age. Now he had to be approximately ninety-five. He provided much valuable information on villages that no longer existed on our route and said he wanted to go to England by *ndege* (bird, i.e.

aeroplane) though he knew absolutely nothing of England. He didn't even know where Bagamoyo or Lake Tanganyika were. Even that they were part of Tanzania.

Back at the camp, writing my journal, I heard Christine very coolly say: 'George, keep very still now! Don't stand up or make sharp movements!'

I froze in place until I heard further instructions. Christine can be trusted in the most dangerous situations.

'Move away now, but keep low and move slowly.'

I did so, slow-waddling like a duck until I reached the cooking fire, then turned to see a green boomslang snake which had been in the tree above slide down the tent to just where I had been sitting and wriggle into the grass. Boomslang are blunt-faced and pretty with big black round pupils. From three to six feet long, they are one of Africa's most venomous snakes. After a bite, without anti-venom, death is certain: progressive internal bleeding leads to all organs failing, respiratory arrest and severe brain haemorrhage.

Thank you, Christine.

16

Unyaturu: Land of Here – and a Queen of the Bees

Camp at Ikasi. We were relieved to come to the end of the Wagogo tribal land. Locals in this tight-knit community – a land known as the 'Land of Here' – the Wanyaturu tribe, had originally migrated to the region now called Tanzania from Ethiopia. While following buffalo and locating the animals' tracks, they would loudly call to others '*Turu* (Here)!' Then in a war with the Maasai, hunting the Maasai by their footprints, again they shouted to each other, 'Here!' 'Here!' until they found the hidden Maasai and massacred them. After this the Maasai referred to them as Wanyaturu – 'The People of Here'.

They were friendly and we set up camp under a huge baobab tree at the edge of Ikasi. Buzzing hordes of bees worried us, but locals dismissed our fears, and otherwise it was a perfectly shaded and secluded spot.

'This is perfect,' I said.

Then Andy suddenly jerked twice as if shot and began running, waving his straw hat about his head and face. What was happening? Then I felt as if I'd been walloped hard on the ear by a swung cricket bat. Another smack on the cheek. Sharp intolerable pain! We were being stung! What by? *Bees!* I ran in crazed panic until I reached long grass stalks and crouched down, keeping perfectly still. Now the donkeys began bucking and kicking, biting at their legs, and galloped away. It was definitely bees – though they stopped chasing us once we were out of their area. This was a warning! Christine, however, was standing by the tents unstung, and Yoshi had run off instantly. When I – or Andy – attempted to return, bees warningly buzzed around my ears. We would have to move camp.

I carefully stood and shouted directions to Christine who slowly dismantled our tents and dragged the heavy panniers away from bees. Why wasn't Christine being stung? She later told me she was visualising undulating blue sea waves. Did these African bees pick up her thoughts? She was definitely the Queen of Bees!

Setting off again, we headed for Bahi Swamp. On the way Christine told me how the women she had met, particularly the younger ones, were often fearful of their husbands. From what she was told, their lives were difficult, defined by their gender; many had been sexually abused by uncles and brothers from an early age, some even made to sleep with older men who believed that having sex with young female virgins would protect them from AIDS. Payment was made to parents for marriage to an older man, and marriage was often to protect them from other abuse. But the man would take many wives, and if they were barren they would be discarded…

Bahi Swamp was not an orthodox swamp, more like a seascape when the tide is out. There was a long sandy shore with enormous crusted salt patches and above it a misty pale blue horizon with clusters of curly white cloud. The white glare of sunlight off salt patches gave the impression of a vast shimmering body of water, but there was little liquid! In opposition on the left, approximately one to two miles away rose the level Rift ridge. We bush-camped at a solitary palm at the edge of the swamp – in the middle of nowhere, though we would have to be careful of wild animals at night since there was a grass-crushed elephant trail towards the swamp.

Guinea fowl cackling in a nearby tree flew off and led us a merry dance as we tried to shoot them for supper. We returned at dusk when we heard a deep lion growl. Then at night, we saw what we thought were clouds of smoke rising off the surface of the swamp, drifting toward us. Then these billows emitted a loud whining nose as they ravenously fell over our bodies and began biting. Mosquitoes! Stinging us raw. We slapped at them, trying to protect our faces, but they came in multitudes. Andy, Christine and I staked the donkeys on short ropes close to the tents, fuelled the wood fire and left kerosene lamps burning outside to deter hyenas and lions before we jumped into our tents and zipped up. We found numerous live mosquitoes on us and spent part of the night killing them by torchlight and covering our swollen bites with antiseptic cream. The long-suffering donkeys, eyes already bitten sore by flies, bucked, bit, kicked out and rolled around outside our tents as the mosquitoes turned on them. Nothing we could do. Mosquitoes were still biting when we left next day at 10am.

Twelve miles through flattened land to Majiri (place of many *ngiri* – warthogs). Travelling in the opposite direction were four donkeys led by two men in a hurry. Much later a running youth with a short sword clenched in his hand said his four donkeys had been stolen and he was trying to catch the thieves. Two giraffes undulated through sparse trees; a mother rhino and her youngster in the far woods, genetically cursed with bad eyesight, stood protectively still. Numerous animal trails: leopard, hyena, baboon prints; a fast-moving monkey jumped out of a tree, startling us, and disappeared. Now the tsetse began biting – and Speke, Burton and Stanley sat in unison. Livingstone's hoof suffering after a stone injury. Hoof rot!

Yoshi was another problem. After a two-and-a-half-mile trek, we reached the bottom of Rift ridge and now needed to push the donkeys up; we had been told it would be an ascent of 800 feet to the plateau. Speke, protesting, knocked off his bags and we rushed to stop them rolling downhill. Yoshi then refused to move, said he thought he had pleurisy in his right lung. I told him to turn back if he felt ill; twenty minutes downhill and one hour would get him back to the village of Majiri where he could be helped.

Andy, exasperated, said, 'We're going on. Stay here if you want.'

Christine just glared with disgust.

We left Yoshi slumped against his rucksack, his eyes gratefully closed, sure he was just feigning illness. One of the scouts on duty at the Rift came to help, and he was given a lift on a bicycle that day to the village of Majiri and safety.

It was a total of thirteen miles to Heka, high and lonely. We camped under an isolated tree inhabited by bush babies whose large eyes could reflect light at night – giant white orbs suspended in branches. Unfortunately, as it was still daylight when we arrived, Heka started to become crowded with traders arriving to sell goats. Two Wabaibaig carrying spears stared open-mouthed at their first sight of white people and we were soon beset by crowds of gaping, giggling Wagogo looking for gifts. A delegation of schoolteachers then appeared, wanting a rundown on our journey and making clear the differences in our culture and our expectations: 'Is it true you've come to find treasure?' 'Do you have special machines to detect dollars Stanley buried en route?'

Help! We needed to get away!

*

20 April. According to my map, reaching Ujamaa Chikola was seven miles, but after three and a half miles we arrived in the tiny habitation of Chikola. Camped under baobabs. Earwigs and jumping black beetles leaving nasty smell behind, purply armour-plated ones nibbling at tent with sharp jaws, spitting out acid when molested – great holes in tent inner. Forced to crush bugs as purple beetles turreted like ancient castles persistently trailed back if tossed away...

*

Evening. Orion, the hunter's constellation, stalking the sky, cicadas echoing the imagined sound of hot stars. Then began slapping ankles. *Siafu!* Not again! A seething trail of ants from the bottom of a tree where they temporarily lived in holes. We collected dry grass and set up a line of fire, cutting off the bloodthirsty hordes, but despite the flames they tenaciously broke through. In the absolute darkness, with failing Tanzanian torches, ants were running up our legs. With smoke from our fire and brandished sticks, our eyes were streaming. Eventually, after about an hour, they finally did retreat. But very shortly afterwards Burton was wildly stamping, as ants had circled back and were attempting to eat him! Released, Burton galloped off in panic, bucking and rolling on the ground to crush the clinging ants. We sprinkled a trail of salt around poor Burton (having restaked him elsewhere) and the tents, but it was a restless night! We fell out of our tents only when we heard Burton loosen his stake and trot around camp searching for juicy grass.

We broke camp; we wouldn't be able to defeat the *siafu* again. We needed to get away. I had a large burn blister on my arm, Andy one on his back. Beetles must have spat acid at us while we were unaware. Last night, they were scrabbling over the tent eating the cotton inner, burrowing into the ground beneath the tent where we lay our heads, singing to get in, a continuous sizzling sound keeping us awake. I now discovered fleas! Locals caught them off chickens and livestock and passed them on in the long grass... The seven plagues of Egypt!

Twelve miles to newly created Idodyandole (meaning Sticky Fingers, as there was plentiful honey in the trees). Burton was surging forth, hurrying it seemed for no reason, butting me on the buttocks until I discovered biting tsetse were speeding him through the high grasses against which he knocked them off. They bit us instead. Many ticks on our arms coming off the grass. A honey bird was chattering madly, a shrill insistent peal, wildly flying back and forth, beckoning us towards honey and sticky fingers. This bird loved beeswax, and the honey badger would follow the bird's cries to a hive, cleverly smearing musk on its own back so the bees would attack it there – where its armour plating meant the stings had no effect. The badger then greedily stole all the honey and left a reward of beeswax for the bird.

Idodyandole was perched on an incline, the Maunguro River beneath. Square-built mud-block houses, some with porches. We camped beneath a shady mimosa tree and it was merely a ten-minute stroll to collect water from the clean river.

Approximately 422.50 miles now covered. Only another 800 to go…

17

Ukimbu: Land of the Beginning – and an Ambush

The people who inhabited this part of the country were known as the Wakimbu tribe, originally Wanyamwezi from Chimbuko village – *Chimbuko* in Kikimbu meaning 'origin' or 'source', 'beginnings'. As the tribe migrated north, they retained their original tribal name, the land of their beginning.

The day was very hot. Stanley had named this area the Magunda Mkali, 'the hot field', as his porters complained of the excessive heat and thirst they suffered during its transit because water was scarce. But the country then, in 1871, was more populous and water plentiful so his title was inappropriate.

In contrast, a cold evening. Answering each other from different parts of the bush, jackals split the night with high-pitched sharp yaps. We organised maize for the donkeys and Stanley suddenly kicked out with both hind legs and walloped my septic-fingered hand, which immediately swelled up. I felt that Stanley had fractured the little bones near my tendon. How would I now lift the bags? How would

I cut through thickets? I was forced to give myself hot and cold soaks in our canvas bucket and supported my useless hand with a bandage tied around my neck. I went to bed with it soaking in the bucket, but because of discomfort I eventually had to bandage it and had a bad sleep with a nightmare of building a fortress against marauding lions who haunted the streets of a small town...

Woke to a painful hand. Underwent the ritual of bucket-soaking again and cursed poor Stanley. Smeared ointment on a blister, iodine on my mysterious septic finger. Christine wasn't well either. She had found blood in her stool and told me she'd had diarrhoea twice and was feeling constantly tired. Was this caused by a parasite? Flagyl to treat it was an arduous experience, but I felt probably necessary. Andy too was vomiting...

Next morning, Andy was feeling sick again, Christine was weak from diarrhoea. I decided I would have to feed her flagyl. We forged on, however, despite our injuries and illnesses. Burton kept up a fair speed, chased by tsetse, and steered clear of any *siafu* trails; Speke had become addicted to sniffing the ground. Meadows of white, blue, yellow wildflowers and the garnet-coloured ones that Livingstone loved to munch, all wafting out a cinnamon smell. The land seemed to undulate ahead of us in a series of never-ending ridges. Early in the afternoon we veered slightly west and reached a path leading to a baobab and a hole in the ground – a well!

We'd only walked nine miles and were completely knackered but felt sure this was the site of Ilowelia, so we organised a bush camp. Bees swarmed around us – *Oh no, not again!* – so we had to move away. Women were collecting water – grey-white – in calabashes among the bees but said there was better water further ahead.

'Very far?' we asked.

'No, very near.'

'So why do you collect water here, if it's better further on?'

They smiled nervously. Clearly they were afraid we would take all their water. Once again, it brought home to us how water was seen throughout Africa as a valuable resource, one that needed not to be wasted or shared too freely.

I decided we would camp and recoup under a sparse tree near the waterhole. While getting our tents and goods organised, we were approached by a curious older woman. '*Salaama jamaani* (Peace, our family),' she called. '*Unatoka wapi* (You are from where)?'

We sang out a typical Swahili answer: '*Kule* (Over there, or Far)!'

'*Unasema kule? Kule siyo mbali. Hata karibu sana!* (You said far? Over there is not far. Or even very near!) *Wapi* (Where)?' she insisted.

She'd got us. '*Uingereza* (England),' we replied.

She laughed a cackling laugh and we joined in. Why not! She pulled up water. '*Kazi ngumu sana* (Work is very hard),' she said.

'*Lakini maisha ni ngumu, mama* (But life is hard, Mother),' we responded.

'*Haya.*' (An expression meaning that she agreed.)

Christine announced I was irritable in the morning, hurrying everyone up. Though we had passed an uneventful night I somehow felt a sense of urgency. Nevertheless, it was 10.20 by the time we left. Livingstone surprisingly raced to keep up behind Burton. We realised he was armed with forethought from his past experiences and felt more protected between the other donkeys – safest between their flicking ears, snorting breath and whisking tails that drove biting *ndorobo* (tsetse) away.

Impenetrable thickets swallowed up the path! We detoured around and picked it up again. Several burnt-rubber smells indicated the presence of leopard. After eight miles we reached non-existent Muale and the tree from which the area took its name. A pool of water we found had been fouled by animals, so we continued to follow a dry seasonal river until we came to a previously dug waterhole in the dry riverbed. We bush-camped a quarter mile away near an eight-foot-tall anthill – *mchwa*, ordinary harmless ants. Away from the water we were thus avoiding dangerous animals that could arrive to drink at the waterhole.

We had learned from locals on the way that a lion had killed a giraffe nearby a few days ago, so I practically chopped down a whole tree and created a blazing fire in preparation and staked the donkeys near to us. Seeing bees living in a hollow of a tree very close to our camp, we successfully smoked them out with burning leaves and collected the honeycombs. 'Sorry!' I apologised to the air. Christine heated these gently in a saucepan, so larvae, dead bees, maggots would come to the top and could be skimmed off. We poured the honey over the groundnuts we carried and devoured the fragrant sweetness, spitting out wax and larvae.

Woke late to discover busy *siafu* trailing around our

tents and cold ashes on a food mission and we found their humped earth burrows. We had to move, for tonight the *siafu* would edge towards the tents, searching the trampled grass for dropped food. Disappearing into bushes for a toilet break I almost bumped into a giraffe nibbling at tall leaves. Where did it come from? I raised my crepe-bandaged hand in friendliness and, swooping its long neck and head in slow motion, it attempted to butt me. I ran behind a tree. The graceful swinging neck could have killed me! The giraffe followed at an elegant pace and attempted another butt around the tree. A big bull can weigh a ton and stand eighteen feet tall. I didn't know whether this was male or female. It threw out its fragile stilt-like legs trying to hit me from both sides but was so slow I could easily dodge and run to another tree. We went from tree to tree.

'Andy!' I hollered, though it was more of a screech.

Andy and Christine appeared at the border of our tents beside the donkeys and threw rocks at the giraffe which thankfully undulated off like dried grass in wind.

'Thank you, Andy and Christine,' I gasped, 'I owe you.'

Giraffes are mute. No pain or passion can make them emit a whisper. Their hearts are as large as oil drums in order to pump blood to distant heads, the arteries in the long neck fitted with large valves to prevent their brains exploding under pressure when they lower their heads low to the ground and stoop splay-legged to drink.

And that's when tall Abdullah appeared out of the bush, his body bandaged in a bedraggled loincloth, clutching an Arab-style self-loading rifle he had made himself. Abdullah was a hunter/poacher and had spent most his life alone in the bush and most importantly knew the way and locations of water. We agreed to pay him 350 shillings to guide us. As we were staying the night, he chopped thick branches, made a rope and secured the branches like a raft up a tree. This was a platform on which he would sleep.

We woke at 6.15am to the trumpeting of an elephant herd 200 yards away. It seemed to be a favourite gathering place. They moved off by the time we washed and began to dismantle the camp. Permeating drizzle, grey blanket of clouds. Freezing! We all wore pullovers, waterproofs and gaiters. Abdullah held a stick horizontally in front of him to keep back wet grass and clinging ticks from whipping into his face. We copied him, also pulling tarpaulins over the donkeys to keep them and our goods dry, and to deter biting flies.

On the old track heading west-north-west, a welcome baobab acting as a signpost, we found the road blocked by a ten-strong line of men. Robbers armed with bows and arrows, spears and *pangas*. 'Sasa rafiki, nipe vitu (Now, friend, give me your goods),' one of them said. Abdullah, who never spoke much, had already levelled his rifle at them.

'Chris, get in the bushes,' I instructed. 'Andy, guns!' Fortunately, we were already carrying our shotgun and rifle that day because of possible carnivores; normally they were strapped across the top of the panniers. 'Abdullah...!'

As we moved quickly behind bushes an arrow thunked into the ground by my feet. Then a hail of arrows. The men had disappeared off the track and were now hidden in the bush. We fired, hoping we were shooting above their heads and that the sound of firearms would discourage them. But arrows kept flying our way, plus a few wobbly spears.

'Keep firing!' I yelled to Andy. Christine, I hoped, was well covered. Abdullah didn't require instruction. He kept calmly loading, aiming and firing his old rifle. We didn't deliberately aim – just kept firing until the flight of arrows and spears lessened and stopped.

Abdullah smiled. '*Wamekimbia* (They have run away).'

We gathered together, shocked by the suddenness, the noise and that anyone would want to kill us.

'Are they mad, Abdullah? They could see we had guns,' commented Andy.

'*Wanataka kujaribu* (They wanted to try),' answered Abdullah.

We passed what used to be settlements: six miles to Mwanakondo (Child of Kondo – the first person to live there) and a mile distance, Mwanakivisuka (Child of Kivisuka). Water was from a *chemchem* (spring), and Abdullah said this was also known as Nyambogi. There was no such place as Stanley's Unyambogi, nor was there, or ever has been a Wanyambogi tribe. I found Stanley's mileages here when matched to the ground extremely puzzling – and the disappearing villages had not helped our calculations. Stanley's *Kiti* (meaning 'Seat') no longer existed, but the site of Msalalo did. And from our Maunguru River camps to Msalalo, Stanley wrote it took him fifty-plus miles. We did it in approximately thirty!

Jungly bush camps in the middle of nowhere, dripping with growths and impenetrable thickets. The donkeys were ecstatic, surrounded by lush grass. This was all-embracing nature and I loved it! The more secluded and deep-nested, the more I liked the situation. Since the beginning of memory no snow had settled in this African forest. Only rain laced the leaves. A fevered heat crept under the skin; mosquitoes multiplied in puddles; frogs and cicadas ripped their throats; and unexpected carnivores left muddy steps.

I remembered being in Devon, slowly learning to love the fresh grass and hedgerows. A Devon butcher wanted to teach me to fire a shotgun using tin cans as targets so we could go pigeon shooting together. Unfortunately, whenever he left me in a field and set off to scare pigeons towards me I would forget about shooting and become engrossed in something like a red-spotted toadstool I'd discovered; the pigeons would pass overhead unharmed! I was always daydreaming and noticing how leaves curled and hedges filled, the vibrancy of living things. Time had slowed and I was writing poetry. Interestingly, Totleigh Barton, the house in Devon that became the first centre of the Arvon Foundation's creative writing establishments, was also known locally in Devon brogue as Tot-ley. Apparently it sat on two ley lines…

*

We found hyenas had closely passed by our camp and zebras had grazed ten yards away, wide elephant trails like man-made paths, giraffe prints looking prehistoric. Christine's face just missed a giant yellow-and-black-spotted spider. Her hair ruined its web.

Abdullah was busy using baobabs and other prominent trees as landmarks and asked, 'As we walk in the bush now, can people see us on TV in England?' He picked a particular leaf, bit a piece out, folded it and blew, making a sharp resonant sound. A reedbuck antelope stepped out of the bush in front of us. '*Piga!*' he ordered, meaning 'Shoot!' I did, and the reedbuck dropped. We barbecued the sweet meat and couldn't eat it all. Abdullah stuffed it into a holdall he carried.

We bush-camped at defunct Msalalo, an idyllic deep-gladed spot where we could relax. Water was from an underground stream one and a quarter miles away. Normally we had learnt to camp well away from water so avoiding mosquitoes and wild animals, and walked a quarter to one mile to a river bed to dig a waterhole if we had to.

Abdullah prepared poison to put on his arrows for hunting game. He took cherry-like roots from a tree and boiled them into a sticky liquid, testing it out on a few drops of his own blood: if the blood turned black the poison was ready to use.

Approximately 449.50 miles now covered.

Four in the morning and the roar of two lions jolted me and Christine awake. This lion row would continue until they made a kill. When their mouths were full of meat they didn't roar. Their present roars sounded like, 'I'm hungry! I am hunting here!' This was initially a big, loud roar which began to diminish in a series of short drumbeats, 'Unh, unh, unh,' warning 'Here, here, here.' Then silence.

Lions could sniff prey up to a distance of two miles and could eat up to forty pounds of meat. They were often found with their heads in the belly cavity of a killed animal and always began eating from the rear, so that the front quarters and head remained intact. They preferred the testicles and heart, the liver, sweetbreads, and any foetus they could find. 'When a lion kills a man,' Chief Fundikira of Unyanyembe (Tabora) told the explorer Burton, 'he will eat, in order, the buttocks, the backs of the thighs, the flesh of the upper arms, and then sometimes as a final delicacy, the face and tongue.'

These lions had been behind us at a greenish waterhole thick as pease pudding. Although they were now upwind, we couldn't be sure they hadn't caught a whiff of the donkeys. So Andy and I sat on armed watch together until 7am, listening to the roars moving from our left to our right, getting further away then returning to our left. We couldn't be sure they weren't sometimes no more than ten yards away, crouched low in the grass watching us.

Abdullah later told us that a woman had recently been seized by a lion while walking to her home, actually in a town. Given the opportunity, and contrary to popular belief that only old and weak lions would eat humans, all lions could attack people – and humans were the easiest and weakest prey, so female lions in Tanzania taught their cubs to hunt human meat. 'Many man-eaters, but we cannot shoot them all. They are very clever, and Tanzania very big...' He told us of a male and female lion that were killing cows in a nearby village. The female would leap over the thorn stockade, kill a cow and with one paw bat the carcass over the stockade to the waiting male. Unencumbered, she could then easily make her escape.

*

Andy wants to discuss night-watch situation. Says getting over-tired. Why now does he have to do most of the watches? (But he volunteered!) Says, 'It's not fair!' 'Life isn't fair,' I reply. 'You'll get your come-uppance,' he threatens, 'bully!' He has hidden truth from himself (self-evident to me) that without his and Christine's help I couldn't do the expedition. If I tell him, fear he will begin taking advantage and things will deteriorate further. Our survival is hanging by a thread. I know he would rather stop now.

I've got to hold this thing together...

*

Andy's words kept me awake: perhaps I am being a bully. And it is possible this is contributing to his tiredness. It is only fair that I share the watches. I will tell him and also apologise.

The expected terrors of the journey from Idodyandole – clouds of tsetse, lions, impassable thickets stretching to the horizon, bogs, and all-enveloping man-swallowing grass – had not been forthcoming. The 'hot field' – Magunda – had not proved particularly *kali* (fierce). The trek had been fairly straightforward, although without a guide it would have taken us thrice as long.

Only twelve miles to Itagata now, its name meaning 'completely clean', which sounded promising. It was comprised of many rectangular mud-built thatched houses lining the road, one shop and a popular *pombe* house for preparing beer from honey. Itagata is roughly 120 miles from Tabora – a town I was looking forward to reaching.

The inhabitants of Itagata were mostly Wanyamwezi. Here we learnt that the old Arab path later refurbished by the Germans would take us past all the villages on Stanley's route, though his Welled Ngaraiso and Kusuri no longer existed. In any event, Stanley's first village was known in the past as Ngaraiswa. It meant 'hats of grass', commemorating a battle during which the attacking Wanyamwezi wore such hats as camouflage while encircling their enemy through the long grass. We would then pass the village of the Chief of Kirurumo, Iwosia (*Iwozia* means 'rot'), so named as it was the site of another battle in the 1800s in which the Wanyamwezi left defeated bodies on the field to rot. Further on there was a river known locally as Zengavahala (girl with ripe breasts) and I assumed quite possibly that this was his River Nghwhalah.

We made camp and Abdullah inexplicably disappeared during the night, presumably into the honey-beer dens of Itagata. This was inevitable, but I would miss him terribly. For much of our trek had not been as bad as we had feared – but our main anxieties were in finding the right path, which could be lost in this wilderness, and Abdullah had been enormously helpful in knowing the right way to go.

Waking, and once again Africa punched us below the belt – mysterious aches and pains, throbbing head, shivers up and down my body and nausea. I was so weak I attempted to spend the day sleeping in the tent. Could hardly sit up straight or think clearly.

Andy confided in Christine, 'I know I'm failing George. I can see it in the way he looks at me.' And his excuse: 'How could I know the bloody sun would be so strong! I just go beetroot red and freckly. Sun is not my thing. Everything is so difficult. I can't be bothered to shave – too much trouble to find the mirror. When I go to a village to be on my own, I get pestered with people asking things of me. I can't bear it!'

Christine, in turn, was critical. 'I think he cares more for the donkeys than he cares for me! Constantly asking me if I've checked their eyes, their hooves, any new cuts. Should we treat them? etc., etc.'

Andy woke me from a long sleep of the dead which had somewhat improved my condition, though I felt in my solar plexus as if I'd been back-kicked by a donkey. He took my temperature. Yesterday, it was above normal, today it was one degree below.

We headed into Itagata to watch a village trial. At the very end of the village under a clump of old trees behind a positioned school desk was the *Katibu*, who had been called from the larger town of Mgandu to preside as judge. Beside him were seated four CCM officials also from Mgandu. Three old women stood before them. The rest of the villagers squatted on the ground in a half circle.

The women had been accused of being *wachawi* (witches) and, after denying the charges, had to remain silent as villagers with increasing frenzy took it in turn to stand and throw out accusations: of the women taking what they wanted – like a joint of meat – without paying and making threats to use their power if stopped; of using *dawa* (medicine) to kill, or to stop a woman from giving birth unless paying them for expensive *dawa*. Last year the *Katibu* was told two men had died by slowly withering away. 'Withering away' is usually attributed to witchcraft. And only last month a boy whose legs had begun to wither accidentally fell into a wood fire and was burnt to death. The women were also accused of killing children that had gone missing. One man stood to say: 'On the mountain a baby can be heard crying, crying. We can hear its voice, but it cannot be found.'

The trial continued for three and a half hours. Finally, the *Katibu* stood up to be heard above the furore: '*Wachawi* don't exist anymore. We live in modern times and practise democracy. We cannot victimise people, etc., etc.'

But faced with angry villagers, he was forced to pronounce a sentence that would mollify the crowd and protect the three accused. All three women were banished from the village and, more crucially, their tribe. They were doomed to wander, to be *masikini* (poor) until, if they lived, they somehow reached Dar es Salaam where they could make money by selling their bodies. If the women had stayed, the *Katibu* knew they would be beaten to death. Could my stomach aches be due to witchcraft? Have we offended someone? I will have to drink more boiled *ndulele* water!

Having got rid of the alleged witches the whole village then attended their simple-structured Christian church.

We headed toward Chona River and Lake, my body moving without me. I kept breaking into cold sweats and waves of gushing nausea. On two occasions I almost blacked out and put my hand forward to soften my fall to the ground. Waves of blackness. Surely we had to rest when ill, as unlike Stanley we could not ride on an ass or be carried in a hammock.

We thankfully halted at an unoccupied loggers' camp: three huts constructed roughly out of logs, vibrating with fleas and bed bugs. I only just managed to lift off the donkey panniers, my strength gone, and slumped to the ground for a while before putting up tents for the new bush camp. Seized with stomach cramps again… rushed too late into the bush. Had to wash myself by torchlight, juggling revolver, torch and soap, treading on thorns and being unmercifully eaten by mosquitoes and small biting flies.

Surprisingly, by the next morning I felt well again; the flagyl I had taken had obviously worked and I had enjoyed a deep sleep. The following night it was Christine's turn to rush into the bushes while I kept watch, and in the morning she was feeling tired and groggy. Blessed with good fortune and feeling well, Andy had arisen early and had shot a klipspringer (a small antelope) which we ate stewed in cumin. Maps and notes, maps and notes... All Christine and I wanted to do was to snooze in the shade. Flies biting, smaller *mpani* climbing into eyes, caterpillars crawling persistently up legs, sun scorching the shade away, wood smoke ruining eyes... Whatever I'd said before, forget it. Ah... the delights of nature...

Near Chona Lake three little old men with white hair, beards and tattered clothes – just like Snow White's companions – visited us. One presented us with a bony young chicken like a gangly pigeon. This was obviously a great sacrifice on their part, which we could not accept. We said, please take it back and let it grow and think of us when you eat it. They smiled, relieved to be released from rules of hospitality. Why didn't they grow rice in the paddy of the lake? The hippos, they replied. Of course!

Our way to Tabora passed Chaya Lake, which supposedly is three by two and a quarter miles in size and full of catfish and cavorting hippos. The path ahead was covered in tall grasses and was merely a shallow bog. We had to walk through it with the sure knowledge that the donkeys would definitely buck their panniers into the muck, so we would have to carry the panniers ourselves.

And for a substantial distance. How would we do that? Over such a long stretch?

Andy had the bright idea of us carrying them slung over poles supported on both our shoulders. We could do it in four relays, a pannier at a time. 'That's brilliant, Andy!' I said, chopping at tree branches for poles. A smile crept onto Andy's face and I realised then that I had not volubly given enough credit to either Christine or Andy, too focused on completing the task we had set ourselves.

Water was up to our knees. It was not saline, so probably riddled with bilharzia. We waded in mud and slippery weeds, splashing and stumbling into underwater holes, shoulders chafing and aching, the heavy panniers swaying at each jolt. We had a morbid fear of falling and dropping the panniers into the bog. This kept us upright.

Surprisingly the donkeys followed us across in a line without being bidden! Finally, finally… At a collection of corrugated-roofed circular shacks I called out toward the huts to check our route, and disturbed a naked mama washing herself over a bucket. She initially started up, clutching her heavy breasts, and then realising the futility of continuing to heft up such weights, let them drop to answer my questions.

18

Unyamwezi: Land of the Moon – and the Tembe of Livingstone

Struck with mental lethargy on monotonous marches. Days petrify and rot in place. Despite daydreaming, chats about food and sometimes Christine and I pausing in shade for Andy and donkeys to catch us up we become somnambulists. Is it effect of featureless flat miombo woodland? Is undulating desert this way? Our bodies aching, mouths dry, eyes screwed up against permanent glare, brains numbed with effort at our attempts to rise out of hypnotic depression. Christine confides in Andy, she's just hanging on. Fulfils tasks only by huge act of concentration, eyes unable to cope with daily glare, her body has given up – feels great, creeping inertia... There is no end. We're doomed to be ever-moving, to wander forever through forests, make fires, search for water, prepare camps and be ever alert for wild beasts. I personally think, no regrets... no regrets... Spiritual experience, a clear view of affairs I hoped to capture in African bush where I could not have been closer to basic Nature, is elusive...

*

Unyamwezi: Land of the Moon – and the Tembe of Livingstone

The region of Unyamwezi was situated in the west and when the moon set in the west, it was swallowed up by land, thus leading to the overall tribal name for this region. We were told that Wanyamwezi chiefs, when they began their rule, were not allowed to cut their hair or to shave until an elephant died in their region. They travelled to the site and sat on the dead elephant's back. The *mganga* (witch doctor) would arrive, shave off the chief's hair and place it in the elephant's mouth. This ceremony assured the chief that his rule would be strong.

We arrived at Tura 5.30pm. The place was referred to locally as *Itura* which meant 'drunken fighting'. A tight habitation of tiny houses, a Muslim praying house where a small group were rhythmically chanting, a water tower and *shambas* of corn, millet, *papai*, limes and unripe bananas. At the CCM Office we discovered that the chairman was in jail for taking bribes. Christine was very sick and weak, vomiting and stomach cramps. She would have to go to bed and commence a treatment of flagyl and tetracycline. Thank the Lord we were a walking hospital or else we could be in a bad way.

In the middle of the night, Burton brayed loudly: 'Thief!' We quickly unzipped the tents – and whoever it was had disappeared. Nothing had been stolen. Burton was an excellent watch, and tomorrow would have a reward of cassava!

It was twenty-four miles to Kizengi village. We worried that the donkeys couldn't make it this far. We'd been told, however, that we could camp at the halfway mark in the forest beside a green-covered pool of water. We eventually found it in the early afternoon: not a pool, but a lake – a grass-filled shallow bog permeated all around by buffalo and hippo prints. We bush-camped in a glade among a network of animal trails and built a large fire. Despite lowing buffalo and howling hyena from the swamp, and although we suspected our camp was surrounded by inquisitive animals, we passed an untroubled night.

*

Young naked cattle herders in Kizengi unusually didn't understand a word of our Kiswahili, unable or unwilling to speak it themselves, but seemed extremely friendly – they were Wasukuma nomads with large shells strung around their necks. Stinking of cow shit they were supposed to be experts in bush medicine. An old man guided us toward the only large shade trees by decrepit old white brick buildings which appeared like monoliths beside the mud native huts of Kizengi. This was part of a defunct sisal factory previously making rope and the grand estate manager's house was nearby – the Malongwe Estate. The outbuildings were now used as living quarters, and one as the CCM Office.

A plump middle-aged woman who enthusiastically greeted us in poor English was African from Zaire. Dressed in brand new T-shirt, skirt and white plimsolls, bouncy as a spring lamb, Jacqueline told us that her late husband, Henry George Jarvis, was from London and owned the vast sisal factory. She had met him in Zaire, married him and travelled to Tanganyika. With no children, she was now lonely living in her spacious European building, accompanied only by her bristling old retainer of sixty-six, a man named Simon. 'I will cook you supper,' she promised.

She kept her promise. We ate a glorious supper of chicken, sweet potato and lemon cabbage to night drumming and singing accompanied by hyenas. The Wasukuma who predominated here had perpetual parties during the dry season, the young men drumming to attract unattached women. They eventually paired off and worked out between them the bride prices for their marriage. This was the time to wed and multiply and be ready for agricultural work when the rains arrived. I lay down my head to hear for the third night running singing insects coming from the ground under our tents. The large armour-plated acid-spitting beetles emitted long buzzing rasps throughout the night. These, whatever they were, babbled in almost human tones. I used telepathy to tell them to shut up so we could sleep, and they immediately clammed up!

Next day, children brought us water from the river in exchange for balloons, and a young lad brought us three catfish, still writhing and gaping, long whiskers aquiver. We would now partake of Stanley's 'mud fish'. He wrote, 'Probably, if I had my choice, being, when occasion demands it rather fastidious in my tastes, I would not select mud fish.' We did, and they tasted like rock salmon.

Bidding a fond farewell to Jacqueline and Simon – who insisted on walking with us for a mile – we made for the Nyahua River bridge, then trekked eleven miles through the never-ending sameness of a *miombo* (dwarf acacia) wood to a deep waterhole with good water beside a small logging camp hut 250 yards further among the acacia trees. Here we bush-camped.

And here Andy got lost! He walked off the path and was immediately swallowed by the trees, losing sight of us and feeling completely lost. Within *miombo* woods there was no point of recognition: everything looked the same. We had planned for such an occasion by each wearing shrill whistles, but Andy eventually related that he was blowing continuously and Christine and I heard nothing! The woods had absorbed the sound. I stepped off the path with trepidation, depending on my compass and pacing not to get lost, and found the neat log house with four made-up wooden beds, a smoking fire and full bucket of water: the loggers had to be out cutting down trees. Of Andy there was no sign.

'Logging camp' sounded grand. What it usually comprised was a rough timber hut near water from which four or five men could go out and chop down trees. They trimmed them of branches and carried the trunks back to camp where they sliced the log into planks. No machinery – all was done by hand. When the group had enough planks they transported them into towns for sale. They received 900 shillings for each log and could easily cut and square up a tree per day. A good wage for Tanzania.

I paced back to the path, trying my whistle as an experiment, and found Christine – who had heard nothing. Then we waited anxiously on the path until a flustered Andy, blessed with luck, broke through the dense trees at its edge an hour later. 'Bloody hell,' he muttered, 'these trees all look the same. I've been going around in circles.'

535.50 miles covered.

Tall and ancient *mihama* (palms) marked the site of Rubuga. All was overgrown wilderness. There would be no people until Kigwa eighteen miles west. We couldn't find water and as the donkeys were getting restless we decided to trek a mile further to a large yellow-lily-covered pond in a swamp, then headed a further quarter mile into dense woodland so we wouldn't be plagued at night by mosquitoes which bred in the water, and bush-camped. We were immediately dive-bombed by our friendly but kamikaze *mpani*. However many we killed – and we could rub out eight to ten in one go – hundreds more were eager to replace them. We had to sit in our beekeepers' hats, and still they managed to crawl under.

At 9pm there was a great squawking of birds all around us, a great crunching of wood and undergrowth fifteen yards from where we sat. The birds became maniacal. We froze. Could it be an elephant? After ten minutes the birds fell absolutely silent. We banked up the fire, left kerosene lamps out and went to bed, rising once in the night to refuel the fire.

Burton sauntered up to me and stood to attention, awaiting orders and to be loaded: he became known from then on as Sergeant Major Burton. I gave him a nose-pat and piece of pumpkin. Leisurely breakfast of boiled peas – yes, just peas! Immediately we hit the path and found fresh prints of a large leopard. That was what disturbed the birds last night we realised, not an elephant! It had to have been sitting high in a tree when we arrived. What we had heard was the leopard leaping off his high perch and possibly knocking a rotted branch to the ground.

As we neared Kigwa, which was a burnt wasteland when Stanley camped there, we concluded that wood-chopping had to be the new big business for we could see denuded hills, tree stumps, and charcoal being made and sold on the paths. We had completed eighteen miles. Well done, donks! We camped under a thick clump of mango trees near the only waterhole, led there by the chairman, the old chief's son.

Kigwa had an extensive camp for refugees from Burundi, Zaire and South Africa, and a delegation headed by the military camp commander woke us early in the morning.

'This is a restricted area, you will have to move,' he ordered. 'You cannot stay here another day.'

I pointed out that we were in the village, not in his camp – and we had permission from the Prime Minister. Additionally, the path led right through the middle of his camp! Where was the logic? If his camp was so incredibly sensitive, either he should move the village and path or re-site the camp in the woods where no one would see it.

After traipsing through luminous entangled greenery, we reached the large *Ujamaa* village of Miumba (also known as Kinamagi) and asked for Ngulati Saidi Fundikira. Fundikira (which meant 'to finally be on top') was a descendant of the Chief of Unyamwezi and Unyanyembe and a d*iwan* – a councillor of Tabora. His young son said he had gone to grind corn but would return in the afternoon.

We asked both locals and then Fundikira if they knew the location of Stanley's 'Shiza', which we thought could have been Kigwa. It was on Stanley's route and it had become an obsession for me to discover all of Stanley's villages. Fundikira didn't know. Or of anyone named Shiza, until he suddenly grabbed my arm and said, 'I have remembered. Shiza is —' And at that moment a garrulous

Unyamwezi: Land of the Moon – and the Tembe of Livingstone

local arrived like a land mine and destroyed Fundikira's memory for good.

It was freezing! We left with an escort of cow-shit-begrimed kids. At the top of a hill we viewed the parched plain of Tabora dotted with many mud houses and modern high-rise stone buildings. We encountered dilapidated lorries trailing clouds of hot dust. And were disorientated by the sight of a rushing train, an aeroplane that had just taken off swooping skyward 400 yards to our left. We were somehow lost on the tiny Tabora airport landing strip, the donkeys halted by a deep drainage ditch. We circled to the control tower much to the surprise of the returning fire engine.

Sizzling on the runway, we were pointed the two miles to Kwikuru where the Sultan's Palace here was a mere nonsensical mud pile. Our tents under a mango tree were surrounded by noisy kids. We utilised them for water-carrying to quieten them down.

Mangoes were not indigenous but introduced to Africa by Arabs and Indians, and Unyamyembe – the 'Land of the Mangoes' – was incorporated in this region. *Nyembe* (mango) was also the name of the founding chief. Locals told us the history of the succession: how his two sons, Mkosi and Mkelemi, had argued. Mkelemi decided to resolve the situation by killing Mkosi. To do this, he dug a pit in the middle of his house and planted sharpened stakes, covering up the pit and placing a stool over the top. He then lured Mkosi there and offered him the stool. Mkosi had fallen onto the stakes but not died immediately, so Mkelemi had decided to finish him off with an axe, only for his brother to revive enough to stab upwards with a knife, killing Mkelemi, ripping into his stomach, spilling out his entrails. At the same instant the axe split Mkosi's skull…

We gratefully bought Double Cola drinks from a lad sitting on a stool under a mango tree, right on a junction providing the old path to Kwihara, the place where Stanley stayed. With a large notice showing the way to 'Livingstone Tembe'. The landscape began to become green and lush with date palms and mango trees. We would go to Kwihara!

The Tembe was surrounded by old mango trees. Though referred to as Livingstone's house it was in fact where Stanley returned with Livingstone, after meeting him in Ujiji. It was here they finally parted, Stanley to travel to England and Livingstone returning to Ujiji. The original house had collapsed and this was an exact replica built by the British in 1956.

It now functioned as a broken-down museum. On the front door veranda a half-naked local had lit a fire and was busy smashing a great hole in its floor.

'Are you the *askari*?' we asked.

He mumbled grumbling under his breath and walked away, his split trouser legs fanning out billows of dust. Christine sheltered under a tree with the donkeys gathered around her while Andy and I walked to the back of this rectangular structure and discovered an open door leading into a central unroofed courtyard. Here, dozing, lay Shomari, the caretaker from the Cultural Office. He immediately insisted we should stay in the house and began unlocking all the doors.

'The animals will stay in the covered riding donkey stables.'

We noticed all the areas were labelled. The rooms were large and empty, dusty earth floors except for one room which was filled with scattered, decaying, dust-covered Livingstone and Stanley expedition artefacts, the most significant being a lock of Livingstone's hair. I could have taken this; Shomari wouldn't have cared. This was the proper museum within this historical replica, and we were really surprised we could camp inside. We decided we wouldn't use the rooms but would pitch our tents under a small awning in the central courtyard, close to the donkeys.

The man on the front porch, we learned, was named Abedi and was mentally disturbed. He lived on the veranda. The house was beautiful and for Tanzania extremely well preserved except for poor Abedi permanently knocking earth-shuddering holes in the porch floor.

A car full of German tourists arrived and received a shock to find us camped in the courtyard and myself shaving with a mirror attached to the central mango tree.

19

Tabora: the Sleepy Town

On winding path through tall grass, interweaving clumps of mango trees and ascending saddle between Malolo and Kwihara hills. On 5 June 1985 we sight Tabora town. Kazeh Hill, which Stanley was told did not exist, is slightly to our right – the 'old Tabora', where Burton, Speke and Grant stayed is covered in houses tumbling leftwards down to the plain and what is now main market.

According to Sir Richard Burton, during famine tribes migrated to Tabora region because of abundance of mangoes. Watutsi migrant women lined the hill route into Tabora, clapping hands and chanting, 'Kazeh! Kazeh!' – their greeting for hunters and heroes – and the name stuck.

Landscape almost verging on denuded and bleak. Pinky-brown colour like tender human skin overexposed to harsh light. Only myriad-leafed mango trees save it. Tabora is slow and sleepy. Doesn't have freneticism and movement of Morogoro and Dodoma. Only 100,000 inhabitants – perhaps that's the reason. We trek through native back yards, squawking chickens, naked children, over-made-up females giving a lascivious eye and wiggling buttock.

*

There was a British presence in the town of Tabora and the British High Commissioner had offered us a house there, provided we contributed towards electricity and water. The compound was run by Chris Rumbelow-Pierce, who we had previously met in Dar es Salaam, and to our surprise he was extremely cold with us. He said he had no extra space on the compound. Even if there was, he said he would expect us to pay rent. For some reason he wanted us out of his office as fast as possible. Well, well…

And we were supposedly a 'British' expedition.

We looked elsewhere, and an Indian, Surat, showed us three empty rooms in a private hospital compound we could occupy for three weeks, while a Tanzanian manager of Texco Textiles offered us an apartment in a newly built block of workers' flats for as long as we liked. The donkeys could safely be accommodated in the fenced Sabasaba Stadium, though we had first to repair large holes in the wire fence. The stadium was now disused, although a miniature railway track overgrown with weeds circled its interior. The donkeys would have to get used to the track. We also needed to fix up a tarpaulin for shade and borrow a metal bath for water from the Railway Club.

It would do.

For Stanley Tabora was the main Arab settlement in Central Africa. It sat in the middle of the Rift plateau, a 3,943-foot-high oasis in a harsh tsetse-ridden *miombo* wasteland. It contained 5,000 people. The white *gellabia*-dressed Arabs (mostly Omani), living in immense luxury in Tabora and every one of them owning harems of black concubines, were to become preoccupied with the actions of Chieftain Mirambo (meaning 'corpse') of Uyoweh.

Formerly a Mnaymwezi trader for slaves and ivory, Mirambo had gradually enriched himself and become a warlord. He headed a gang of robbers and forcibly seized the throne of Uyoweh (a vast region that incorporated Tabora), then began a widespread war destroying populations and stealing their goods. He turned against his supporters, the Arabs, and prevented free passage through *his* country to Ujiji. It was in Stanley's interest to join the Arabs and fight Mirambo. But in Kwihara he fell into a malarial coma which lasted seven days. Shaw, who had also been ill but attended Stanley, miscalculated the dates of the coma by a week; Stanley commented of Shaw that 'fever was rapidly destroying his memory, and indeed his reason'.

As Stanley recovered Shaw worsened. On 13 August a caravan arrived from the coast and reported that Farquhar and his cook were dead. Stanley had readily abandoned Farquhar in Africa with only Jako to tend him, having only just written of African conditions: 'It is an erroneous supposition to think that Livingstone, any more than any other energetic man of his calibre, can travel through Africa without some sort of an escort…'

On the way to battle with Mirambo at Uyoweh Shaw fell behind and collapsed in the forest.

Men were dispatched to carry him on their backs. Stanley, having met up with the Arab army of 2,255 men, also collapsed with fever and was carried in a hammock. Villages were attacked and burnt while Stanley perspired under blankets. Then Mirambo turned the tables, successfully ambushing an Arab group. The rest of the Arabs favoured a retreat as Mirambo was speedily approaching. Forty-three of Stanley's men deserted. The Arabs returned to Tabora, Stanley to Kwihara.

Mirambo attacked Tabora on 22 August, mutilating the fallen bodies: he would cut off the skin of the forehead, lower part of the face, the forepart of the nose, the fat over the stomach and abdomen, the genital organs, and lastly a bit from each heel to be prepared as a potion mixed into *ugali* or rice and eaten as protection against bullets.

Tabora was in uproar and hundreds of refugees crowded into Kwihara. Stanley recruited 150 more assistants, posted sentries and cleared the area surrounding his house. Mirambo eventually withdrew from Tabora, and though suffering defeats he remained ever-present as a fearsome prospect.

Stanley decided as his men were reluctant to face Mirambo, he would detour southward and then curve north-westward to Ujiji, so avoiding the areas in which Mirambo would be present. This was a 400-mile detour which we would have faithfully followed had we not learnt that this route was now designated as an uninhabited sleeping sickness area.

Andy wrote down a numbered list of tasks we needed to complete in Tabora:

1. Decide on our accommodation. (We had to stay two weeks in Kwihara, walking a total of two miles per day in and out of Tabora.)
2. Donkeys have been offered:
   - Kipalapala Ball Centre (an unfenced desert).
   - The abattoir (a tremendous blood lake to fall into! No!).

- The Sabasaba Stadium (fence will take two days to repair. Put up tarp. And borrow tin bath).
3. Donkeys – organise veterinarians to test blood, stool, skin samples. Check respiration, eyes, heartbeat. After several days, suitable injection against sleeping sickness for Speke, Samorin for others (Speke had a reaction to Samorin) and drench all with Panacur for worms. (Every day, the donkeys required at least two hours for us to refill their water, feed them with bran and brush them down!)
4. Repair torn panniers – stitch on leather at bottom.
    - Make new ankle straps.
    - Replace ankle ropes.
    - Make new nosebags from sacking.
5. Repair canvas bucket. Attach leather support.
6. Make mosquito-netted room to hang from trees.
7. Buy new glass for kerosene lamp.
8. Repair worn boots.
9. Replace, if possible, broken tent zips.
10. G to write journal and requested articles by Tanzania Tourist Corporation.
11. C to prepare list of supplies needed for next section. Weigh and pack into insect-proof containers.
12. Make *biltong*. Ask Game Department for permission to shoot buffalo or zebra. We need forty-eight kilograms to dry down to twelve kilograms.
13. Write letters to donkey sanctuary, Ministry of Agriculture, airlines regarding import restrictions and getting donkeys to England.
14. Seek advice on sleeping sickness from research centre in Tabora.

15. Have our blood, stool, urine checked at hospital.
16. Christine to have ECG test because of erratic heartbeat – tachycardia.
17. Stock up on any drugs.
18. Send photographs and press release to *Sunday Telegraph*.

We began with the local vets, and here Speke almost died on us. He had a bad reaction to the sleeping sickness drug Berenil; it affected his central nervous system making him sway, fall over, his eyes dull and tongue paralysed. He couldn't eat or swallow successfully. If an animal didn't eat, it died! A visiting English vet, Dr Connor from Kenya, immediately stated, 'Berenil! I've seen the same thing in horses I've injected. They usually die.' Christine constantly pushed mashed paw-paw into Speke's mouth and sugared water, gently massaging his throat until he swallowed. After three days and injections of Penbritin penicillin to clean the system, which we asked the veterinarians to give, he miraculously rose again and slowly became the cheeky Speke we knew so well. Strictly no Berenil for Speke or the other donkeys in future!

The week before we left Tabora, brown-eyed Paula burst into our lives.

A highly voluble woman, her short skirt constricting ample thighs, a long white scarf trailing ostentatiously from her hair, and obligatory owl-like sunglasses, she announced imperially to the centre of the room in the British compound, 'Hi, I'm Paula Parke. I'm a journalist!'

This wasn't quite true. She was actually desperate to break into journalism and, while staying in the British compound, had been trying to meet one of the Wasukuma vigilante groups (*SunguSungu*) to write on how they were unofficially superseding the inefficient local police force. The Regional Administration Officer had refused to see her or give permission for any interviews. We offered her a consoling coffee. Immediately recovering from her frustrations, she kicked off her shoes, displaced Christine from her seat on the sofa and collapsed cross-legged in Christine's place, liberally exposing her knickers. 'I speak fluent Kiswahili, you guys. Spent three years in a Kenyan village... Hey, I can interview you guys, can't I?'

Paula had been a Peace Corps worker and had accompanied her boyfriend (who was with well-paying UNICEF) to Tanzania. She was interested in coming with us for a few days to take photographs and in the hope of writing her story on the *SunguSungu*, hopefully for the Associated Press. We planned to take a rucksack in order to carry Paula's goods as well as the extra food we would need for her, and she could sleep in Andy's tent while he voluntarily slept outside on a tarpaulin beside the fire. She would be with us for two or three days and ahead was a point where a side road suitable for traffic entered one of the villages we would pass through so she could be picked up again there.

On the last evening before leaving she panicked. She said she wanted to return after one day. But there was no pick-up point after a day's trek! I tempted her with the *SunguSungu*; we would be passing their cattle camps. But her notion that only she knew the right way of going about things overcame logic. She said she would walk the eight miles out of Isunuka village. I rejected this irresponsible tactic. She said she would elicit help from villagers. I said she couldn't involve them: they would misconstrue her actions, particularly the men.

'I don't want to discuss this!' she stormed, stamping her foot. 'What I do is none of your affair. I'm not part of your expedition. I'm a journalist!'

I pointed out she was a guest on my expedition and would have to be sensitive to the way we did things. I merely wanted a simple reassurance from her that she would not cause me and the expedition any problem.

'We'll discuss it tomorrow. I'm just not prepared to talk about it any more. I'm not part of your control system. You can't dominate me. I act as I like.' She broke down in tears. 'I can make you guys famous!' she spat out, ignoring everything I had said and flounced back to the British compound.

Collecting our donkeys from the stadium, we noticed the railway line and miniature signals were clearly exposed now all the grass had been eaten, but there was no train! We trekked over the hills to Kwihara, intending to complete fourteen and three-quarter miles to Isunuka. Paula hardly acknowledged me and trailed to the rear of our line loudly calling out to passers-by and jabbering to them in very bad Kiswahili, which began to grate on my nerves. At the Livingstone Tembe we hailed Shomari, who waved, and Abedi who was reclining flat on the porch beside an ever-increasing mountain of rubble and wood ash. Paula wanted us to stop while she changed the film in her camera. This was impossible with the donkeys so she would have to catch us up.

Shomari agreed to escort her.

PART FOUR – FINALLY FREE FROM GAME SCOUTS

We used the same track as Stanley, which led over a saddle to an expansive view of rolling slopes, rocky outcrops, clusters of thatched houses and the buff Ntalikwa Hills in the background. Exposed was a creamy blue Mediterranean sky which had only started to be seen once we had ascended the Rift. We descended to Migwengwe (Stanley's Mkwenke where he camped) and passed through it. Officially it was not a village; it possessed no CCM Office, and during implementation of *Ujamaa*, the inhabitants were meant to move to the new village of Ntalikwa, three miles south-west, but the villagers refused to leave and Migwengwe continued as an unofficial settlement. Migwengwe was a species of *miombo* tree; the roots were boiled to make an antiseptic mouthwash and a drink for stomach pains.

From Migwengwe we curved by rocky hills through groves of cashew nut trees to the *Ujamaa* Ntalikwa, the land fast becoming desert as locals had over-cultivated a narrow area of the land and decimated trees as fuel to dry their tobacco, although the area was designated as Forest Reserve, so it was illegal to fell trees.

Paula in her tight jeans, plimsolls and thick rolls of sock, mindlessly taking photographs, was continually falling behind. At one stage she became lost until a local found her and showed her the right track again.

She was furious. 'I thought you had to keep to the pace of the slowest person,' she exploded.

I had previously explained our predicament with donkeys. If we stopped they would either buck off their panniers or sit in protest. She needed to keep up. Andy's shoulders were being pulled apart with the weight of her rucksack as Paula had wanted us to also carry her camera and tape recorder. I took over the rucksack from Andy. And Paula decided she wanted her water bottle, which was inside. I undid it. We waited while she slowly glugged down the water.

'Can we put it away now?' Andy asked. She ignored him and walked away. We waited for a while longer.

'Close it, Andy!' I ordered.

As he did so, she casually strode over. 'I want to put my water bottle away now!' she insisted, grimly holding it out.

'Carry it!' Andy said.

She threw it on the ground and turned her back on us, arms folded. This was getting petty.

Isunuka (meaning 'to spy') was once a large village of 160 families. The villagers exhausted the land by over-farming. Now only seven scattered houses were hidden away in the far corners of a scrubby area. Most locals relocated in 1974 to Ntalikwa, and Wasukuma cattle herders moved in. The Wasukuma comprised the largest cow-owning tribe in Tanzania. In their own region, Shinyanga, there was little grazing land to satisfy the whole tribe and large areas were taken by government aid schemes to grow cotton, further reducing pasture areas. Apart from the cows and goats the Wasukuma traditionally grew sweet potatoes and made *matobolwa*. Their dress was basic and they lived cheaply. Like locusts desertifying their own land, they had become nomads, forced to move ever further south with cattle and goats. Using anti-sleeping-sickness drugs they were able to take their cattle into tsetse-infested areas, and could sell beef and milk to towns like Mpanda – that previously had no cattle – for far higher prices.

Desertification of the land was a serious matter and

Rukwa Region for example had introduced by-laws banning Wasukuma moving cattle along their roads. If caught they were heavily fined and moved away. So they remained suspicious of strangers, thinking them officials. Thus they provided little useful information to us, sometimes even denying knowledge of Kiswahili. Two hundred Wasukuma families were secreted in the Isunuka area. Some of these Wasukuma were also the vigilante *SunguSungu*, but Paula was too exhausted from the trek to interview them.

We camped near the herders, under a huge mango tree within walking distance of a well containing milky water. From her rucksack Paula brought out an orange for each of us, then on the pretext of collecting firewood she devoured four in the privacy of the well. Asking if there was anything she could do and then being given a task such as pumping water, she immediately languished and begged Andy's assistance.

At one stage she stood up and announced, 'I'm going over to talk to the cattle herders.'

She returned after an hour. The Tanzanians would misinterpret this; it was bar-girl behaviour. It made us look bad. After supper Paula began to relax and we were having a halfway normal conversation when she suddenly announced she had arranged with the cattle herders to be escorted eight miles to the road and would be leaving at six in the morning.

'It's out of your hands, George. There's nothing you can do,' she smirked.

Lord, the lass was deranged! She truly did not understand she could be raped and killed. In the bush we had become a self-contained ruthless team determined to let no one thing deter us from our purpose. We were a ship at sea, and she could not accept she was merely a passenger.

I exploded, 'Take all your stuff out of Andy's tent and get out then. You will sleep beside the cattle herders. And you can be escorted from there. I don't want any of us to be disturbed in the morning.'

'I will not. I will stay right here!' She slapped the ground.

'You can't stay here. This is my camp, and I don't want you.'

'You don't own the land, George. I can go where I want and stay where I want. If you want me to leave, you'll have to pick me up and throw me out. D'you hear me?'

'I'll say this once: it would make no difference to me if you were a man or a woman, a ten-foot giant or a three-year-old child. You are deliberately disturbing this expedition like a whining mosquito. So you will not stay in this camp tonight.'

'Oh, you're just like Stanley…!'

Andy returned to find Paula sitting on her bundled goods, calmly attempting to justify her behaviour. 'It's difficult, you see, for an outsider to fit in with you three… You have your own rules…'

I asked Christine and Andy to make a decision. Perhaps I'd been too harsh. Andy said he wanted to discuss the matter with the cattle herders. He returned to report the cattle herders thought she was foolish in not continuing with us. They were worried about escorting her. As we were with the government, if anything happened they would be held responsible. Good. I was relieved that they were worried.

Floods of tears from Paula. 'I don't want to go over to

the cattle herders... You guys... you don't understand their culture and what they'll think...'

Andy volunteered, 'They won't do anything, I assure you.'

'It's not what they'll do. It's what they'll be saying to me all night.'

I interrupted. 'Paula, stop being precious. You knew all this when you strolled over to chat to them. You've been in enough bars and discos in Kenya to know the rules.'

'And what will you do if I stay with you? Beat me if I don't behave?'

'I think Paula should leave now!' Andy declared.

'It's obvious, Paula is too much of an individual to travel with us,' added Christine.

'That's your decision?' I asked.

'That's it.'

'Have I been fair, Paula?'

'Yes.'

Andy spoke again to the cattle herders and Paula trailed over carrying her white-wrapped bundle like a dispirited Santa Claus. I wasn't sure she'd be fine, but that was her choice.

By morning she was gone. We met her again very much later when our expedition was over in Dar es Salaam at the Kilimanjaro Hotel swimming pool. Her image had changed. She was now in a prim blouse and skirt, an au pair, escorting a child.

'Well done, you guys,' she said, 'I couldn't do it!'

We spent our time in Isunuka chatting with the cattle herders about potions to frighten off lion and hyena. One of them reported that Paula had held court in the early morning telling them about her work as a freelance journalist. 'Like your Queenie Victory of England,' he harrumphed like a hippo.

Approximately 606.75 miles covered. We were slowly getting there.

We trekked ten and a half miles to the medium-sized village of Kasekera with a group of chattering Wasukuma women carrying large containers of rotting *dagaa* on their heads. Donkey Burton would stop and stare into the distance, dreaming. Then would nip Livingstone's buttocks when he attempted to usurp him and take the lead crossing the dry Wala and Kasisi riverbeds. Originally the indigenous inhabitants of this refused to fight alongside other Wanyamwezi. Villages nearby made fun of their cowardice and so gave the settlement its name: Kasekera ('to mock'). Now there were only seventeen Wanyamwezi families left, swamped by the secretive Wasukuma and a hundred other refugee families from Burundi, Zaire and Malawi, who grew tobacco as a cash crop.

To the donkeys' delight, the village had a crystal-clear underground spring flowing into a granite basin full of frogs. Tempted, the thirsty hot donkeys all galloped wildly to the water, causing panic. Two cattle herders, who had never seen donkeys before, sprang into trees. A group of children and a woman collecting water scattered howling into the bush. Only the cows remained unconcernedly drinking.

*

Third week of September. Because of the inaccuracy of our maps, what should have been an easy eight miles to the small village of Mole turned into a frustrating and sweaty fourteen. We all became easily tired; every day there was something to do. I knew it would be difficult eventually to explain to people in England what we found to do that kept us so occupied. And the stress! It was incredibly humid. We were told the rains were imminent. We hoped they would fail and spare us the mud and muck we would have to trail through. Andy was not feeling well; his urine was dark orange and he had no appetite. I was desperately lacking medical knowledge. He could be suffering hepatitis B which could occur after a bad bout of malaria, or long-term infestation, when his liver was weakened. I needed help! After Mole, another six miles would bring us close to a road where it might be possible to get a logging lorry to take Andy to a Moravian mission hospital that was ten miles further on. This was our last opportunity for medical treatment before we set off for the 150-mile-distant town of Mpanda. As a final resort I would have to dose Andy's delirium with explorer Stanley's well-tried remedy: carefully measured portions of quinine!

We wasted an hour in largish Tutuo, while Andy and I scurried about looking for a campsite with a sufficient quantity of dried grass. We were led off by insistent locals to survey what they described as 'a green valley and very clean drinking water'. This as we expected, but hoped against, was a wild goose chase to view coarse stalks and a filthy pit of stagnant liquid. We returned and sat to collect our wits. We could never find a suitable shade tree as they had been cut down for firewood, charcoal, or to clear the land for planting. If we did find shade we discovered corrugated cultivated earth beneath, requiring hot work with a borrowed hoe to level the ground.

Then local children (mobs of them) descended to gape and giggle and attempt to steal. Long after adults had left, the kids remained. Christine, I was happy to acknowledge, was happy to face the bush, to step into the wild and be independent even if it was so full of discomfort. Her indomitable spirit and dislike of bullshit was probably one of the reasons we got on. Andy, however, was swaying.

Afternoon. After killing a venomous boomslang with a stick (it fell amongst us from a tree, looking as innocuous as a slim green bootlace), Andy and I trekked into the centre of Tutuo to purchase a live duck from a chatty, gesticulating owner with one arm. He insisted on showing us his wild watchdogs in the shed. He demonstrated how the furry half-starved beasts wouldn't harm him by pushing his face into theirs. They would have torn our arms off! He fed them on *ugali* and *mchicha* (kale) or sweet potato leaves. So they were vegetarians, but they snatched the duck out of Andy's hands and tore it apart. Not to worry, he brought another live one out, dangling it upside down by its legs and in between affectionate strokes from his stump began bargaining all over again.

We had been given an official warning from the Sleeping Sickness Research Centre in Tabora, but despite this region being designated an uninhabited sleeping sickness area, there were villages full of people who had refused official requests to move. And tsetse, though present and biting, up to now had been more numerous in other parts of the bush. Anyway, we had no possible alternative route if we were to faithfully follow Stanley.

PART FIVE –

INTO THE LAND OF SLEEPING SICKNESS

20

Ugunda: Land of Deserted Villages

On to Igalula, which in Stanley's time was the seat of Chief Mumeta of the Wagunda tribe. He died in 1927 aged ninety. The Wagunda were a Wanyamwezi clan, and so the area was and still is referred to as *Ugunda*, a general name for this cultivated region.

Igalula meant 'to change', because the Wagunda changed their place of settlement so many times. Because villagers refused *Ujamaa* status and were forcibly removed, Igalula was not however classified as a village.

After a mile we reached a fork in a red dirt road and turned our faces south-south-westward following Stanley's detour towards the direction of the present-day western frontier town of Mpanda. At the head of this road was a prominent sign which read:

Warning.
200 miles to Mpanda.
Before driving on this road, make sure you have enough water, food and petrol, and that your vehicle is in good condition. You should be prepared for any

eventuality. The road is rough, and in disrepair. The region is inhabited by wild animals.

A sharp blue sky, the white glare bursting blood vessels in the whites of our eyes. Scattered *miombo* woodland, grey anthills like granite stalagmites. Although we didn't see cattle, we occasionally heard the jingle of cow bells. We passed date palms, *mkoche* (doum palms). They possessed sweet orange fruits looking like small pineapples, which elephants and baboons loved to eat. Plentiful mango fruits, hanging like swollen green kidneys from branches, just beginning to blush red, uneatable until the end of November.

Igalula was at the top of a shallow hill. A path was lined with great shade trees. There were no houses! Doum palms rattled and squeaked like winches as we continued on to the outskirts of this area. With great relief we finally saw several broken-down houses, but the place was deserted – and we needed to ask where we could go for the ever-essential water.

A one-eyed man and a sulky-looking woman with a swollen top lip reluctantly appeared in an open doorway of one of the broken-down houses and leaned on a tree.

Our desperate questions were answered in lazy monosyllables.

'We need to camp near the water. Could you tell us where it is?'

'It is near...'

'Where?'

'Over there...' The woman waved into the sky.

'Where, exactly?'

'On the path...'

'What path?'

'The one over there...' Again, a vague waft of the hand.

Hot and exhausted, we felt like jumping on both and throttling the information out of them. We were reaching the end of our tether.

'And the old road to Koga River is where?' we asked.

'There...' This time neither bothered to wave or nod toward a general area, merely stared fixedly at us.

We'd had enough! No longer polite, we fired questions at them, interrogating them as an officious African would do: Who were they? What were they doing? etc., etc. Her body sagged and his smile dropped away, replaced by a lip-twitch of fear and uncertainty. Clearly they should not have been here...

'You will show us the water!' we demanded.

Now they fell in beside us, leading us to a shallow depression with milky water in the middle of a flat, empty area. A large herd of cows was in the distance, and near the water was a thorn stockade.

'Wasukuma?' we asked. One-eye nodded his head.

In 1973 there had been 2,500 houses in Igalula. The villagers were suddenly forced to move because of *Ujamaa* and Igalula became a ghost settlement. Later, a few returned. One was Ali Zaidi Teketela, now the unauthorised headman of the settlement. But only sixteen Wagunda families now inhabited the area.

'There were too many people in the new villages, not enough land to farm and the soil was bad,' he said when we found him in the only solid house existing. 'The people were suffering hunger. There was American relief aid of yellow maize, but this gave diarrhoea and blood. I did not want to stay and be ill.'

Was his life better now? we asked Ali Zaidi.

'Ha, *wapi*?' He laughed. 'We are *masikini, bwana* (poor, mister)!' With this ubiquitous complaint he launched into a familiar Tanzanian lament: there was only so much land that could be worked with two hands.

Nyerere's *Ujamaa* policy, it seemed to me, had two faces. It purported to create order out of the scattered population of Tanzania, to concentrate them in new villages, close to main roads and communication, serviced by schools, dispensaries and supervised by the political party. But by abolishing the chief system and moving people of one tribe out of their old region and allowing them to intermix with other tribes in large *Ujamaa* villages, the policy was also attempting a forced integration and a dissolving of tribalism. And, of course, by gathering people into accessible and controlled villages, a proper census could be taken and taxes levied.

Income tax in low-salaried Tanzania was high – thirty-three per cent. And in 1984 just as we started our expedition a 'Development Tax' of 200 shillings a year was introduced, to be paid by each person over eighteen. People had since been asking, 'What development?'

Ali Zaidi said we needed an expert guide to show us waterholes on the way to Iswangala, our next destination, thirty-one and a quarter miles distant. There were no settlements or known water on the way and fourteen years had passed since a Land Rover had attempted to use the road. It was now a ruin.

There could be water, he told us, fifteen miles away at

Milala, a dead village where the Wasukuma had dug holes in a dry pond bed to find water for their cattle. Once these men left, however, elephants stamped the holes into a muddy mass which soon baked hard. After that, there was no water for twenty miles. His words left us agog with fear.

We had camped very near to Ali Zaidi's solitary mud house close to a water source, and at the crack of dawn young loud-mouthed locals came to sell us bran for the donkeys. Christine, about to unzip the tent door, froze and sat back down in the tent as a long grey snake slithered over our dome tent, down to the ground, and then rose three to four feet to reach the branch of our mango-shade tree. We let it go. The Kinyamwezi name for this snake is *Nhangalukwi*. We believed it could have been a black mamba, in which case the black colour was only seen inside its open mouth. You could unknowingly carry it in firewood and it wouldn't hurt you unless you attacked or accidentally trod on it. The male snake grew to five feet and was an inch in diameter. It lived on insects and frogs and its bite was deadly; death would occur after half an hour.

'Welcome, welcome,' Ali said, as a huge communal mound of steaming *ugali* was brought out on a wooden tray for breakfast. There were also two small bowls, one with boiled-up tomatoes in water and flour, and one with chopped cassava leaves in water and flour. A bowl of milky water was first passed around and everyone – there were five family members – dipped their filthy hands into the water, rinsed, and passed the water on. Then they ravenously dug into the *ugali* with their right hands.

We said, thank you; we were full.

PART FIVE – INTO THE LAND OF SLEEPING SICKNESS

A local lad named Thebit said he would guide us to the waterholes. 'I want 2,000 shillings!' he demanded. We laughed. His face fell. '200 shillings!' we said. He instantly accepted.

7am. Overcast. Boom of hornbills. Baboons trooped speedily across the ground. Although we were downwind, we nevertheless startled a relaxing young impala. Tsetse! The donkeys charged crazily about. After sixteen miles we reached the deserted settlement of Milala. Here there were clay-dug waterholes and a couple of scraggly mango trees for shade. Thebit raced forward and disappeared into bushes. We discovered two roughly put-together log shelters with wooden beds. Thebit had claimed a bed and spread out his meagre possessions in such a way that even should we have wanted to we couldn't have squeezed ourselves inside the tiny structure. We were in any event afraid of fleas. He sat on a wooden bed expectantly frozen until we passed. He had taken to making rafts in the trees like Abdullah where he spent the night. When we led the donkeys to the waterhole, Thebit nervously sped past balancing a large calabash on his shoulder.

*

Now without donkeys, explorer Stanley could walk unhindered. His account perfectly illustrates the ignorance at the time concerning cause of fevers: '...fever is frequent in this region of extensive forests and flat plains, owing to the imperfect drainage provided by nature... the poison of the dead and decaying vegetation is inhaled into the system...' Stanley doesn't mention mosquitoes!

Milala is lion territory. Have to be extra alert with donkeys. Two chattering birds pick at Livingstone's back till it bleeds (finding mites?).

Humidity – rains creeping closer; mpani *flies distracting. Andy not feeling too good, walking around with dripping shirt on head, got one* mpani *caught in eye. Could only remove it hours later covered in white pus. Accurately sight revolver and rifle by shooting at old newspaper target hung in branches. Work out mileages. Yet again! At night slinky low hissing of rustling grass, rhythmic, long-drawn-out breaths, make us grab guns. Leopard? No. Merely seething heat and normal collective emission from* mchwa *(ants) in their earth burrows. Christine thinks: Oh, for a woman to have a laugh over ridiculous situation I'm in! Christine has filth from cooking etc under nails (something I know she can't stand), discomfort, danger and is endlessly putting up with it – sometimes even enjoying it! Today she spotted another single red bloom, like a lily leaping out of the mud, twelve inches high…*

*

We left after a fall of rain had ceased. One would think that without sun the day would remain pleasant, but no. A mass of newly hatched flies (because of the rain, said Thebit) crawled over our faces and bare arms. Then a horror squadron of tsetse! Insect spray did not keep them off. Thebit forged ahead for devious reasons of his own – perhaps to collect honey.

According to our map, we were now coming into the Ugalla River Game Reserve – an overgrown area with a

PART FIVE – INTO THE LAND OF SLEEPING SICKNESS

concentrated animal migration that naturally flowed across our path. We were obviously nervous.

Christine whispered to me, 'Will we be all right?'

I replied, 'Of course.' But we really didn't know what we could encounter.

Ugalla means the 'Land of the Feather Hats'. It got its name from the warlike Wagalla tribe, who had claimed the territory south of the river. The Wagalla had trekked westward from Tanga, fighting all the way. Their original tribal name had been *Wasegeju*, meaning the people who tucked up their clothes for freedom of movement or who 'girded up their loins'. They habitually wore tall hats of gaudy bird feathers (*ngalla*) to strike fear into their superstitious enemies. Thebit told us that, like the Maasai, the Wagalla now refused to cultivate land or even keep domestic animals. They preferred to live wild in the forests.

'They don't like people to get near. They'll shoot at them with arrows. Their work is to fight and kill animals for meat,' he added.

This did not help our nerves!

Another three and a half miles brought us to a deserted area, which may have been, according to his timing, where Stanley camped under a giant sycamore (thirty-eight feet in circumference) beside a large pool of water, '*ziwani*'. Here he displayed his lordly magnanimity: 'I talked with my people as to my friends and equals… stretched on my carpet [*yes, a real carpet*] smoking my short meerschaum.'

There was now no water in the camp and the tree had long gone, but under a cloudy sky the donkeys were at least speeding along. And without the blazing heat and blinding sun, we ourselves had no need to dwell on our water bottles.

Honey-filled hives in the trees; bunches of bees sitting outside hives on tree branches preparing to swarm; dried-up flat bogs; desolate burnt areas of woodland; blackened trees remained standing without leaves. We were continuously flicking away flies with switches cut from bushes when Andy shouted he'd seen a dark shape lumber across the path.

'Where?'

'About 400 yards.'

We saw one shape unfold into two shapes. 'It's giraffes!' Christine exclaimed. 'They're taking young leaves from the trees.'

I was wary. However cute, they were still wild animals as I had learned to my cost! We were thirty yards downwind of them before they heard us and balletically galloped in slow motion through the woods, their necks swaying like flexible bamboo. Then they deliberately went off in opposite directions, to confound us in case we were hunting them.

Another deserted settlement. Mwanamskie. The donkeys were tired and slumped to the ground. Thebit sat under a tree looking gloomy. There was no water! We had no alternative but to continue.

Up with the groaning donkeys for an extra three and a quarter miles more to Iswangala, the site of Stanley's Manyara, now a small logging camp. Bush camp for the night.

Iswangala ceased being a Wagunda village in 1962 when the area was designated a Forest Reserve. Its name meant 'to set out and profit', these being instructions originally issued from the village of Igalula – then the tribal centre of Ugunda. Stanley had named it Manyara, because Manyara was the ruling chief at the time.

PART FIVE – INTO THE LAND OF SLEEPING SICKNESS

The waterhole had a rainbow of oil floating on the surface. Had to douse Andy with water buckets again; it was looking possible that he might not finish the journey. I was so terrified of making a mistake. It was far worse than I ever imagined, and Christine and Andy were relying on me. I know they thought me bloody-minded with my orders and demands, but I couldn't help it. I had to be this way if we were all to survive and complete the journey.

In some weird way, I felt I had to permanently show I was madder than the Tanzanians and more ruthless. They'd given me a nickname, *bwana nyati* (Mr Buffalo) because I butted through situations. This, to them, was a compliment. They admired mindless strength. Christine said, 'This is rubbish!' as witnessed by her list of my illnesses. 'You are just being a stubborn perfectionist!' she declared. And I had to admit I had been constantly ill.

Approximately 667.25 miles covered. More than halfway...

From his Ziwani camp to Iswangala Stanley was sorely attacked by *mbungo* (tsetse) or what he calls *'panga-*fly' (sword-fly). On the road his caravan came upon a man dead of smallpox and to give an idea of the mad warfare tearing the land apart at the time I quote Stanley: 'He was one of Oseto's gang of marauders... in the service of Mkasiwa of Unyanyembe, hunting the guerrillas of Mirambo... they had left their comrade to perish in the road... it was a frequent thing to discover a skeleton or a skull on the roadside. Almost every day we saw one, sometimes two, of these relics...'

At night a series of grating drawn-out nasal blasts from my donkey Stanley pierced my thick sleep, his rasps totally unlike his normal nostril-clearing snorts. We all stumbled out of the tents, guns glued to our hands, to see an elephant at a hundred yards crunching through grass and bush, searching for fragrant *doum* fruits under the palms. Hearing us, the elephant moved slowly off.

Stanley instantly calmed. Henceforth he was chosen as our wild-animal watchdog while Burton was our man-watcher. Stanley's snort was just like that from a wounded sable antelope that we once approached: a signal of aggression and ready fighting spirit.

To prevent further incidents we decided to restake the donkeys closer to our tents, surmising that our human scent – and the blazing fire which we had piled high with logs – would act as a buffer between further elephant incursions and the donkeys. But Stanley grated again, this time accompanied by snarls, fighting snorts and kicking hooves. Out of our tents again.

Hyenas! They had never made a sound. A hyena was gripping tight with its claws and sliding down Stanley's back, ripping it badly, as he bucked and viciously struck double back-kicks at other hyenas. Speke and Livingstone were both kicking furiously – hyenas somersaulting into the air. There were so many hyena around us and the donkeys that we were powerless to use our guns, not wanting to mistakenly shoot the donkeys. Instead we edged into the hot stink of hyena, risking sharp flying hooves striking us in the head and at each opportunity swung the butts of our guns at the determined crook-backed creatures until the hyenas finally slunk into the darkness.

Hyena always hunt in packs and rarely show themselves by day, resting in their lairs, down holes and in inaccessible natural burrows. Females are larger and stronger than males and have developed a clitoris as large as the male penis, also a sham scrotum so it is difficult to tell the sexes apart. But it's a myth that the hyena is hermaphrodite. They are though cannibalistic and possibly female dominance has evolved to protect cubs from voracious fathers. They have the strongest jaws in the animal kingdom; the only bone they can't crack is an elephant's skull! We concluded that the ugly creatures had waited for us to fall asleep and had silently sloped in from the dark side of the camp to attack. They must have picked out Livingstone first as he was the oldest and therefore most vulnerable. But they had miscalculated Stanley's loyalty. Sturdy Stanley had always stood protectively beside Livingstone. His ankle rope was also broken; he must have pulled at it until it snapped in order to go to Livingstone's aid.

We retied brave Stanley and Livingstone, banked up the fire and inspected Stanley's wounds, but there was nothing we could do for him in the dark.

Christine whispered, 'I was not much use in that fight. I got out my gas-gun but was too scared to use it. We were downwind, and it might have gassed me.'

We hardly slept, checking on the donkeys throughout the night. In daylight, Stanley's scars looked much worse; the hyena's sharp claws had gouged deep cuts going down his flank. We washed and sprayed his wounds with tetracycline-gentian violet, stuck on an antiseptic dressing and injected him with more tetracycline.

Andy seemed disheartened. He said of the hyena battle, 'I just follow George these days. I copy him. That's all I can do.'

Our bodies swimming in insecticide against tsetse, we departed in a haze of murmuring flies. Our arms and necks were swollen and on fire. Tsetse had bitten us on the face until we felt like weeping. We had never known them so bad.

Far ahead of us in the heat haze we saw what we thought were humans, moving in and out of trees, behaving so oddly as to appear suspicious. I loosened my revolver in its holster, while Andy loaded a buckshot cartridge into the shotgun. As we approached, two men dodged into the trees and two others came toward us. One was a giant, holding a huge cudgel in one hand and a *panga* in the other.

'If something happens,' I told Christine, 'fall flat on the ground and roll out of the way.'

A rock almost hit Andy. Then a spear! Arrows!

We dashed behind bushes and fired from there. The giant and his mate had disappeared, but now someone was firing a gun at us. Tree bark flew into the air. We dodged low from tree to tree firing back. Then it stopped. We saw a rag waving above the bushes.

The cudgel man stepped out and walked toward us.

'*Salaama* (Peace),' he said.

I certainly hoped so. '*Salaama tu* (Only peace),' I replied.

'You are moving house?' he asked.

I studied him closely. He was serious. 'No, we are walking to Ujiji.'

He deliberated. 'A long *safari*.'

'Yes.'

'Walk in peace.' He stood aside and we moved on, though I was walking backwards, my hand still on my gun trigger until we were safely past. What was all that about? We were never to know.

We crossed the river and warily entered Ukonongo tribal territory.

21

Ukonongo: Land of Iron Hoes

Daylight hours were the safe times. Baboons slithered from their trees; spring-footed impalas hiccupped and silently interweaved bushes like floating elves; heavy-bodied warthogs with a line of babies minced by on tiptoe, stiff-as-a-stick tails held vertical; a baby elephant bathed while its mother stood protectively on the bank. Along the grey river: buck bent to drink; marabou storks took, it seemed, painful aged steps; pelicans yawned fish down their swollen throats; geese in loving pairs sat cushioned on the water and wide-feathered black storks cloaked the banks.

*

On the other side of the river was a crude log shelter used by honey-gatherers and river fishermen who caught and smoke-dried huge catfish for sale. This river flowed into the River Ugalla to the north-west, and then into the great Malagarasi which spilled into Lake Tanganyika.

There were numerous dishevelled fishermen crammed in the timber shelter who emerged to greet us. They said we must be careful of lions. The lions were as many as herds of goats. Thebit immediately headed to the log shelter. We nodded wisely at the fishermen. We were now used to exaggerations.

The tribe in this area, a Wanyamwezi clan, were known as *fundi* (craftsmen), experts in the smelting of iron. They made hoes of a certain sharp-pointed design called *konongo* in Kinyamwezi. These iron hoes were so highly prized they were often included in a bride price, e.g. two to three cows and five to six hoes.

The cropped, grassy area was spread out for miles like groomed parkland, with a river running through it teeming with fish, hippopotami and crocodiles. It reminded me of a safe Regent's Park, yet – warned by the fisherman of lions in the area – I kept turning to look behind. Somehow I felt as if we were being spied on.

In all, sixteen and three-quarter miles to the Koga River and our sixteenth bush camp. It was now 2 October. We spent the afternoon cleaning and treating a tightly secured Stanley's wounds and injecting him with more tetracycline. The wound was by his shoulder and had opened up as he walked, making us worried about the possibility of tetanus and rabies: there was no tetanus antitoxin for animals in these parts of Tanzania and we no longer had any injectable penicillin. Instead, we had to give Stanley a series of five painful injections of tetracycline. By the end of it he would hate us!

We haltered his head to a tree to prevent biting, and lassooed his back leg and stretched it tight until suspended in mid-air, then secured it to a tree stump so he was on three legs and could neither bite nor kick us. Then I slapped

Stanley hard on the rump to numb the area and plunged just the needle into his flesh. The difficult part then was to screw the syringe to the base of the needle as Stanley threw himself about, squeeze in the solution and withdraw quickly, all in rhythm with his attempted bucks and kicks. Unfortunately, these antiquated needles were all that were available to us, as provided by Tanzanian vets.

Over supper Christine inadvertently caught two yellow burning globes in her torchlight looking like lanterns. They flashed twice and she realised that they were large blinking eyes surveying our camp and the tethered donkeys. The one thing that gave wild animals away in darkness was their eyes when a light was shone in their direction. With experience you could even tell the type of animal from the shape and size of the eyes, distance apart and height from the ground. These large eyes were of a low-lying lion! Caught out, it stood up and slunk slowly away. It didn't return, so we eventually climbed into our tents. This was an animal that had haunted my dreams since childhood.

At 3am we were alerted by Stanley snorting aggressively, a stamping of hooves. I had been in a deep sleep. I struggled for my boots, ignored my clothes and tumbled out naked, the shotgun which Andy had cleaned that day and loaded already in my tight grasp along with a searching torch.

Stanley was rearing up, front hooves whipping the air, while a lioness crouched in the grass, staring, no more than fifty feet away. Its eyes darted to me, daring.

'Come out with the revolver, Chris,' I whispered. 'It's a lion. A big one.' I did not take my eyes away from the lion or raise my voice in case I encouraged it. Mosquitoes began biting my back and buttocks, but I had to concentrate. The donkeys were becoming hysterical, tugging at their tethers. The lion began to crawl forward.

'Shoot!' shouted Andy. Thirty feet. Twenty. I pointed and shot. Nothing happened. Just a click of the trigger. There was a piece of rag hanging from the barrel. Andy had forgotten and left it in.

'Bloody hell!' I exclaimed. The gun could have blown up in my face. All this happened in milliseconds. The lioness was very near.

'Shall I shoot?' Christine was standing by me now, with the revolver. With a revolver there is as much chance of missing as of hitting. The shotgun was the best bet. Bitten to distraction, I was furious. Anger at Andy took over. I would throttle the beast with my bare hands, snap its jaws apart, squelch out its eyes. I revelled in rage. Mosquitoes kept biting, but I no longer felt them. I no longer experienced panic or a need to destroy the lion. And I knew that it was also aware of this shift. At ten feet I tore out the rag and fired over the lion's head. 'You missed!' said Andy. I almost felt like shooting him!

The animal stood, its heavy stomach hanging almost to the ground (had it already eaten?), peered at us disdainfully, turned sedately and strode away, slowly swallowed up by the darkness. But we could not rest.

'Look!' Christine said. Her torch had picked out two more lionesses, crouched patiently on our left a mere ten-foot distance away, one more at our front, one on the right, and two others further back.

'One more there! Look, one more!' Andy began discovering eyes and groups of eyes like grounded constellations. No wonder the donkeys were agitated. The lions *were* like herds of goats. The fishermen had been absolutely right. Crouched low to the ground the lions crawled forward, huge heads rising every now and then to survey the way, then continued to advance in stops and starts, until I fired over their heads. They then stood revealing themselves, almost shrugging their shoulders with cool indifference and luxuriously pranced to the edge of the black. To begin all over again!

They were teasing us, playing 'Grandmother's Footsteps'. Eventually we all had to fire. And destroyed the night with bangs, flashes of light, shouted exclamations, lion grunts and purrs. I wasted countless cartridges. We all shot above the lions' heads. Then powerful roars that rattled our eardrums and loosened the depths of our stomachs. Two more lions passed close to our camp strolling to the river for water. Fifteen minutes later they returned, still roaring loudly. But they were making such a reverberating din it was obvious these were not hunting signals. They had gorged themselves on warm bloody meat, distended their bellies with water and meant no harm to the donkeys.

Until the next time.

Illuminated by firelight, dressed only in unlaced boots, mosquitoes feeding from my buttocks, fear had flown. Never again would a lion worry me. To subvert a phrase: the only thing to fear was yourself. A weary crumbling away of darkness and the dawn's slow seeping light brought us relief.

Christine in our tent admonished me. 'It was an accident. Andy didn't do it purposely. You're giving him too much to do, you realise. He can't cope.'

'I know, I know,' I said. 'It *was* an accident and I'll

apologise for my mood when I'm up, but you have to realise that we're short-handed.'

A fisherman in tattered shorts, body gleaming with water reeking of stale fish, brought us a gift of a five-foot-long catfish which was so fresh it was jerkingly alive. He wanted to hear our news. All the fishermen knew we had been attacked by lions. They hadn't thought we would be alive in the morning.

Tall as the fish he carried, the heavy weight hanging on a yoke over his wet shoulder, the fisherman slapped the fish to set it jiggling, wafting watery-fish smells toward us. 'Big like a human! Big as a man!' he described.

His name was Idi and he jangled on the spot with nervous energy, insisting on showing us a disused hunter's camp past the hippos' graveyard of massive bleached bones, remnants of unsuccessful hippo wars. Though very gregarious, bull hippos fought frequently and more fiercely than most other animals, inflicting frightful wounds with their teeth; hippos could very likely die from their wounds after a fierce battle. Males threatened each other by displaying wide-open jaws showing the interior of their mouth and teeth.

We were unable to refuse Idi. He had snared us with his mind-capturing monologues and constant hypnotic movements. Finding animals was his true job, not handling fish, but there was no one to employ him. He walked us off our feet, spinning on the spot, tugging and patting, showering us in fish scales, encircling us in pungent reeks of aged fish. *Bwana mkubwa* – 'Mr Big'; I had been elevated – 'you will give me your address! Perhaps you will come and hunt and make a camp. I will work for you.' He hammered his thin chest in recommendation. 'I know this place. I know all the animals.' He windmilled, then balanced on one leg, arms outstretched like a floating undernourished octopus.

Teasing lions came again and again on every night but kept outside the prickly thorn circle we had newly constructed, afraid of catching thorns in their paws. We undoubtedly felt trapped and besieged on our now narrow area of land and could not wait to leave.

We trod a steady upward incline for the whole thirteen miles to our next bush camp – our seventeenth now. We were entirely in unpopulated, uncultivated land now, truly in the bush. We had to dig for water which dribbled out at a snail pace. Parched bees swarmed over our faces searching out drops of perspiration. We hardly dared move. I wrote in slow motion as they crawled over my hands. And I began to enjoy the idea of these fierce creatures drinking from us, being dependent and looking humble and helpless. We were happily having a symbiotic relationship. They were too tired from thirst to buzz. I liked the little creatures desperately hovering in the heat. They found my soaked canvas bucket after I'd washed, and swarmed into it until it was black with moving bees. Thebit was still with us, but he looked drained and I believe regretted ever stepping into this lion-infested area.

Andy asked him, 'Are you used to walking in the bush?'

'Very much so,' he replied, but he took every opportunity to sit. Perhaps this was bush technique.

Approximately 708 miles covered. The early watch chilled us to the bone. I had to wear a jumper. Thebit clambered down from his timber perch in the trees and informed us that an old lion passed by our track at roughly 2am. He saw it hesitate, glance at our crackling fires and decide to continue.

*

Thick dusty sand on track. Prints of jackal like a dog's; delicate steps of reedbuck; giraffe like a large cow but elongated; close beside it smaller prints of its young; sandy swirl of snake; sable antelope droppings like small black olives; fresh hyena prints, cruel-looking dug-in steps and stool turning calcium-white in sun, evidence of bone-crunching; large round pads of elephant crinkled and creased like old parchment, always crossing our tracks never following them. Donkeys' hooves slipped, sunk, kicked up dust – found it hard-going.

7 October 1985. Bush camp 18. Dug for water again. So slow leaking through. Collect enough for donkeys and tea. No washing away sweat and dirt. Bees seeking moisture between fingers. As write, have to be extra careful not to accidentally crush one. In tent Christine complains of itching on toes. I check. Discover a jigger has laid eggs under nails of her big, second and third toes, eating into flesh. Carefully cut into toes with razor blade. With sharpened matchstick roll fragile sac of eggs out together with female jigger. Ensuring that I don't puncture else it leaks into wound and Christine's toes would become infected. Disinfect with iodine the devoured half-inch hole...

*

We kept watch, two fires going, Thebit up in the trees. At 7.15am I spotted huddles of guinea fowl on the path. I shot and missed. And multitudes of tsetse descended. The more we killed the more appeared. We realised the shot had attracted them, but it would not have been the sound. The vibrations through air? My forehead came up in lumps, my eyes blurred. Round timber hives were hanging in the trees, placed there by local honey-gatherers, looking like giant cotton reels. They were made from hollowed *miombo* trunks with a half-inch diameter hole for bees to enter. A potion of pounded leaves was placed inside to attract the bees and the hives were hung in December, then the honey collected April/May.

Time stood still. I kept peering at my wristwatch to find it had hardly moved, kept picking out features ahead and guessing how long it would take to reach them. The walk was interminable. And as always around midday in desolate places we all became morbidly introspective; a kind of melancholia descended.

Six and a half miles from Inyonga, after walking a total of seventeen miles, we witnessed the utter desolation of a growing village: trees mown down as if with a scythe; earth dug up and folded into furrows; new buildings being thatched or sapling frame-shaped houses being coated and filled with lumps of mud; smoking *pombe* houses being built around the alcoholic brewing-fires – but no tsetse, thank God. With our blood boiling, throats like the bottom of a budgie's cage, we headed for the waterhole, passing colourful crowds of people and groups of drumming men.

Andy walked the three miles to the local hospital on Mpunze Hill, where Thebit regularly had his blood tested for sleeping sickness. Construction had commenced ten years ago, but the uncompleted building was only opened officially on 1 July 1985. It was not yet properly functioning as a hospital. There was no water and the staff were waiting for Norwegian aid to dig a bore hole. Why was the hospital built so far away from the village? Andy asked. The doctor told Andy that the hospital was part of a government scheme to move the whole village of Inyonga to the hill.

'Why?'

'As an exercise,' he replied casually.

'So, only the hospital is left here now,' Andy affirmed.

'Only we are left,' he agreed. 'Now, we travel a mile to a swamp every time we want water and have to carry it back on our heads.'

Apart from a blood test (positive), they could do nothing for Andy's malaria. They had no equipment or medicine but lots of information on sleeping sickness. It seemed that in 1924 a Regional Health Officer moved all bush settlements towards Inyonga – a tsetse-free area – because of sleeping sickness. Symptoms appeared four to fourteen days after an infective bite: recurrent fever, either insomnia or desire to sleep for twenty-four hours, confused speech, no appetite, schizophrenia and confusion. The doctor personally recommended taking a dose of chloroquine – the hospital didn't possess any – which could possibly kill the parasite and would at least delay its activity. We were horrified. We were about to spend at least two months and six weeks in a sleeping sickness area!

We took a course of our nausea-inducing chloroquine immediately and hoped the chloroquine would rid us of any trypanosomiasis (sleeping sickness parasites) in our blood, but it had quite a serious reaction on my system. I was out for the count – nausea, vomiting, unable to focus my eyes, headache and eye-ache. It felt like being seasick on a see-sawing ship in a storm. Christine was slightly nauseous and Andy felt nothing at all. Still, he'd had so much chloroquine he would be immune. Livingstone was sleeping sprawled just outside our tent door like a watchdog.

In my present state, only six and a half miles to the new *Ujamaa* Utende ('to rest') was quite enough and very appropriate. Unfortunately, this was not to be. The scattered huts of the original Utende that Stanley had visited had been moved eighteen miles away, near Ifumya Hill, because of sleeping sickness. We would have to go there tomorrow, blast it!

We discovered a new lump on Speke's backbone. This could be the reason he'd been bucking off his panniers in the morning.

After eighteen miles of trekking in bushy heat the Thebit-promised water was invisible.

We couldn't find it.

'Where is it?' we called to Thebit. We and especially the donkeys were desperate for water.

'As far as a shout,' Thebit replied. He helpfully added, 'from the path', unable to calculate in miles or minutes.

We found what he intended: cracked earth which in the rains became a swamp, and dug a deep hole in the dried ground with sharpened sticks and waited for a clay-like mixture of milky goo to slowly ooze out. Every half hour we collected a canvas bucket full. Thirsty butterflies and bees immediately fluttered and buzzed around the liquid; it was amazing how they sensed it seeping out of the ground. Did they smell the water?

We bush-camped (number 19 now, would it never

PART FIVE – INTO THE LAND OF SLEEPING SICKNESS

ever end?) at the site of the 'original' Utende. Stanley had written: 'From the hill and ridge of Utende sloped a forest for miles and miles westerly, which was terminated by a grand and smooth-topped ridge rising 500 or 600 feet above the plain.' This was what was now known as the Kanono Escarpment, an arm of the Great Rift.

The donkeys were dog-tired of walking through the humidity (like wading in boiled water) and deep dust on the path. Stanley was dragging behind, his head hanging low to the ground. He was not losing weight or appetite but appeared slow and sleepy and his breathing, when we had stopped, was at twice the rate of the others'. Lungworm? Sleeping sickness? Or reaction to his wounds? We hoped to find out in the sizeable town of Mpanda sixty miles away – if there were worthwhile vets and good enough microscopes to check stool and blood.

At night we lit three fires, built a thorn stockade and kept the donkeys tied close to the tents. I walked into the bush to look for a toilet space, gripping my paper roll – and got lost in the dark, no landmarks to guide me.

Desperately I called out. Nothing. I wandered about like a sleepwalker searching for some kind of identification. And my heart seized as I suddenly saw grazing black buffalo all around me – fifteen of them, the most feared wild animals in Africa. Though looking like innocuous English bullocks, African buffalo were notoriously fierce and always sought revenge. They could chase you until you climbed a tree and would urinate onto their spinning tail to splash you. Their urine would itch so badly that you would probably fall out of the tree, and they would then gore and trample you to death. If you lay in a narrow hollow hoping to escape their horns, they would lick you. Their tongue was like sandpaper and could take off your skin. There are stories of hunters wounding a buffalo and it would disappear only to follow the hunter for miles and attack him while his back was turned. Buffalo, we had been told, always attacked from behind.

My head filled with terrifying stories and instinctively I fell to my knees. It just happened, possibly because of fear. The buffalo roamed close to my lowered body. They were all around me contentedly tugging at tufts of grass. Because I was on all fours I realised they thought me another grazing beast. I crept out of their circle, reluctant to straighten, and stumbling about found myself miraculously back in our camp.

We left early the following morning and trekked another thirteen miles to the place where Stanley had camped close to the Kanono Escarpment. We saw prowling leopard prints in the sandy road. White heat crawled under our skin and within minutes left our flimsy clothes sodden. We tried not to look at our watches. Burton in the lead stopped suddenly, shying, and began to reverse. His head was twitching nervously from side to side. He'd smelt a predator. I took out my revolver and walked in front of him to reassure and he warily strode on looking intently to the left. Nothing sprung out at us. We continued for half a mile and Burton relaxed. I was pleased to replace the heavy .357 magnum revolver back in its holster.

Burton the donkey, I imagined, was very much like his namesake: aggressive, single-minded, selfish, haughty, but also a daydreamer. Our Sergeant Major donkey chuntered through obstacles like a bull in a china shop but also stopped now and then, wandered off and peered dreamily into the distance while the others passed him by. In the mornings if we allowed him a portion of time for dreaming and didn't bother him then that day he gave of his best. Stanley was still dragging along. He began to sit, encouraging Speke until we were travelling at a snail pace. Burton began to lead the donkeys into the bushes causing chaos, and sedate Livingstone galloped forward like a spring lamb. We decided it was a donkey conspiracy, an attempt at safari sabotage.

Reaching the River Msima, we found it bone dry! Searching for water, Andy and I left Christine with the donkeys and fast-walked a mile downriver. Nothing. We surprised a lioness who sprang out of the grass thirty feet from us, stared fixedly at us and then turned and ran off. Our hearts took fifteen minutes to return to normal beat. A strange wind howled down from the escarpment, rattling the brittle doum palm leaves like rabid flaps of multitudinous prehistoric birds. Spat-out fibrous stones large as mortars bore witness to elephant presence. The Escarpment was dense with poignant autumnal-coloured trees. We drew breath and thought of English winters.

Collecting Christine we made another bush camp sixty feet up a gentle breeze-blown slope beside a clear trickling mountain stream. It was so unexpected to find water that didn't need to be pumped clean that I placed my palms in the cool water and splashed it onto my face, then bent and drank straight out of the stream like a donkey. Conditions were idyllic. Donkeys had their wounds treated, eyes washed out with saline solution, and seemed happy with the fresh grass. I shot a guinea fowl which Christine stewed,

A man collecting wood appears and encourages us

George, Ruger always to hand, has studied his map and insists we complete Stanley's route to the end

Christine cleans a cormorant for supper

Unfinished carving of our names on a large rock at Mpwapwa

The treacherous Bahi Swamp, now like a sandy seashore when the tide is out

Recent lion footprints at Mpwapwa

Journey's end; in Ujiji

The donkeys have been well trained for the journey by air to their new home in Nairobi

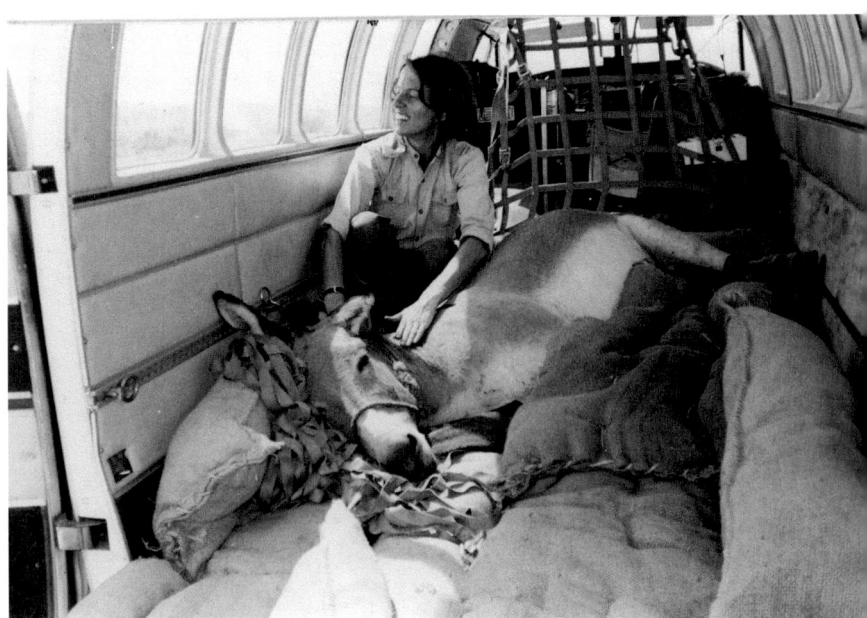

and we ate this with *ugali* and bloated ourselves on slices of sour mango in a salt, chilli and lemon juice marinade. Mango compote for pudding and mugfuls of lemon juice in water.

In the middle of nowhere an individual dressed in a stained smock clambered up the hill, surprising us. But he was not aggressive. Wearing a greasy slouch hat on his head with a tinkling bell attached, carrying a staff, and over one shoulder a bow and quiver of arrows, he asked us, 'Is there water?' He had just walked thirty miles from Inyonga with a herd of cattle. They were clearly visible down below. He was Msukuma, and would rest on the Rift for the night, leave at 2am and be in Katumba before nightfall the next day to sell cows to the Burundi Refugee Camp.

We left at 7.30 the following morning to walk fourteen miles after a night of fitful sleep.

The clouds were clear, but sun and tsetse struck. Huddles of guinea fowl were tempting us from the bushes. Warthogs strode past unafraid. Pushing up the gradual incline we reached the top of the Escarpment – a land of candelabra and extensive *miombo* trees swallowing up and shrouding the heights.

22

Onward to Mpanda – Through the Land of the Hunters

The warlike Waluwila originally came from the Congo. They fought numerous battles and vacated their conquered villages many times, before finally seizing and settling in this portion of land which stretched sixty miles to Mpanda. The Wabende were the tribe now living in the area dominated by the town of Mpanda.

After six miles we reached the deserted site of Mwaru village. It had once been the seat of the fierce Sub-Chief of the Waluwila, Ka-mlambo. A Tanzanian had told us, 'To hear his name was to think of death.' On the map the village was named Masigo which meant 'thickets', and the area, generously sprouting with *mihama* trees, was still surrounded by impenetrable thickets that once provided a natural defence against Ka-mlambo's enemies. Sleeping sickness finally defeated this village and in 1924 the villagers moved twenty-five miles to Uruwira.

A passing caravan from Ufipa (Simbawanga) – seems they were as frequent as the 31 bus from Camden Town to Chelsea – informed the camped Stanley that there was a white man in Urua. Livingstone? (Urua was a district of the Congo that bordered Lake Tanganyika.) It was also in this Mwaru village that Stanley, on his way back to Tabora with Livingstone, first received news of Shaw's death in Kwihara of *homa* (fever) many months previously. Stanley seemed completely unaffected, agreeing with Livingstone that excessive alcohol must have caused Shaw's death.

In the museum at the Livingstone Tembe, Kwihara, there is a letter dated 13 October 1956 from Alfred George Robinson to the London Missionary Society (Robinson was employed by the British Government of Tanganyika in 1925 to overhaul the German railways).

At that time he had spoken to the old caretaker at the Livingstone Tembe and reported his conversation thus: 'I was at this house when Bwanas Stanley and Shaw arrived with their safari in June, remained here about three months and left in September. They were on their journey to find *Bwana magunga* (Mr doctor) Livingstone at Udjiji. Bwana Shaw was very sick and wanted to remain here, but Bwana Stanley, who was *Kali sana kabisa* (completely fierce) insisted that Shaw should go on. We found him a donkey on which he rode and the safari left. About a week later, Shaw returned and was so ill that I had to lift him off his donkey. I then made him up a bed at the corner of the verandah as it was too hot for him in the house. He was ill only a few days when he took his own life by shooting himself.' Robinson comments, 'I can find no mention by Stanley of Shaw taking his own life, but the caretaker assures me it was so.' The caretaker showed Robinson where he had buried Shaw in the jungle among tall grass covered by large stones placed there by Livingstone and Stanley. Those rocks marking Shaw's burial place were put there in 1872 and with the passing of years had disappeared.

We carried on to the Mugele River. That night, Burton kicked out at us and the other donkeys to protect his food in the tight thorn stockade we had put together encircling all of us (it usually took an hour to chop branches to construct this). No sooner were the donkeys safely tethered than echoing ghoul-like yowls and looping cries haunted the night. Numerous hyena! A cacophony of manic shrieks, wails and bloodthirsty yells enveloped our camp, shrinking our souls. In the dark, evil slashes of yellow eyes.

*

20 October. A sandy path, tsetse and *miombo* again. To break the monotony and keep ourselves amused we called out to each other in our well-versed positions beside the donkeys, describing imagined sketches and giggling inanely at our ridiculous inventions. We began, speaking as in the *Dragnet* TV series:

Christine: 'Three travellers in the depths of the dark interior...'

Andy: 'Trudging the heat and dust of their bones into African soil...'

George: 'Their mission – a mystery; their intentions unknown, their identities lost...'

All of us: 'In featureless, impenetrable, interminable *miombo*.'

We circumnavigated a rotting bridge and crossed over the dry River Kavisama.

We headed for an old White Fathers' Catholic mission

established in 1889 and still funded by Rome, as were all the other missions on our route. The African padre, in white cassock and red rugby socks, smoking local tobacco wrapped in newspaper, readily gave us permission to camp under a grove of trees nearby. When he turned to leave, his underpants glinted red in the slit of his cassock, a slash of red to match his socks!

Victuals for sale poured into our camp: chickens, eggs, *mchicha*, tomatoes, onions, bananas, *matoke* (plantains), cabbage, groundnuts, *papai*, sweet potatoes and cassava. A treasure trove grown in the rich-earth bed of the wide river! Unfortunately, we also had CCM officials and *Katibu* swagger over like Mafiosi. 'Come to the office!' they ordered. 'We wish to ask you questions. We have a small job to do.' The chairman leant toward us and whispered conspiratorially, 'We need you.' *You'll be lucky*, we thought, having become hard with experience. We first set up camp, washed and drank a coffee before we even began to think of anything else. We were aware our politeness had gradually faded.

Stanley had been forced to stay here for three days as one of his men suffered acute dysentery and a disease of the limb which caused him to tremble and sprawl helplessly. Stanley spent his time mending his own shoes, repairing thorn-torn clothes and hunting in the forest. He saw for his first time a small herd of wild elephants.

He commented, 'The destruction which a herd makes in a forest is simply tremendous.'

This is an ecological argument used today in Africa to justify slaughter, euphemistically referred to as *culling*, and animal restriction in small game parks which almost become desert-like because of elephant activity. Previously without the interference of man, elephants were able to roam freely on well-trodden seasonal migration routes stretching over extensive territories. Whatever they devoured and destroyed in one area regenerated by the time they returned again. With wholesale slaughter for ivory that took place before and during Stanley's time, elephants restricted themselves to ever-narrowing forest areas for safety. With larger concentrations, an imbalance naturally occurred, and because of present ivory poaching, the need for timber and the overpopulated cultivation of more and more forest lands, elephant populations were now slowly diminishing.

When ready, we went over to the CCM office to face the menacing officials. Andy was armed with a thick file of correspondence and press cuttings. Before they had a chance to speak I said, 'I would like to show you something. Andy! The file!' I tantalisingly shuffled the contents, then casually revealed letters of authority from the Prime Minister's Office and a press photograph of us with Edward Sokoine.

The *Katibu* jumped to attention like a private. The frozen *mwenyekiti* handled the cutting with reverence. 'Ah, you have met Sokoine.' His head nodded at me like a drunken metronome. In my best Humphrey Bogart voice I spoke to his nose. 'We need to speak to old men of the village. Please arrange for them to see us tomorrow. We also have a small job to do.' They exploded into action, criss-crossing each other in their eagerness to show how helpful they were.

At our camp the padre of the peeping red underpants

told us that in the late 1800s Mirambo invaded Uruwira and at *Maji Moto* ('Hot Water' – site of a hot spring) killed two White Fathers and a friar. He had their faces skinned and made into masks.

Bidding the friendly padre farewell in the morning, we headed to Songambele, where we found lush riverine vegetation and rivers running with water. An hour after Uruwira, we were forced to ford the Shula River which flowed south-east. Stanley very often got his river-flow directions wrong. This river, he said, went 'north-west'. Did he possess a faulty compass or was he relying on what he was told?

We continued through a green landscape onto the new *Ujamaa* Songambele village, a large tight-knit area whose name meant to 'move forwards', and camped under eucalyptus trees.

The Wabende were also originally from the Congo and Burundi. Travelling south from Uhha – a region east of Ujiji – they hunted to survive and made their own self-loading firearms, bullets and powder, and before claiming a woman in marriage they had to present a home-made gun to the in-laws. In Stanley's time, there was no Mpanda town, though the river was always known as the River Mpanda and there was always an *Mpanda ndogo* settlement (little Mpanda) beside the water. When settlers moved to present-day Mpanda from Mpanda Ndogo they carried the name with them – Land of the Hunters.

We reached Mpanda after a short day up and down conical hills. The town consisted of a squashed collection of very many untidy low buildings widely scattered over a rise overlooking dusty hills and valleys. Despite green patches marking the rivers, the rest of the land was dry-brown earth and scrub. Corrugated-iron roofs and a cramped layout gave it a rugged lawless look. We cut through town to the top of the hill and temporarily camped under trees in what locals called the Forest Nursery.

In Stanley's time the Mpanda area was a main stopping place on the ivory route to what had become Northern Zambia. In British times, Mpanda was a bustling gold mining town which illegally persisted. Until recently it was famous for a series of armed robberies involving so many deaths that people barricaded themselves inside their houses. Then the Wasukuma *SunguSungu* began vigorously hunting down law breakers and robberies ceased.

Mpanda is a Kibende word for a children's disease which was common in Mpanda Ndogo, the settlement on the river before Mpanda town was established. It affected children under two years of age. The symptoms were a throbbing fontanel, which if left untreated would sink inward, a sure sign the child would soon die. Medicine men treated it with herbs. To us, this sounded like the effects of severe dehydration.

Approximately 425.50 miles remaining. When will it finish?

The District Commissioner was out supervising the coming elections. While waiting for the Commissioner to grant us accommodation in The Rest House, we investigated the small shops owned mostly by Arabs, and the large enclosed market where everything seemed to cost three times as much as anywhere else. In one shop a scrawny young Indian held court, huddled in a recess of his gloomy emporium: long wooden shelves up to the high ceiling stacked with mildewed cloth, age-old body oils and unguents. On the floor various cardboard containers were filled with unlabelled cans, crumbling macaroni, rocklike clumps of solidified milk powder, nylon brushes, fibreglass-tasting biscuits, and Tanzanian shampoos that burnt the hair out of your scalp. Well-dressed Tanzanians came and went selling their own items, picking up bribes, and walking off with goods without paying. The reason was clear: the Indian had a small wooden box filled with gold. He was allowed to be the main gold dealer in town and was reputed to clear £5,000 per week, which made its way to foreign bank accounts. He talked to us in spasms of American jargon hardly listening to what we said in return, his eyes flitting snakelike around his premises.

'Hell, it's a tough safari, guys. A hell of a journey.'

No one knew of the River Mpokwa and settlement where Stanley camped – our next objective. But examining an old, featureless, black and white map in the dusty Department of Lands, I finally caught the name Mpokwa on a faded scrawl of river seven miles west of Mpanda. No village – just 'Mpokwa'. I guessed it was possible there may in the past have existed a temporary family settlement. If there were it was correctly situated in Utanda, a Wabende clan district, and it tallied with Stanley's general description and correctly with his distances.

The rest house was full, so we moved into an empty Moravian missionaries' tumbledown modern house situated unfortunately in the very middle of bustling Mpanda. The donkeys were tethered outside until we could find them a more suitable home. Local children tormented our helpless donkeys, first throwing dust and eventually stones. Each time a donkey brayed they imitated it for hours, falling about in squeals of delight. Then they began throwing stones at Christine, so I broke the padlock on the adjoining garage door and ushered the donkeys inside well away from the crowd before I found cause to shoot someone.

Meanwhile Andy had befriended a Norwegian aid water engineer, Tor, who lived on the edge of town. He said we could stay in his neighbouring uninhabited newly built house – provided we put together all the packaged IKEA furniture. By it was an unused football field for the donkeys.

Mpanda for us seemed to be accursed. I was getting progressively weaker, and no sooner had I rid myself of amoebic dysentery than I contracted bacyllic dysentery. Christine had *giardiasis* (similar to amoebic dysentery) and the donkeys needed attention: Stanley had somehow torn off the skin above his hoof, and Burton was limping after cutting his hoof on stray corrugated iron.

Andy had been slowly deteriorating and became clumsy and dangerously forgetful. He was failing to spot the donkeys' ills; he did not check the knots on ropes when tying the donkeys, so they came loose; did not straighten bent stakes, enabling them to be easily pulled out of the ground; dropped items and left them; did not finish off tasks. In Mpanda, he'd reached his zenith. He'd left hanging keys on public display in the front door, twice left our front door unlocked and forgot donkey ropes in the football field. He would never admit his mistakes but always found fault with everyone but himself. When caught out, he said in his defence, 'I can't help it… I'm doing my best.'

Of course, I'm no angel. I am bitterly afraid of making the wrong decisions and I certainly cannot hold my temper. If it was not for Christine's intervention, I felt sure the expedition would have collapsed by now.

With rains flooding the rivers and washing together all the infected muck the tap waters ran black. People were dropping like flies with intestinal problems. Typhoid was only just kept at bay. Every day we saw at least two bodies wrapped in stained sheets, arms lolling out the sides, being carried through the town's streets to a doctor.

Because of Andy's inability to cope right now, we hired a donkey herder: dour, hippo-shaped Clemence. Walking with tiny pigeon-toed steps, marked out by luminous blue socks rolled up over his trouser bottoms, he carried a long metal rod which he used as a walking stick and to wave directions at the donkeys, seemingly afraid to make personal contact.

Burton developed a septic ear from a bite. We injected him with tetracycline, and after a series of hot compresses squeezed out all the pus. Two days later, Clemence minced to our Norwegian-built house to tell us that Burton had fallen and could not get up. He had attempted to stand several times. And he had a piece of gut protruding from his anus. We rushed to the football field to find Burton flat on the ground finding it difficult to breathe successfully. His rectum was protruding out of his anus covered in blood. His breathing was rapid and rasping. The other donkeys were braying in a tight huddle. Burton looked up at me pleading, 'Make me better – you've done it before.' There was nothing I could do except utter his name and gently stroke his neck. I felt completely useless. In panic we

PART FIVE – INTO THE LAND OF SLEEPING SICKNESS

looked for a vet, but he was away and no one knew where. His assistant? No one knew. We sped to the hospital and a nurse we questioned said it was a prolapse of the rectum; we had to push it back. We returned to find Burton dead!

Clemence said his eyes had filmed over fast; the whole incident had happened in an hour. Flies settled in a mass on Burton's anus, on his open eyes, and injured ear. I turned to Christine and cried my heart out. Although I may not have showed it, I loved Burton very much.

Eventually, we found the vet, who was stunned at the speed of Burton's demise and said he would perform an autopsy to determine cause of death. We unceremoniously dragged Burton's tough little body out of the fenced field and onto the back of the vet's pick-up. The vet discovered that Burton had died of poisoning; his stomach and intestines were scarred and a muddy-brown virulent liquid smelling of organophosphate crop-spray lay in his stomach. This could only have been deliberate…

My heart went out of the trip at this point. I had wanted us all to finish together uninjured and triumphant. Now there would be no triumph. Dependable Sergeant Major Burton, who had trusted me implicitly, had gone, suddenly collapsed and died in agony. While loving and trusting humans most of all, he had been deliberately poisoned. Why? Because of a personal grudge against us, general resentment against *wazungu* or, in the vet's opinion, purely malicious curiosity to see how an animal would die of organophosphate poisoning.

My depression over Burton persisted for days. Burton, my donkey!

11 January 1986. Left Mpanda very early – minus Burton. And minus the items inside his panniers except for the valuable water pump now carried by Stanley. This north-north-westward turn-around now definitely felt like the last leg of our journey, heading upward toward Ujiji. I thought we had stayed long enough to miss the coming rains. Stanley completed this last stretch in the dry season, but it seemed as if we were travelling at the height of the rains. A grey overcast sky heavy as concrete releasing a constant fine drizzle. We undulated through water-sodden vegetation and woodland to cross countless swollen streams. After only fifty yards our trousers had soaked through like blotting paper, their heavy weight stuck to our legs from the thighs down. We waded the Msangu River, which practically melted our socks in our boots, sucking them forward to tangle our toes. Then the marshy Ntumbi Stream. We ducked under bushes and into a dim tunnel of head-high matted grass and shrubs, where bent in the darkness we eventually scrabbled to open light.

We continued through *miombo* – trees struck by lightning lying in swathes, white splintered flesh cruelly exposed – until we reached foothills and a small temporary settlement named Mguibwa. Yawning figures emerged from the gloom of their log huts and two young women began to fan up their sleeping fire.

We sat for a short break. They offered us *ugali* and *dagaa* for breakfast, but we declined. We asked about Itaga – Chief Imrera's village, where Stanley camped. They replied,

PART FIVE – INTO THE LAND OF SLEEPING SICKNESS

'No! Itaba further on was the chief's village!' So Stanley was referring to Itaba as Itaga and must have camped there. 'Itaga is only half a mile from here. It is the name of the river and small settlement that was there long, long ago.'

Itaba, behind a hill, also no longer existed. It seemed both Stanley and our modern maps were wrong; Itaga and Itaba's positions had been reversed. This was not surprising as early map makers worked from explorers' accounts, and to this day, apart from aerial photographs, new maps were being produced which merely repeated and compounded original mistakes.

We headed directly north to another rise in the escarpment, through two miles of knee-high black bogs and sharp grasses rising above our heads which sliced like razors when gripped. Flashes of light split the sky and the thunderstorm rolled toward us. Just as we began to climb the escarpment rain spat its flashing wet venom onto our heads. The drumming force drove us into the ground. We had been walking for eleven hours and this was the last intended hour. The donkeys were speeding on, hoping perhaps to out-walk the wetness.

The almost vertical track uphill had become a rushing stream washing over our boot tops. Two thin black snakes emerged right at our feet. We leapt instinctively to one side and they slid away with the rush of water. Our lungs were knocking against our ribs, knees and tendons locked tight. We paused for a back-stretching rest, looking down into a valley set in granite. Apart from what was pouring out of the sky, the nearest other water source was the River Rugufu. In the distant past this was a rest spot constructed by Arabs from Ujiji. We squelched to this place, making camp 200 yards before the river. An excuse for our low mileage for the day was that we were absolutely exhausted. From here on, as no villages existed, Stanley made bush camps all the way to Uvinza district. We were following the same route, though now Katumba Refugee Camp had been set up on our way.

We had walked twenty-five miles. At the edge of our hearing was a continuous rumbling that was not thunder. It became louder and shuddered the air. Suddenly the ground began to tremble. The sound took hold of my feet, my body, and filled my head with chaos. Unable to speak, jaw clenched tight, juddering on the spot, I watched outlines of Andy, Christine and the trees blur into layers. The little light shattered into small particles. My eyes would not keep still. Stunned at our vulnerability I pressed my palms helplessly on the shifting ground, willing it to stop. It grumbled once more, a deep rattling of the earth's molars. Then all was still. Life settled into place. We breathed aloud with relief. Andy chuckled. An earth tremor! Because of unstable fault planes releasing sudden energy to the earth's crust (the earth in these Rift regions, it seemed, was still coming to fruition) this movement was very common to the area and caused no destruction. The world was as it was. It had not changed. Yet beneath our feet? No, the world would never be quite the same again or feel as safe.

Leaderless next day without Burton, Livingstone and Speke took it in turns to lead. Walking at slow donkey pace the donkeys had fallen back into their normal speed which was extremely tiring at less than two miles per hour. I'd forgotten how tiring. I ended up with my brain closed down, almost sleepwalking to the endless plodding

PART FIVE – INTO THE LAND OF SLEEPING SICKNESS

rhythm. Persistent drizzle until a fat black cloud burst its package over us at mid-morning. We came upon open woodland, with park-like stretches where we were able to keep an eye out for predators but where *dik-dik* safely leapt and sable antelope grazed. Having ascended a gentle hill to an open plain we sighted across it the distinctive flat-topped Mt Ikus. Grey cloud played across its top. There had never been a place to camp there – not that anyone would want to camp in such an exposed place. We were soaked, the maps in my belt soggy and melting. The temperature had dropped dramatically. We looked forward to returning to English brick-built houses and cosy central heating. We began to shiver and this encouraged us to speed up.

On our right we encountered the path to Katumba Refugee Camp (population 85,000), also known to locals as the Burundi Refugee Camp, whose manpower was used by ivory poachers to transport tusks to Mishamo and thereafter Kasekera on Lake Tanganyika to be collected by boats bound for Burundi. Prices paid for the tusks were 1,100 shillings per kilo. We had met many ivory poachers on our journey and knew their hiding places for tusks in the bush.

The camp had been arbitrarily placed in this wilderness merely because the isolated space existed and functioned as a holding camp, keeping the Burundian Hutu tribe well away from being killed by Watutsi in their homeland and vice versa. The long-term refugees in the camp had become accustomed to their fate and were well integrated into Tanzanian life. After all, this was just another district of Africa itself.

Rain was ripping down as we passed the refugee houses.

People ran and hid. The *pombe* house which was vibrating with raised voices fell silent when we were spotted, and we saw figures slipping out the back hurrying to their houses, possibly going to hide stolen goods.

Three braver or drunker souls in linked arms approached us shouting greetings. 'My friends, my friends, any problems? Welcome. This is our village. We are here. Is there a problem? Welcome. This is our village…'

One hollow-mouthed figure splashing us with puddles stalked around in continuous circles. This was *Bwana mganga* (Mr doctor). The barefoot youth in an over-sized tweed jacket with the arms torn off, spatters of pawpaw stuck to his right ear, was *Bwana shamba* (Mr allotments). He insisted on speaking in English. The third, an old man in a black plastic raincoat and nothing else, stood like a petrified tree stump, his large eyes dodging from side to side like traffic signals. He was the *askari*.

We prepared our bush camp at the edge of the gigantic refugee camp. By evening Andy could hardly move his legs; on our long walk, he had adopted a shuffling gait to aid his movements. Each time we stopped he stiffened up and had to swing his hips forward as if he had artificial legs, then tottered the few steps that helped loosen his joints. Now he scrabbled across the floor like a spider, giggling painfully at his ungainly manoeuvring. Only the tendons at the backs of my knees had seized up. Christine was fine! Women seemed to be more resilient. 'Being a Welsh miner's daughter helps,' she joked. 'I'm just glad to be above ground!'

Approximately 390.50 miles remaining.
Almost there.

PART FIVE – INTO THE LAND OF SLEEPING SICKNESS

Thirteen more miles took us to the derelict houses of Ifukutwa. Another thirteen miles to a dip a hundred yards from a mosquito-plagued river at Vikonge Hill, where we decided to bush-camp for the night. Rain erupted, and then stopped after we had gone through the soaking procedure of putting up tents and getting the panniers inside. We had a system, but each time, the discomfort of wearing waterproofs that leaked in African torrents, soggy boots, clammy clothes, handling muddy donkey ropes, finding dry wood, etc. got the better of us and was a time of curses and violent impatience. Walking was naturally hard if you walked over a sustained period of time in sweltering heat crowded by biting insects, but it was after all merely walking and everyone could do it. It was not the strength of calf muscles that pushed you through an expedition but absolute determination, a true sense of duty and old-fashioned pig-headed stubbornness.

The donkeys were stiff too. Speke had cramp in his rear leg and was stretching in involuntary t'ai chi movements, so I rubbed him with camphor and he reclined on the ground like a prize football star.

Ten and a half miles next day to camp beside the Nyamansi river bridge. This entailed a steep climb. Dramatic views of mountains, mists and deep green valleys, but it was impossible to concentrate on taking photographs of these scenes when assisting donkeys to find the best climbing trails. Where we camped was beside a clumsily put-together wooden shelter. I pushed past a hanging grass canopy serving as a flimsy door to disturb a sheet-wrapped bundle lying in the corner that jumped up startled, mouth hanging open, and scurried out trailing the sheet behind it. 'My name is Petronella!' the twig-like woman kept repeating. Not content with the cup of coffee and half cabbage and salt we'd given her, she grabbed handfuls of maize flour from Christine's cooking and ate it raw.

Next morning, we left a well-fed Petronella behind. Eleven and a half miles to the next camp at the Sabaga River. A gradual never-ending uphill path before we descended almost vertically into the beautiful deserted Nkondwe Valley with its pulsing waterfall, painfully green growths and pastures of sharp-bladed grass. 'The colours are so clear!' exclaimed Christine. At the end of the day the climb past the waterfall to the summit caused Livingstone's limp to become pronounced and all the donkeys stopped for breath, with surprised expressions at the uphill trudge over slippery rocks. We were almost bent double, emitting sounds of hoarse breathing; clothes sticking to us; fiery faces and arms lathered with dirt; our tongues manacled; *mpani* flies flocking around eyes and nostrils; tsetse providing sharp injections. After each ten concentrated plods we had to encourage the halted donkeys with weak pushes, clicks of our fat tongues, and dry-lipped whistles that emitted more air than sound. As soon as we reached the top we unloaded with relief and prepared our camp, the donkeys shocked into stillness, their panting lower bellies rising and falling like bellows.

We had begun to realise that walking off into the Amazon, the Sahara or African bush for an extended time away from so-called civilisation was not to live on the *edge* of nature as in huddled country communities in Europe but to be in its *centre*. The European way was in

PART FIVE – INTO THE LAND OF SLEEPING SICKNESS

effect to lead a parallel existence, to witness nature like a voyeur in voluntary glimpses. Approximately 341.50 miles remaining. Would we never finish? I felt I was coming to the end of my energy supplies. Because of severe fever the villages of Mpandule to Lusaka remained a blurred memory. In Mpandule, though, we had met the two old twin brothers aged around eighty years, and established good relations for the future. They were both extremely content and hospitable and couldn't stop offering us food and vegetables, saying like Jewish mothers, 'Eat, eat. You will need your strength.' In the circumstances, a happy encounter.

A gradual descent into the Valley of the Malagarasi. Donkeys were moving slowly. Without Burton to lead they would never reach speeds of two and a half miles per hour again. Their top speed was two miles per hour. Camping beside the River Kanselelwa. A convoluted winding track and lichen-covered, grey sandstone outcrops. Misty scenes like Chinese watercolours. Rain fell as we found a flat area to set up our camp, requiring no clearing with *pangas*. We were 400 yards from the river. There was a tiny dilapidated grass shelter, used by woodcutters collecting fuel for the Uvinza Salt Mines, but the roof had fallen in and the grass walls swayed.

23 January. It was a long way down to a watery feeder of the great River Malagarasi. We came on deserted settlements, the banana and fruit trees left behind taken over by baboon troups. We heard them barking and squawking, and they bounded across our path (darker grey and heavier than we'd ever seen), desperate stragglers scurrying across one by one. It was an extended thirteen

miles to the River Malagarasi, where we set up camp again. The reflected sun in the river was so bright you felt you could burn the tip of your nose if you dipped it into the water.

At night an insect metallically rasped non-stop in the trees. We threw twigs to scare it to another location. It was reputed that many of these insects singing together could perforate the eardrums. A leopard passed our camp, completely ignoring us but startling us enough for us to grab our firearms. There was first a deep repetitive casual clearing of the throat (the famous cough?) and later a heavy purring so loud that it fooled Andy into thinking it was thunder.

23

Uvinza: Land of the Dried Pumpkins

Glare of early light slices into tents; shrill cries of birds sharply striking day awake; insects sawing and buzzing like spinning lathes; dense tension of stillness that comes just before dawn trailing a smell of wood smoke; grass-cropping of grazing donkeys; our lethargic shuffling of pots; wary glances into the encircling green barrier. With the burglarious shift from dawn's pearly-grey to light blue, waving stars having been drained of strength and the prickle of the first drop of sweat, the world slowly returns to shape. We descend through rainforest infested with baboons to the bend of the Malagarasi River and bathing hippopotami, heads like rocks bobbing on the surface. Only nine miles to Uvinza.

*

Salt had always been valuable in the territory now called Tanzania, its price sharply multiplying as it was transported inland; long ago Arab traders would stop in Uviza and exchange slaves for salt.

The manager of the salt factory was English; lonely and isolated, he heartily welcomed us into his comfortable home, very happy to have like-minded people to converse with, providing food, drink and interesting information on the salt. There were fields of pasture for the donkeys. A river full of water!

But Andy and I were well aware that we would have to leave these luxurious comforts to investigate the next part of Stanley's route without our donkeys. Stanley had provided horrific descriptions of crossing over rivers on a tight grass-matted covering through which an entire Arab caravan and thirty-five slaves had sunk without trace, and further on gave an account of his donkeys being pulled into the water and devoured by crocodiles. Though I would be faithful to Stanley, I would not risk our donkeys' lives.

Stanley himself never reached Uvinza, as he readily heeded advice and changed his route out of fear of becoming involved in tribal wars. Instead of taking the usual path (the Arab road) direct to Ujiji, Stanley was forced to cut across the broad path at Mt Sinyongi and head a fair way northeast, eventually circling back to again rejoin the path at the River Mkuti. Stanley commented on the tribe present at that time. 'The Wavinza are worse than the Wagogo, and their greed is more insatiable.'

'We were a rich people. We never lifted a hoe,' said Mzee Safe Halid Mnoza Lulengelule, descended from the first immigrants to arrive there. 'But that was a long time ago. Now we *have* to cultivate.' Not strictly true. Just as in the past the salt supported its inhabitants and discouraged cultivation, so now the large modern factory employed almost the whole of Uvinza town, who had become dependent on its salaries. Cultivation was non-existent and most goods sold in the market arrived from outlying villages.

The Germans established the mine and set up the salt factory in 1904, which after World War One was inherited by the British, who controlled all Tanganyika: the railway line from the coast to the lake, the gold mines at Mpanda, Zambian copper, which was exported via the lake, and the salt at Uvinza.

The principal brine spring was situated at the Ruchugi river crossing at *Pwaga*, meaning 'market', five kilometres north of Uvinza. Burton crossed the ford here twice in 1858. He described it as: 'A settlement of Wavinza containing from forty to fifty beehive huts, tenanted by salt-diggers…'

Here I had to leave Christine behind again. Andy and I planned for a three- to four-day absence and decided to travel by a much shorter way to familiar Mpandule to continue Stanley's north-easterly route; I had to be true to Stanley, even though I didn't want us to be apart. Christine didn't want to be left alone either, but she was not in the bush or in an African village; here she was sheltered by an English environment. And she had work to do, looking after the donkeys as well as having a good rest. But this is something which has haunted me to the present date. Without a father and having a full-time working mother, I sometimes thought when young that my mother would not return to pick me up from school or from the babysitter (usually a friend). The words 'Don't leave me' still unfortunately haunt me.

Andy and I left very early. 'Good luck,' Christine muttered from her slumbers.

From this Mpandule settlement of four houses there was a clear path which led to the River Isinde. There we would discover if we could continue on to the Great Malagarasi; no one was sure if a track existed.

Here we met a line of ragged hive-makers and honey-gatherers from the settlement, about to set off in our own direction. One short gnome-like old man with a worn plastic raincoat down to his ankles, belted with string, had five wives. These were new ones, he emphasised. Others had died or abandoned him and returned to their villages.

We offered coffee. 'Yes, yes. It is very good for this!' He smashed at his trouser-front with clenched fist.

'For what?' we asked.

'This! This…!' He tugged at his flies. 'I must please my wives.'

Obviously caffeine was a viable alternative to rhino horn.

He pointed out his own crops. 'Here we are strong, never hungry; we always grow enough.'

'What if the maize fails?' Andy enquired.

'You see this…!' Tall, easily grown cassava bushes stretched to the distance in neat rows. 'We can leave this in the ground for up to four years. If the maize fails, we dry cassava, grind it to flour and make *ugali*. We are never hungry.'

We trekked an exhausting twenty-one and three-quarter miles to a stream feeding into the River Isinde. Here we camped overnight. Approximately 210 miles remaining. I prayed that it would be over soon.

Next morning we began another long day's trek. A small ascent continued along a well-forested ridge, crossing trickling streams, trending first north-westerly and later north-easterly.

Crossing over Stanley's 'immense sheets of sandstone', huge outcrops towered above us like mushrooms, narrow at the bottom and broad at the top or falling in shelves like overgrown Indonesian jungle temples, only lacking idling baboons to bring them to life. In this poached-out region a single elephant track trailed into the bush. We pointed it out. 'Yes, we know this one,' our companions promptly answered. 'It has no teeth, yet.' Perhaps they meant it was tusk-less? It was infinitely hoped so by me. In the region it had been reported that tusk-less elephants did exist. Their tusks were in place, but they simply did not grow any larger. These were genetic mutants and it was as if they had signalled to each other, 'Stop growing tusks if you want to survive!' Our friends wanted to stop and cook *ugali* for lunch. I urged them on. 'But, *Bwana*, we are tired and hungry.' No, I wanted to jog on. They gave in, thinking me mad.

After some miles Stanley had camped in the forest (probably near the River Ibula). He was anxious to reach the River Malagarasi. Though what he would find there to assist him we couldn't tell. His supplies were low, only one and a half pounds of flour to feed forty-five men. But there was thirty pounds of tea and twenty pounds of sugar. He immediately ordered that every man be given a quart of the well-sweetened drink to keep them co-operative. Yet Stanley's wild goose chase north-easterly, supposedly avoiding Uvinza tribal battles and wilderness, was to cost him dear in cloth tributes paid to village chiefs. Next morning Stanley's men guided him unnecessarily into a long series of descents down rocky gullies into a stony ravine and then over a low ridge.

Eventually he believed he had arrived at the looping Great Malagarasi according to native accounts and Burton's directions. But Stanley's maps clearly showed the Malagarasi was still two long marches away. They camped near a massive rock seventy feet high and fifty yards in diameter, having walked thirteen and a half miles. Try following Stanley's route on a map! It is virtually impossible without further information from either Stanley or local inhabitants… We were forced to continue along the only route that existed, sensibly following the hilltops to make camp at a crystal-clear stream (Ibula River?).

From features seen, we calculated Stanley's camp would have been approximately one mile to the west of ours. To save time we did not erect the tent. At the urging of the hive-makers we used an already prepared but broken-down grass shelter. A mistake! Rain poured through the meagre roof. The hive-makers guiltily rushed into the wet weather and speedily skinned the broad bark off several *miombo* trees. These long, curled lengths supported by poles stuck in the soil served as a canopy to keep us dry. The trio later used the same bark to construct hollow log-shaped hives, which they tied in the trees. They'd inspect and gather honey once bees had inhabited the hives.

A slow start, because of all-pervading rain and tsetse attacking in large numbers; at one point, walking behind me, Andy counted fourteen sitting on my back.

Extensive blue-black mountain ranges. An imperceptible descent through boggy scrubland over sandstone slabs, through dark forest, narrow gullies and

PART FIVE – INTO THE LAND OF SLEEPING SICKNESS

rock outcrops solidly closing in either side. We continued through a green valley and came to a massive bog! Six miles by four, this broad swamp drained into the grass-matted River Isinde ('floating islands of grass'). We had to cross two and a half miles of this swamp to reach Isinde village, which was situated on a narrow strip of dry land one and a half miles long and less than a quarter mile wide, sandwiched between the swamp and the Isinde River. The raging Kawangi River sliced the swamp in half.

There was a native track that cut through the bog, but without the energetic gnomes' guidance we would never have found it. We would either be stalled at the edges or up to our armpits in stinking black mess. Instead, in careful single file we kept balanced on this narrow line, occasionally wading ankle deep in stagnant muck, and after an hour we entered the elongated humid but fertile village.

Outside the present chief's hut we sat on logs swatting flies. He stumbled from his hut to greet us, and before being guided onto a stool by a young man, spun around as if blind and fell to the ground. Helped up he asked in a sing-song voice if we had medicine. He suspected that he was suffering from *malale* (sleeping sickness).

'Many, many people in the village die from it,' he hummed. 'They go crazy, taking off clothes, shouting and wanting to fight.' He paused for breath. If his elbow had not been held tight he would have spun backward and fallen. 'We have to… to tie them with ropes,' he stammered in unconscious sing-song. 'If they go to hospital, they sometimes live, but usually return with half… half a brain.'

'You must see a doctor,' we urged.

He chuckled. 'I am old… old, so will have to be carried

on my bed for two days, before we reach Malagarasi dispensary. Then... then it may not have medicine. If it does, I will be asked to pay a black-market price. How... how can I trust these doctors? No, it is my... my time.'

The name sleeping sickness is a misnomer. It is only in the later and mortal stages of the disease that people keep dropping off to sleep in the day. Initially, with the nervous system affected, patients are unable to sleep at night. If the disease is not caught in its early stages and treated with Pentamidine, which has toxic side effects, the patient dies. Out of the maps of his mind the chief began chanting, tracing our forward route from memory: 'The old, old path to Ujiji. From here it crosses the swamp. It crosses the swamp to the side of the mountains. You leave them to your left, left. It climbs a little, a little. Then it goes on, it goes on, it goes on. You climb up, climb up, climb up. It goes on. You descend, descend, descend, descend. You have arrived.' We later checked his strange directions on detailed maps; the contours of his mind were absolutely A1.

No one in Isinde village knew of the Ihata Island we were heading for. There was an Ipata Island, but it did not fit with explorer Stanley's mileage and description.

'At the meeting of the two rivers,' we asked, 'was there an island?'

'Yes. Izabika. Fishermen live there.'

'Izabika...?' Never heard of it.

'It is right where the two rivers meet...'

We were making a calculated guess that Stanley did cross the Isinde River. So we would too. Much scrawling of native directions and diagrams in the dust with a stick.

PART FIVE – INTO THE LAND OF SLEEPING SICKNESS

And the chief produced the eternal catch: 'The way is through bush and swamp. There is no path. You will need someone to show you.' He called for guides. A youth finally said he'd take us, though we would have to pay a hundred shillings, but his friend also had to come as he was afraid of returning alone. And his friend would also want a hundred shillings. We agreed as long as we left immediately. They just had to collect food from their houses, they said. We accompanied them and sat outside under the shade of a mango tree. An hour passed. We entered the dark interior of their hut to find them squatting with the family, digging their fingers into mounds of *ugali*. We chased them out, their family running around handing them goods, while they giggled nervously.

*

From actual features seen and experienced (our maps wholly inaccurate concerning contour lines etc.) we thought we were now able to work out explorer Stanley's previous route. He'd done this in dry season. From the River Rugufu he passed Mpandule on the same track until the next river, the Ibula. Unaccountably, instead of keeping on a common-sense route up high, he had descended into the tortuous Mgugwisi Ravine, trekked five miles through the gulley, then up again to catch sight of the distinctive Mt Sinyongi – probably his 'triangular mountain with perpendicular sides', where on the summit he sighted with relief Welled Nzogera village. The rest of his route we only puzzled out afterwards, working backwards. Always the case: unable to gather correct information before, only after the event do we find some truth and a clearer picture begins to click into place.

The Isinde, we had been told, was only passable in the dry season. During rain, when the river swelled, the interlocking grass on the surface lost its grip and crossing it was fraught with danger. Once fallen through into deep water the grass would close above your head. When we got to the Isinde canoe ferry, our two young guides asked if we wanted to cross this river or circle the marsh and make directly for the Malagarasi. Indecision haunted us. What did Stanley really do? Bugger it! Common sense decided we would cross! Through a narrow channel cut through the thick grasses, the bark canoes wobbled backward and forward, taking only one person at a time. We couldn't risk walking on the waving slippery grass.

On the other side, bogs! We were instantly stumbling into great mud holes created by night-wandering grass-seeking hippopotami, sinking one minute, ascending rims the next. Boots and trousers soaked, we rolled up our trousers and head-high elephant grass sliced our legs like razors. We waded up to our crotches in black bog water, our cuts stinging, blood running down our legs and smearing the water. Above us huge grey humps of rock protruded into the greenery, vertically striated as if clawed by giant talons. Hunks of rock lay like abstract sculptures as though slapped off the tops of mountains by an angry hand. Black and white fish eagles patrolled anxiously. Humidity and white glare tightly encircled our foreheads. A single *mihama* tree tipped the sky, like a ship's mast.

On high ground where we attempted to roll down our protective trousers, long roots caught our soggy boots, tripping us up, and somehow *siafu* invaded our clothes, wanting to nibble on us as we walked. At 7.30pm, exhausted, we put up our tent for the overnight camp. I collected water to wash the septic muck out of our wounds. Our bleeding legs looked as if they'd been whipped by a cat-o'-nine-tails. There was a hippopotamus trail beside our camp, and throughout the night the hippopotami in the river – a mere twelve feet from our tent – splashed, snorted and blew water in irritation.

Woken by the two lads' coughing. A cold fire and a thick white mist like London fog muzzling everything in silence and inactivity until 8am when it cleared in swirls and sudden broken patches. The two lads were reluctant to move. Stepping off the high ground of our camp we left as soon as possible, slipping and wading through a muddy swamp. Anxiety and panic from the two youths when we reached water up to our waist. This continued for an hour and there seemed to be no likely method of extricating ourselves. Then, fifteen yards away, standing on a narrow ridge of high ground we saw three figures waving directions. We followed their instructions and found ourselves on firm earth. I really didn't know why I was putting us through all this. It was tortuous and people back home wouldn't know at all whether we had followed Stanley faithfully or cheated part of the journey.

But I would know and feel regret at not overcoming this last threshold.

Our young guides instantly announced this was the end of their journey. They didn't want to continue. Then they wouldn't be paid, we told them. They didn't care. They were willing to abandon us in the middle of nowhere.

Sensing my anger, they both dropped the little luggage they carried and with a yell scuttled into the bushes. The three men laughed. They explained they themselves worked at the camp three miles from Izabika Island. What camp? The Hydro. What Hydro? *The* Hydro, they repeated. They would show us and the way to Izabika, but they wanted a hundred shillings. Having saved a hundred shillings from our earlier disrupted deal we readily engaged them.

The Hydro camp was an empty tin shack in the middle of nowhere beside a full river. Our three new guides who guarded it and received a salary from the government did not know what work was meant to be done there. No official had been there in all the years they had lived inside it. In British times we guessed it was probably some kind of recording station measuring the depth and flow of the river. But now…?

We finally reached the River Malagarasi, and Izabika was the first island encountered. From the bank we could see it was flourishing with maize and mango, yet on our map it was marked as a swamp! This provided a whole new perspective to what we had previously dismissed on our maps as uninhabited bog. One of the men asked us to conceal ourselves. He would have to call over the locals with their canoes. If the Izabika villagers, having voluntarily exiled themselves to this island, saw us white men they would be afraid and want to hide away.

Hidden by bushes we heard him hailing the canoes and eventually the chatter of conversation. On the island bank there was a slight brown movement. A solitary bush buck was warily sipping at the river shallows, stopping and looking around at each sip. A lightning flick of a tail and a slap. The buck flew sideways into the river. Instantly its hind leg was seized by a crocodile and the body pulled under again and again. Two other crocodiles slid through the water as the pair were pushed downstream by the fast current. There was no struggle, even though the buck was still alive. Each crocodile bit into it with gaping jaws, grabbing a leg, a mouthful of flesh. Then with jaws clamped tight, they began twisting, twirling in the middle of the river, tearing off bleeding joints. The carcass bobbed and turned lazily then came violently alive as it was again jerked backward and forward by the deadly reptiles. Then it floated out of sight, the red taint in the water diluted to invisibility.

A piercing shout told us we should move out of hiding. We would be ferried across. The canoe was carved from the trunk of a *mihama* tree. I asked our paddler whether there was another island to our right. On the map this was seasonal marsh.

'Yes,' he answered at once. 'It was once the home of a single man named Ntende. The place was referred to as *Mudiantende* (the settlement of Ntende).'

'Not Ihata?' I asked hopefully, desperate to find the island Stanley mentioned in his account and more importantly to orientate ourselves in the bush.

'No.' He had never heard the name.

On this faultless, overgrown island there were six families, mainly eating fish and what they grew. We found most of them lounging in the shade of a large mango tree. The elder amongst them told us about the area.

But first, 'Where was Ihata?'

'The island of Mudiantende was originally known as

Ihata,' he said. My God, that was a quick revelatory answer! Now finally, we could sort out Stanley's route!

'And Misanga?'

It transpired this was the overall name of a group of islands meaning 'many branches', as the islands were formed by several dividing branches of the Malagarasi.

We briefly visited Ihata Island, ferried across in a canoe, then asked the islanders there about a path leading from the Malagarasi north-north-west to Isinga, the settlement of a fierce violent robber Katalambula. On our map this was marked by a single dot meaning a house situated on the old path to Ujiji and known to locals as the *Barabara wa Jerumani* (the road of the Germans) because the Germans had refurbished and marched up and down this track from Bagamoyo to Ujiji. This, together with the *Barabara wa zamani wa Arabu* (the ancient roads of the Arabs), was considered in the same way we view the straight old Roman roads in Britain. But here they had worn away and disappeared.

To track down Stanley's journey, this trip had become an exercise in historical detection about this part of Africa. Wrong facts and differing stories. Tanzania was vast and its population so scattered and intermixed that finding useful information well in advance was in many cases impossible.

The islanders had never heard of Isinga, but said we could walk to the German road through the forest. But there were no paths, they said. We would never find it in the long grass without a guide. We asked could someone show us? It was only a half-hour journey. Knowing smiles and silence which extended for long minutes. I began to feel hairs rise uncomfortably at the back of my neck like premonitions. Heads turned away. Their eyes would not meet ours. What was going on? We volunteered, 'We will pay!' Suddenly all turned keenly toward us with broad smiles and friendship.

We were naturally suspicious. I shouldn't have offered them money. What were they up to? 'For half an hour?' we ridiculed, when they suggested a price. 'Are you so afraid of the bush?' The price slipped to a hundred shillings. Then they agreed. We stood up. But they huddled together in their local language. Further discussion and back up to 150 shillings. We eventually agreed in order to gain time. Just as we were all to set off, seized by sulks they increased it to 200 shillings. Oh, no!

Having eventually crossed over from the island by taking and paddling a canoe ourselves I was grateful to leave Ihata. We then became completely lost on the other side. But using our map to detour around a fair-sized bog we relied on our compass and travelled directly north through endless-looking forest and scrubland, stumbling through brush, using trees as guide posts. I was really worried that we would never find the old German road. I walked sixty-three double paces for every hundred metres, and a hundred metres was equivalent in time to one and a half minutes plus two minutes for every contour line crossed; thankfully we were not climbing or descending.

Finally, joy. We miraculously reached the German road: more a single-track path hidden by grass and thickets. Andy was dumbfounded by my prowess and luck, and I was impressed by Andy's incredible patience and stamina. In this instance he'd surpassed himself. I couldn't help but praise him. 'It's because of my long legs,' he beamed.

We followed this German track north-west to where Stanley's Isinga should have been. Nothing but forest and scuttling animals. A hartebeest loped through the trees. Otherwise, silence. Ravenous tsetse hovered around our heads in clouds, attacking ears, cheeks and attempting to fly into our eyes. Forced by extreme tiredness to make camp in a scrubby forest, we were now looking like crazed men, with swollen, bitten, unshaven faces and hair tangled with twigs. It was again incredible to me how easily our struggling to survive and moments of danger had become just routine, an everyday part of our existence.

One hundred and twenty-nine and a quarter miles remaining. Come on, come on.

24

Uhha: This Land

The Wahha, before their given name, came together from different tribal regions now known as Rwanda, Burundi and the Congo. They settled permanently in Tanzania under one agreed paramount chief. They insisted they were now one integrated group. When outsiders asked what tribe they were from, they proudly displayed their ownership of the new land, in a sense also showing that they would never leave. They replied in Kihha, 'We are the Wahanyenye, the people of this place – Uhha ('This land').

We returned twenty-one miles to Uvinza (easier without guides and following a clear path) to pick up a rested Christine, who exclaimed, 'What on earth have you been doing?!' We had been absent for six days. I was hugely relieved to be with her again. Andy had stalked off to recover in the civilised house of the Englishman.

I hugged Christine. 'You're a brave little creature,' I said.

'I was really worried,' Christine confessed. 'I began imagining the worst that could happen. What would I do if you didn't return? I haven't been able to sleep, woken up by the least noise, always checking on the donkeys. You could have been attacked by wild bandits. You could have been killed and left in the bush to be eaten by carnivores. I know you took your revolver, but the grass is so high in this uninhabited place that if you'd been unexpectedly attacked, you wouldn't have been able to see or have time to shoot. And you forgot the Black Stone. I should have reminded you. I've been blaming myself. You're crazy, you know that!'

I felt that Christine wanted to swear and scream at me, but she had showed such a sense of relief at seeing us alive again that I couldn't help foolishly grinning at her.

'What are you laughing at?!' she shouted. 'It's all right for you, you've got it all planned out. Oh, don't worry about me. How can you be so light-hearted about it?'

Although exhausted I seemed almost exhilarated by the adversity. Even Andy had been stimulated to brighten up.

'I'm sorry we're late,' I said. 'We had a few problems.'

We regrouped and collected the satiated donkeys in order to proceed thirteen miles to Basanza, five miles south-west of Lake Musenya. The humidity caused us to pour with sweat while standing still. Through meandering green vegetation, tight-knit woods, and forest extending as far as the eye could see.

Despite receiving assurances from sub-chiefs that he wouldn't have to pay further *hongo*, Stanley passed countless villages which expected him to give tribute before he could travel on. 'Angry!' Stanley exclaimed. 'Angry is not the word, I was *savage…*'. To avoid further payments, he hired a local guide to lead him secretly through the jungle at night. Finally, they arrived at 'the little lake of Musunya'. Large pools and swampy waterholes crowded with hippopotami were typical of this area. Stanley correctly inferred that in the dry season the lake was a three-quarter-mile circumference; he didn't know that in the rains it extended then and now to just over four miles.

We were frustrated by the lack of information. We could so easily get lost at this late stage. In the fertile *Ujamaa* village of industrious Basanza, ninety miles distant from Ujiji, which had been deliberately set up in 1974 to grow food for the salt workers of Uvinza, we eventually found only one person, a sinewy little man who said he knew the old paths through the forest. The whole area was now a wilderness. Forty miles of bush without paths or tracks. A track was a luxury that we craved. The small hyperactive figure agreed to guide us for the three days of the trek.

But first he said we had to 'understand each other'. Because of wild animals he explained he could not do the journey alone. His brother would have to accompany him, and there would be no one therefore to look after his *shamba*. The wild pigs and baboons would destroy the crops.

'Look in my house. Check, check!' he urged. 'I have many children and wives. They will need money for food when I am gone. Much money…'

'I don't have much.' I quickly stemmed his flow. 'My money was burnt in a bushfire,' I said.

His face melted.

Thinking I was on a winning streak, I continued, 'We are *bin adamu*' – sons of Adam, human beings – 'and must help each other. We are no different…'

'Not different. No.' He crouched on a stool wringing his hands, playing for time. Finally he'd come to a decision. 'You have no money here, but in Kigoma you will use this.' In front of my face he scribbled on his wrist in air.

'This, what?' I asked.

'Your signature. It is white and very powerful. You can enter a big building, write it down and they will give you money. Not so? The signature of a black man is rotten. It does not work in these buildings.' With his slanted beliefs and warped view of banking practices I knew I had lost.

We agreed that he and his brother would guide us for the price of two *debes* (approximately twenty to thirty kilos) of maize flour equivalent to 500 shillings which they would carry, plus his tobacco money of forty shillings. The wives and children were forgotten!

Leaving day; after a quick wash, a chew on strips of *biltong* and a cup of condensed-milk tea, the day fell into shape. We sat on left-over logs of chopped wood and waited for our guide as usual. I stretched my morning aches into the log, finding comfort in its rigidity. We didn't leave until very late, because our small guide arrived at the *Katibu*'s office at 10am instead of 8am. His father was ill and he had again changed the employment conditions. His brother wouldn't now be going! OK, was he finally ready? No! He had to mill his maize first and the *Katibu* had to write him a letter of official permission to leave the village. The impish guide suddenly announced he wanted 800 shillings, with payment in advance. But we had agreed on 500 shillings for two persons. The high-heeled *Katibu* interrupted with a sad face to say we should pay as his poor wives and children would starve.

He had us in his power for otherwise we would have to travel back to Uvinza and take another path, two days would be wasted and we wouldn't be on the old trade route! We turned to the *Katibu* for help. But as expected:

'My friends, there is nothing I can do here – I am defeated. Pay him. Why not? It is nothing to you.'

It was time for me to become wholly Cypriot and think and argue in Byzantine ways: 'As you know, it is not normal to pay in advance. What if he is lying to us and doesn't know the way? He may abandon us in the bush and run away. We are not in a position to chase him…'

'No, no,' the *Katibu* interrupted, 'I will vouch for him. If he does this, we shall have him arrested.'

What I would have loved to say was, if he does this I will return with a sub-machine gun and stitch your smiling face to the wall, but in life you can't always do as you like.

'In that case we shall pay a hundred shillings now and the rest when we reach our destination.'

But the guide wanted it all, so to gain thinking space I went out and purchased a *papai*. Time was passing and I was burning with murderous thoughts. I pricked up slices of pawpaw with my Bowie knife, chewed the *papai* and attempted to smile sweetly.

The yellow-eyed guide broke first. 'I will not go unless I have 800 shillings now!'

'You can have a hundred shillings.'

'No! No!'

I deliberated. Slowly chewed another slice. 'You want it all now?'

'Yes, yes.'

'Hmm… But we did not agree on 800 shillings, it was 500 shillings.'

'I will take 500 shillings!'

'The 500 shillings was for two people. You are on your own. I will give you 250 shillings.'

'No!' he howled.

I paused with a worried look and spat out a *papai* pip. 'This is fair,' I pressed. 'A hundred shillings now, plus your tobacco. The rest when we reach the River Mkuti.'

Agreement. Thank the Lord!

Eighteen miles to the River Uhha Rugufu. The end was in sight now. The track was so overgrown and unused that most of the time creepers and tree stumps were tripping up our boots. I had to be constantly ahead, cutting and treading down low bush and saplings that could rip panniers. We stopped at a large boggy waterhole. From our compass we discovered the guide was taking us on a great northern circle, unnecessarily detouring around a low mountain range. We could easily have gone straight across this over a shallow shoulder. This madness added on an extra seven miles. At this rate we wouldn't reach the river until midnight. The guide raced madly to drink at a murky stream as if desert-parched. We interrogated the greedy twit, and it was obvious he didn't know where he was or where he was going. He hadn't done this journey for ten years.

We stated, 'We could have gone straight from Basanza.'

'But it is bush there.'

'*This* is bush!'

'You do not know the African bush. Sometimes you have to go around to avoid swamps and thickets.'

I pointed out to him that, first, we had walked from Bagamoyo. Second, on my map there were no marked impediments all the way from Basanza to the Rugufu; taking map errors into consideration we had certainly not been aware of any swamps and thickets. Third, though his only worry was getting to water in order to drink, cook and eat *ugali*, my worry was the over-tired, battered donkeys. At water, they would drink first. We came second. Furthermore, if he was feeling tired or thirsty he should return at once as I'd had enough! He grinned sheepishly.

Walking our way by compass direction we again reached the dank, tall, jungly growths along the river and put up our camp as darkness fell. Squawks of baboons and a distant lion roar. I decided we would stay two days for the poor travel-shocked donkeys to rest, and for me to catch up on writing my notes and studying maps.

*

The guide said he'd been vomiting blood – we saw no trace – and I felt this was a strategy to acquire his early release and pay. We mixed up flour and water, mumbled words over it and he drank it. It shut him up but not before his telling me his name in a fit of confidence – Hamisi. 'Now you're better,' we said. And he had to agree, nodding his knobbly head. But he got even! In hesitant apologetic tones he revealed that he only knew the route up to Zeze, a village near the River Sunuzzi. Not to worry though, he said he would find us a local guide in Zeze. I didn't want to discuss it with him. I knew if I continued I would thump him.

We crossed the swollen Rugufu with panniers carried again, hanging on sapling poles balanced on our shoulders. Hamisi, curse his name, was not at all sure of the route. There were no paths. We trudged out of the huge bog he'd led us into and took over with map and compass, climbing onto higher, drier ground to contour beneath Nyakatonge

Hill, razor-sharp elephant grass sprouting in tall clumps and serpentine roots impeding our path. Beds of primitive, scattered rocks and boulders booby-trapped our way and played havoc with the donkeys' weary and tender hooves. We cringed at loud knocks, as they clambered over and hit their forelegs against these obstacles.

For fifteen miles we stumbled on until in sight of the Zeze maize plantations that stretched for miles. Every available piece of land was taken up with tall maize, a waving jungle of green leaves and pendulous elongated cobs. Apparently, buyers came from as far away as Kigoma and Uvinza sixty-seven miles away to purchase Zeze maize cobs. We too loved the young juicy cobs. Unfortunately, local farmers left the maize kernels to harden so they could grind it to flour to make *ugali*.

*

Christine's had enough. Her feet were killing her and she felt light-headed. So did Andy. I encouraged them along by saying it was almost over and my mind choked on the words' emptiness. I was sure everything would be fine once we reached the end, but I could never be sure.

*

The *Katibu* of Zeze, whom we consulted, insisted no paths existed to the River Mkuti (Stanley's next camp) and nobody knew of a way through the wilderness. Our devious guide smiled nervously. There was another village, Nyanganga, only a half hour south-west of Zeze,

PART FIVE – INTO THE LAND OF SLEEPING SICKNESS

the *Katibu* said, perhaps they would know. Could we buy some maize? we asked. The *Katibu* washed his hands of us by rudely saying, 'Ask the corn-growers.' But they wanted three shillings a cob. Cobs were normally given free, and we could have picked up dozens of the fallen ones on our way into the village.

As I refused, Christine erupted, 'Why are you so dogmatic and principled, it's only three rotten shillings. Buy them!'

But for three shillings? 'No!'

We left the maize. Christine continued, 'You could have made my life easier. We could have had instant supper. You're bloody-minded and unreal.'

I was surprised, as Christine didn't often question my judgement. Perhaps I *was* being picky.

Without the likelihood of any guide from Zeze we sent Hamisi ahead to Nyanganga to arrange a guide from there. As always, we were helplessly caught up in a whirlwind of day-to-day events that threatened to engulf whatever we knew or thought we knew of ourselves. This was the closest we came to believing in fate. We were mere mimicking players stumbling through preordained lives. We could so easily disappear and die. We were as nothing.

A clear path balancing the hilltops passed the blackish mire and weak surface trickle of the Sunuzzi. Whatever deep forest once existed here had over the years been cut and the herds of buffalo, giraffe and zebra had either moved on or been decimated. Dark clouds rolled in and coagulated the sky. We heard the approaching rain drumming in the distance and could clearly see it like a grey sheet, a barrier moving toward us. Exposed at the top of a hill, we were hit hard by penetrating drops and painful hailstones. Rumbles and flashes frightened the donkeys. A pouring torrent of ankle-deep water and slimy mud rushed past. Donkeys slipped and slid. We were confronted by an uncrossable bridge of clumsy logs over the now racing river. Nyanganga village was on the other side. We sheltered in a soggy maize patch to collect our thoughts and feed our cold, wet, miserable donkeys the maize cobs we had picked up.

As if by magic, a young woman appeared on the opposite bank and shouted in Kiswahili that there was a crossing further back. Soaking wet in her dull-coloured *kikoi*, rain pouring off her scarf-bound head and face, she ran alongside the river to direct us. At the crossing the river was rapidly rising. Christine crossed with the donkeys; sensing the urgency they obediently followed her. The river was just above her knees. By the time we struggled all the panniers across, the water was sweeping past our hips and we could only just keep our balance, battered by the force of water that was visibly rising.

The woman was urging us on. 'There is more big rain coming,' she cried. 'Cross quickly, cross quickly!'

Christine cried out to her, 'God bless you, Mama.' We never saw her again.

The *Katibu*'s 'half hour' proved to be two hours of soaked misery. We had been forced to detour to Nyanganga. Yet without further directions from this village we would most probably not be able to reach the River Mkuti. Still, tomorrow was a new and wonderful beginning… I could not help the hysterical laugh that overtook me.

Approximately eighty-three miles to go – or less. Wowee!

PART FIVE – INTO THE LAND OF SLEEPING SICKNESS

Hamisi chose this time to inform us that he was possessed by a green genie and wanted to return. He obviously could, but with no additional money! He fumed and spat and asked the *mwenyekiti*'s help. The *mwenyekiti* simply laughed. I was so glad I had chosen donkeys over porters.

*

14 February. The chairman of Nyanganga carried a long-handled spear over his shoulder when we set off at 8am to trek the twelve miles to Matendo village. Most locals we met carried spears to kill wild pigs and baboons that plagued their *shambas*. We forded the river. On the other side wild and rapacious germination! My memories of this day were all of pushing grass stalks out of my face in order to see the ground a few yards ahead, muddy water, and stumbling over uneven ground that punished our well-marinated and tender toes. The slosh of dragging boots and donkey slurps as they fought to extricate their stiletto hooves from fetlock-high mud.

Although somewhat excited at eventually being within reach of the lake I could not summon up out of my exhausted body real enthusiasm. I just knew we were reaching the finish of our journey. That was all. Probably seventy-one miles yet to go.

We passed through Pamira Village where Chief Niamtaga (meaning 'generous') had a second house by a kapok tree. His main village and residence was Lubila, west of the River Mkuti. Here, in this very small village without any amenities, Andy turned pale, began staggering and abruptly collapsed to the ground. We rushed to assist him, the donkeys circling around. It took a couple of buckets from the village tap to revive him, but he was getting worse.

It was fortunate that we'd almost reached the larger Matendo ward. Though populous it didn't have a hospital. But at least it had shops. It was a remnant of civilisation and comfort, and Andy could have a long, deep sleep.

I questioned Andy again as to his deteriorating condition. 'You were brought up on the streets,' he said. 'It must have contributed something. Whatever I did – climbing mountains, fell walking – never lasted more than two weeks. Then we would have a hot shower and end up in the pub, rest and recreation. Well, on this journey there is no rest and it seems to be going on for ever…'

Instead of making directly for the River Mkuti we decided to detour the three miles to Matendo. But we first had to cross a rotting bridge over the River Kibumba. I reckoned the bridge could collapse while bearing the weight of the fully laden donkeys, so we took off their panniers so we could carry them over ourselves and leave the donkeys free to make their own choice. Amazingly, Stanley crossed successfully but Speke and Livingstone stopped dead.

I had to pat and reassure Speke in his every attempt at approaching the broken bridge. He sniffed the jagged planks nervously and turned away. I grabbed his halter, and uttering words of encouragement, demonstrated wide-stanced leaping. Together we galloped over, jumping like idiots!

Livingstone most unusually wouldn't move. We waited. Stanley began to plod back to join his mate. I stopped him with ropes, Christine assisting, then we pulled Livingstone across, and as he trotted towards the waiting Stanley and Speke, both of them brayed a relieved welcome.

25

The Final Push – Ukaranga to Ujiji: Land of the Small Village

Twenty-four miles to Ujiji.

Matendo, known as 'Matendo of the elders', was a large and prosperous village group in the area of Ukaranga, bursting with industrious farming and the NORAD water taps working. Houses were built of mud-fired bricks and thatched with straw. The traditional cone-shaped grass shelters that could be packed together and carried to another place were no more.

Battered senseless and aching in every limb, we asked to stay in the mud-brick CCM Office. It was roofed with corrugated iron. I couldn't face putting up the tents.

Andy just wanted to lie down. I really could not understand how despite our many difficulties we still continued to forge on, obsessive as ever. Accepting our nomadic journey and its problems as normal. In fact, the more the likelihood of dangers on the trek ending the expedition, the more immovable we became. Nothing was impossible! In the bush I personally could forget myself totally – my failures, inadequacies, guilts – and

The Final Push – Ukaranga to Ujiji: Land of the Small Village

become strong and whole all over again. I firmly believed from my own experience that a nomadic lifestyle was what we all once shared before settling into a secure and boring existence. I had grown to love walking through an unfamiliar nature by day and sleeping in an unknown environment in the evening – the differing smells and animals encountered. Like the American Indians and animal migrations we too it seemed once wandered the planet.

The meaning of *Ukaranga* elicited argument and disagreement among the elders, punctuated by one drunk old man squeezing through a small window and falling over the ground-squatting bodies in the crowded CCM hall. Other locals also wanting to attend the discussion managed to climb through the narrow high windows. First, they said, *karanka* was a Kikaranga word for pebbles with which children played. Then one old man said the word was the name of a river in the Congo, from where the Wakaranga first came.

The Wakaranga tribe had been reputed to be *wachawi*. 'Karanka is the name of a potion,' one shouted, 'used by *wachawi*' – black magicians/witches – 'to drug people and turn them into zombies, then force these people to cultivate *shambas* and work as servants...'

Another white-bearded elder returned to pebbles. 'In the past,' he explained, 'when there were wars with spears over possession of land, people used pebbles piled up around trees to denote boundaries between one tribe and another. This area was filled with pebbles.'

An old lady to whom others deferred now stood up and there was silence. Leaning on her stick, she chanted

PART FIVE – INTO THE LAND OF SLEEPING SICKNESS

a rote-learned history of ancient borders: 'To follow the border begin from the hill Mukulwa in Heru. Then pass Karanga, where pebbles placed there by God surround the land. After, you will reach the one tree named *kalembera* where people liked to rest when crossing the border. Then *ninakabeja*, the place of the mother of Chief Kabeya on the hill of Pamira... etc.'

Completely uncheckable but fascinating to listen to and to imagine the traditional verbal pictures painted of the Ukaranga border.

I discovered a weakness in myself: that I had a liking for older Tanzanians who had achieved a kind of nobility, for the simplicity and innocence of an age I hadn't experienced. Who knows, perhaps all along I had unknowingly been experiencing it on this trip... Overall we decided Ukaranga distinctly meant 'place of pebbles'.

In Chief Niamtaga's village, in anticipation of meeting Dr Livingstone in Ujiji the following day, Stanley requested Selim to lay out his new flannel suit, to oil his boots, chalk his helmet and fold a new *puggaree* (headband) around it. We in Matendo treated ourselves to a cheap delicious-looking body-building chicken. We painlessly chopped its head off and Christine cleaned and fried it. And, to follow, tongue-prickling pineapple.

Sadly, we had no hope of reaching Ujiji on the morrow, weighed down with the depressing information that the old path from Simbo to Ujiji was impassable. In Mpanda and Uvinza, we had been informed we could easily cross the Luiche River. Now we were told that the bridge over the river with its huge metal gaps would be impossible for the donkeys. We had therefore to stop in the *Ujamaa* Simbo,

The Final Push – Ukaranga to Ujiji: Land of the Small Village

the last village before Ujiji, and ask the villagers for definite information.

We pushed on, thirteen and a half miles westward, to Simbo, where Chief Niamtaga frequently travelled to preside at tribal meetings. In 1876, in order to gain control of Niamtaga's territory, the newly elected Chief of Uvinza murdered him.

The Ukaranga landscape comprised wide views of rolling green hills, pastures scattered with dwarf trees extending to blue-hazed mountains. Up on high ground Christine had readied our battered but reliable Canon camera. Around the corner of the hill was the exact spot approximately ten and a half miles distant from the lake where Burton and Speke (14 February 1858) first sighted from up high the Lake of Tanganyika. Overhead, a sudden storm was beginning to break, darkening the land with shadow and spoiling any thought of photographs. Barely perceptible in the sudden downpour, the lake became a stringy line of grey on the horizon. Rain pelted down. The lake disappeared. Africa won again.

The rain stopped as we reached the outskirts of Simbo. Arab-style, rectangular-shaped, mud-constructed thatched houses abounded as in Bagamoyo. The isolated CCM Office overlooked the Luiche Valley and the old path leading to Ujiji.

The chairman and elders in white *gellabias* and *mtobo* (lace skull caps) came out to meet us. They explained that the old route to Ujiji was usually not used at this time if the rains were heavy. The River Luiche emptied into a large swamp – oh no, not again – and the path would become obliterated by growth. It was easy to become bogged down. The only way over the river, villagers informed us, was by the high metal rail bridge with large gaps in the floor. But we could try, they said. It was February. The rainy season was from October to May, but rains were unpredictable and fickle and the worst downpours would usually be in April or May. In the dry season it was simple to walk over the caked bog and wade the river. But during the full *masika* people preferred to avoid any flooding, clambered down the shallow hills and detoured around to Kigoma, which was further away, and then entered Ujiji – a long and circuitous way round. Despite present wet weather we didn't want to detour to Kigoma. This was not Stanley's route. We decided to stay until Andy and I, without the donkeys, would investigate the professed bog for ourselves. I hoped Andy would have sufficiently recovered by then.

Christine was pleased to be finishing the expedition and that she had successfully managed to do so. Andy was completely neutral. I just felt glad not to have cheated – other than that I took it for granted that we had almost reached Ujiji. A very large village (almost a town) and the end of our expedition.

'Don't hang about doing nothing. The donkeys need un-entangling,' I said to Christine, engrossed in the stars; I couldn't help myself. 'Pump water or do something useful.'

Christine burst out, 'You're never satisfied! Either with what Andy and I have achieved, or with anything!' I knew this was part of my character. 'You may make a marvellous leader,' she said. 'You have natural instincts about the route, reactions to characters we meet on the journey and you know how to get people to help us. Africans love you!

The Final Push – Ukaranga to Ujiji: Land of the Small Village

But… all you do is moan. You're always dissatisfied. Don't know how to enjoy the moment!'

She eventually admitted that I was as hard on myself as I was on others.

Although I saw myself as a warrior, she viewed me as soft and tender. A knight without armour excited by quests and projects. Christine had loyally supported me in following my dream, though to keep herself together she would occasionally whisper to herself, 'It will end! It will end!'

A dark night. We peered miserably over the valley to the flickering lights of the Kigoma suburbs, the largest town approximately three miles from Ujiji. And before it, the fires and kerosene lamps of Ujiji itself! For us it was ten and a half miles away. So near, and yet so bloody far. A cliché but so true. Hard to believe that such problems could exist over so innocuous a part of the route at such a late stage.

And then we discovered that what we had been told was not true! The paths had *not* been flooded out. The rain had so far fallen lightly this year, and the donkeys could make it, especially over the River Luiche! We were so relieved. We could be true to Stanley's route after all, without any detouring. And Andy seemed to have recovered somewhat.

This was to be our last night before Ujiji. We had aged four years since leaving London in January 1982 on our peripatetic journey. Andy was then twenty-one. He was now twenty-five, almost twenty-six. I was feeling old. And faithful, trusting donkey Burton was not with us to share the expedition's end…

26

Arrival in Ujiji

The Ka- prefix in Kiswahili denotes a small thing. Once a man with his wife lived alone by a tall *mawesi* tree beside the lake. There were no other people in the area. A son was born, named Kajiji – the name usually given in those times to the first-born of a couple living alone away from other settlements. He was the possible beginnings of a new village, a biological time bomb – growing evidence. The settlement expanded and the area became known as Ukajiji – Land of the Small Village. It eventually grew even more in size so that it could no longer be known as Ukajiji. And as people found the word easier to pronounce it became 'Ujiji'.

*

Early morning. 18 February 1986. The day was overcast but hot and sticky as we set off to bustling Ujiji, 2,500 feet above sea level, bordering Lake Tanganyika – the terminus of the old caravan route from the coast. Lying in the Great Rift Valley fault, Tanganyika is the second-deepest freshwater lake in the world (only surpassed by Lake Baikal in Russia).

Arrival in Ujiji

The lake is 420 miles long, approximately thirty miles wide and in parts deeper than 4,700 feet. It is also rich in fish with more than 250 different species at the time we were on its shore.

A census taken in 1990 calculated that there were 10,000 people living in Ujiji. In Livingstone's time in 1871, many Arabs chose to live at the end of the caravan route because of its flourishing slave market, and I would have guessed the population to have been very much less than 5,000.

A winding, hilly road and rolling grass all the way. Bogs had dried out. Locals trailed past with goods on their heads to be sold in the Ujiji marketplace. We turned off onto an isolated track and into the bush. At the very broad River Luiche we unloaded the panniers and carried them over. We slid and sat in the mud, laughing at our useless selves. The donkeys were crossed at an easier, narrower alternative with less steep, slippery banks. We rose to the top of a hill on the old slave trail, and I felt a thrill at the broad lake like a spreading sea gleaming below us. We descended to a grand lengthy row of ancient mango trees; past the collapsed White Fathers' house, its galvanised-iron roof already taken by locals; the present working seminary; the crumbling and empty German Usagara Company building; a still-bustling secondary school; to the shanty suburbs of Ujiji town and through the busy market where oiled slaves were once sold. Men once fetched thirty rupees and women forty rupees because they bore children.

The houses were set close together in tumbledown rows, the snaking earth-dusty streets narrow. Black goats said to bring luck wandered the streets disturbed only by occasional bicycles and handcarts ferrying goods from the lake. Most houses were thatched and had unbroken glass windows. Each had an Arab-style raised stoop at the front in which to recline in the shadows of the eaves and take the air.

We had finally arrived!

*

Men in white *kanzu* (*gellabias*); women completely shrouded in black *boui boui* (an Arab head-to-toe gown; also the word for spider); shops with Arab names; open-air coffee shops as in Sudan with grizzled old men sitting on benches set in a square sipping from miniature bowl-shaped cups; but everyone's features were African.

Crowds formed behind us, screaming kids running back and forth seized with hysteria. Someone directed us the wrong way into an earth street of eroded gulleys and corrugations. Maize plots beside each house, banana palms and *mawesi*, mango and coconut trees – compounds surrounded by tall bamboo fencing to delineate ownership. This was the renowned Mnazi Moja Street where a solitary coconut palm once stood close to the old mosque where Livingstone's grass church was reputed to have been.

'Livingstone Street?' I found myself shouting above the noise.

A hand pointed left. We swept into a straight sandy earth road sloping down toward the glistening distant waters of the lake.

We reached the place from where explorer Stanley, dressed in his Sunday best, first sighted the 'port' of Ujiji below him. There was no port as such now or in Stanley's

Arrival in Ujiji

day. It was merely part of the sandy shoreline, a shallow creek set among tall reeds and waterlilies. Four or five large flat-bottomed fishing boats lay lazily moored. Others were on shore, balanced on their sides to be caulked. Not far off was the unused newly built Customs House and tents of the elite Tanzanian Field Force, based here to stop smuggling and in readiness for when trade restrictions with Zaire across the lake were officially lifted. There was no coastguard, no helicopters, and no policing boat-patrols, so the idea of customs checks along its extensive shores was ludicrous.

The Livingstone Monument (the alleged site where Stanley and Livingstone met) was on a hill overlooking the lake, enclosed by a high brick wall. Much to our surprise the corrugated-iron main gate swung open as we approached. We anticipated problems as we had been told the armed *askari* (who was missing) let no one enter without official written permission or money.

We filed inside the empty, spacious enclosure with its basic garden lawn sloping down into thick vegetation. The donkeys immediately pounced on the plump grass beside a stocky stone monument carrying the carved name of David Livingstone, below it a map of Africa with a cross cutting through the middle of the continent, and to its right a brass plaque which simply stated:

Under a mango tree / which then stood here /
HENRY M. STANLEY met DAVID LIVINGSTONE
10 November 1871

Thank God it was over!

We took photographs. For Christine and Andy it was definitely time to stop. Christine breathed a sigh of relief at finally ceasing all movement, but felt extremely proud to have completed the journey and put up with extreme conditions. She loved living outdoors. Andy seemed exhausted and non-interested. He had come to detest everything African.

What was uppermost in my head was infinite relief that we had reached our destination as one intact human team. But I could not stop learned routines; I was once again investigating our new surroundings and thinking of finding future food for the donkeys who had buried their heads in the juicy grass. Where would we erect our tents?

The monument was erected by the Government of Tanganyika Territory and the brass plaque contributed by the Royal Geographical Society in 1927. Apparently at Bujumburu, Burundi, there was a stone twice the size of the one at Ujiji stating that Stanley and Livingstone met there on 25 November 1871.

Nine yards from the monument here was a smallish, low, stone-stand with another plate in English and Kiswahili:

On February 14th 1858, Burton and Speke reached Ujiji whence they explored Lake Tanganyika.

A newly built red-brick building, locked up and empty, was meant to be a museum but the Cultural Officer had wasted all the donated money. In the shade of an old mango tree we sat and peered down beyond the heavy-leafed branches to placid portions of the silvered lake. In early morning without flaring sun the lake would be blue. Since 1871 it had receded

300 yards. In distant haze just visible were the mountains of Zaire. An idyllic spot, fervent with growth and cooled by lake breezes. I fell to thinking: bearing in mind the lake had receded, was the present monument marking the site where they met or where Livingstone moored his boat?

We hadn't finished yet, though, by a long chalk. We had to establish whether the donkeys could roam in this green two-acre area – most of the land taken up by the absent *askari*'s maize and banana crop. We would see if we could move our goods and ourselves into the empty museum building; purchase charcoal; borrow a *jiko* (a raised, circular metal support for charcoal); shop for fresh vegetables in the market; begin writing reports asked for by various Tanzanian institutions; write my own digest; arrange for the donkeys to be flown to Europe and plan flights for ourselves (I gratefully had *Sunday Telegraph* money stashed in the bank); find if possible a typewriter and carbon paper, etc., etc.

Seemingly impossible to achieve in the land of *hamna* (there is none) and *kesho* (tomorrow).

Tomorrow, I was reminded, we would have to meet regional officials and gain their permission to stay, otherwise we would have to begin the usual saga of finding a grassy environment at the edges of town and constructing fences to keep the donkeys safe. The *askari* finally appeared and approached to say that he had been informed of our imminent arrival by the Regional Cultural Officer. We were welcome to stay.

'The museum is locked!' I explained. 'Where is the key?'

'The contractor has it.'

'Could we get it?'

PART FIVE – INTO THE LAND OF SLEEPING SICKNESS

'You could try.'

'Where is he living?'

'Between here and Kigoma.' Kigoma was a full day's walk away.

The contractor would not give up the key. He hadn't yet been paid and didn't trust the region to pay him. In the meantime we pitched our tents under a mango tree at the monument and began to wash from a hosepipe. A party of German tourists appeared, having gained entry by paying a bribe in lieu of written permission.

'You can camp here?' they eagerly asked. We explained our situation – our trek!

'But this is an anticlimax, no?' they said.

We agreed.

They promptly left, and soon after returned with a crate of beer, loaves of bread and a large tin of processed cheese. The *askari* found us tables and chairs, and we celebrated under a shadowed umbrella of mango, while fifteen feet away the solid monument stood to attention and grazing donkeys moved around in a slow dance, picking at delicate grass tips.

*

Three days later, after much persuasion, we got the key to the museum building from the contractor. Inside was a cavernous dark hall and two small rooms. A year ago, the Prime Minister's Office had ordered a toilet and electricity to be ready for our arrival, but nothing had been done. We had to find beds, tables, chairs and kerosene lamps. Outside, down in the maize patch, we dug a deep hole

Arrival in Ujiji

for toilet duty. Water was from the hosepipe fixed to a tap which we kept turned on to help the grass grow. The donkeys loved the area and ran free amongst the greenery. They would put on weight.

Bird calls, mourning doves, the sounds of fishermen bringing up their catch to sell in the market, the gabble of mamas filing past the enclosed monument with empty containers on their heads to fill with the fish they bought at lake-edge while it was still cheap. We joined them down the sandy slope, and at a boatful of just-caught fish tried three of the varieties Stanley mentioned: sangala, kuhe and a type of eel. Women were scrubbing clothes on the shore, or bent over full buckets and *sufurias* (saucepans) of collected lake water.

The monument *askari* kept loading and reloading his AK-47, clicking a blunt bayonet into place. He slouched to the monument when visitors arrived, dragging his gun behind him on the gravel and stood there sweating and scratching his chest.

'Can you tell us something about this?' visitors politely asked.

He chewed his lip in concentration and stumbled forward a few steps. 'This…' throwing out his arm. 'This thing, this…'

'Yes, yes?' visitors gasped in expectation.

'…is a stone,' he concluded and, turning, shuffled back down the steps.

It seemed his wife and two children were also living at the monument in a corrugated-iron shanty shed, but he had sent them away at our arrival in order to first establish how accommodating we were.

PART FIVE – INTO THE LAND OF SLEEPING SICKNESS

*

The President was coming! The President was coming!

Still thought of as the President, though Mwinyi had taken over, Nyerere was to arrive to make a speech of welcome for our arrival! How did we know? The road overnight had been miraculously resurfaced and potholes filled. In Kigoma, filth had been cleaned up and there was a 'plant a tree' campaign in operation. Children had been made to leave school and place embedded lines of cut-off tree branches into earth on either side of the road, which at first glance looked like an avenue of young planted saplings.

The President arrived amidst much fanfare but stayed only an hour in the course of which he gave his speech. Children were organised to sing for him and because of the shortness of time had to be hurried. We ourselves were not in time to attend his speech and were forced to water our donkeys at the lake where everybody washed clothes, their bodies, watered cows and goats and used it as drinking water.

Because there was now no *askari* we kept watch outside at night with loaded shotgun and rifle. Across the road our Arab neighbours were caught in their beds and robbed with machine guns. The doors were smashed down and shots fired into the bed to scare them. Robbers chopped off a man's head last night at the Regional Block. The body was still lying in the road today as vehicles drove past.

'Why?' we asked the police.

'We are looking for fingermarks,' they replied.

Tense with fear we stopped three suspicious pistol-armed figures slinking about outside our walls. Our

Arrival in Ujiji

shotgun was aimed at a man's chest. One ran off shouting, 'Police!' Were they police or was he calling for help? The remaining ones cowered.

'Identity cards!' we requested. They refused to show them. One kept whipping a dark police cap from his pocket and placing it on his head like a *Monty Python* sketch every time his colleague stated they were police. 'Tie them up, Andy!' I instructed. The cap-wearer fell poleaxed flat into the mud, beer fumes rising off his besuited body. One trembling man finally let us see his identity card. They *were* police! May the Lord preserve us! But what were they doing near the monument?

*

CNN arrived to film us. For them we rehearsed a typical scene from our journey on the old slave road. At the secondary school, children came out to voluntarily sing and they were filmed as a matter of course but didn't actually appear in the final version on American TV.

Andy's malaria was occurring with increasing frequency; he had never fully recovered, and it was decided I would cut down his tasks and at the very earliest opportunity he should return to London for treatment.

Alert for Andy's imminent collapse, I fell ill myself. I was ashamed for this to happen after making such a fuss about Andy's irresponsibility, and also at the very end of the trek. I had a terrible nauseous fever and spent time in bed. Thinking it malaria, I took a course of chloroquine which made me much worse. I was weak as a baby and lost control of my body. I could not stand unaided. Andy arranged for a lift to take me to a mission hospital run by the Sisters of Mercy. I had to stagger to the car, half dragged with one arm around Andy's neck and one arm around Christine. At the hospital there was no electricity, only kerosene lamps.

Christine was allowed to stay and offered a bed. We were there four days and I genuinely thought I would die. All I could remember was a hazy glow of kerosene light as sisters regularly checked on me. They were becoming extremely worried; nothing had shown in the blood. Then Sister Maria rushed in with the medical handbook she had been consulting throughout the night. She had prayed desperately, and it had miraculously fallen open at a page on *Borrelia Duttoni* (Lyme disease), which she thought I must have and which was easily treated with tetracycline. *Borrelia* was passed on by ticks. I vaguely remembered I had swiped a blood-swollen tick off a donkey and it had burst. My hand, already covered in cuts and bush scratches, became smeared in infected donkey blood. I had caught the disease from that. Now speedily injected, within two days I was as good as new!

The donkeys were in paradise, getting fatter by the minute. When in the wild with risks of predators, lack of food and water, their movement confined, they were calmer. Now, in a secure compound, no predators for miles, masses of food, total freedom, they fought viciously over every morsel of food.

It seemed a witchcraft battle had broken out in Mwangongo two miles past Gombe Stream where Jane Goodall undertook her chimpanzee research. I was interested in interviewing Jane Goodall and in writing an

Arrival in Ujiji

article on her chimpanzees for the popular Kenyan *South West Magazine* which concentrated on African animals, so headed there in a boat with a businessman who was trying to control the situation. Jane was sitting on the ground surrounded by her chimps when I arrived. She was impressed with our expedition, but I was disappointed to discover she was absent most of the time thereafter and depended on Tanzanian assistants to collect her information.

The village of Mwangongo, however, was in mortal fear and nobody could sleep as people fell ill in the night and died mysteriously. Villagers were also bewitched like zombies, and in the morning found themselves exhausted and covered in mud or by the lake, arms smeared with fish scales and slime. Children disappeared, beasts attacked villagers and then transformed back into humans. It was claimed an evil businessman from the village was responsible (the businessman in the boat) and that he had to regularly kill (especially one of his relatives) and enslave workers in order to keep his riches. The desperate villagers pooled together money and recruited their own witch doctors from Zaire – *kamchape* (exorcists) to defeat this evil.

The news editor of the *Sunday Telegraph* could not understand it when I phoned and dictated a story on the witchcraft wars. I had to hold the phone outside Omari's window so he could hear the *kamchape*'s drumming and witches' screams, as from those who were being killed or neutered.

'We'll print it,' he said, 'but I doubt anyone will believe it!'

We would not be able to go home soon, however. Our three remaining donkeys, shaggy Livingstone, dependable Stanley and cheeky Speke, were historically famous for their trek. To return them to Bagamoyo (a perilous railway journey in cattle trucks, many of which became derailed) would be to sentence them to a life of drudgery, carrying loaded coconuts and being mistreated. In other parts of Tanzania, they would be immediately turned into sausage meat. They deserved a grassy pension and I decided to somehow transport them to England. I had visions of living with my donkeys in the Devon countryside. I wrote to the Ministry of Agriculture explaining our predicament. They replied that donkeys were classed under 'equines' and so could not enter England because of the fear of East African horse sickness, which equines transmitted to each other. Donkeys were definitely not horses and according to our information at the time did not suffer this sickness, catch it, or pass it on, but according to the ministry's rule book… Stubbornly I wrote to the then Prime Minister, Mrs Thatcher, and to His Royal Highness the Duke of Edinburgh, pleading for help.

Mrs Thatcher was unable to assist but His Royal Highness took the trouble to inform me that there was a home in Nairobi that could take our donkeys if we could get them there. Other than that, 'Would Ireland do?' Obviously, the nearest and easiest place to make for was Nairobi. I wished to find a settled place where they would not have to work again for the rest of their lives.

We desperately wanted to leave Tanzania to locate the donkeys in a safe place. The Missionary Aviation Fellowship (MAF) said that for a fee they could fly us to Nairobi. With

Arrival in Ujiji

RSPCA donations and money I had saved myself I could just make it. They would have to take out all their aircraft seats to make space for our donkeys.

Approximately six months were spent in Ujiji making and unmaking donkey crates. We had to tempt the donkeys into crates with a trail of corn kernels and thereafter train them to lie down and stay down for three hours, while feeding them treats of *papai* as they could, if rising, kick at the fuselage.

At the end of the six months, at the beginning of September 1986, we made our way to the small, seemingly abandoned airfield of Ujiji. Collapsing the trained donkeys into a large cargo net Andy, myself and four Tanzanian volunteers carried each donkey into the aeroplane and onto the floor, where they obediently lay throughout the flight.

Sprawled untidily amongst defecating donkeys who lay down peacefully as if expecting to be fed further dainties, I felt airsick the whole 775-mile journey to Nairobi (if during the flight one of the donkeys had got up, proving a risk to the small aeroplane, the pilots would have immediately 'put them down' with a humane killer). After three hours – Nairobi was only an hour away, but we were on a circuitous route – we arrived at a Nairobi airstrip.

Unloading the boisterous donkeys I knew we would have to find temporary accommodation for us all, we hoped, at the Kenya Society for the Prevention of Cruelty to Animals (KSPCA). I had their telephone number ready in my shirt pocket.

The customs official who poked his nose into the entrance of the plane staggered back at the smell. 'Oh, you have brought camels!' he said.

PART FIVE – INTO THE LAND OF SLEEPING SICKNESS

After we arrived in Kenya, the KSPCA temporarily lodged the donkeys without payment, and we stayed for a night. No one at the KSPCA could confirm whether Pam Savage in Nairobi (owner of the donkey home found for us by the Duke of Edinburgh) was to take on an additional companion for Speke as had been agreed. And she herself was away in Australia at this time.

The donkeys after their trials and illnesses which we had successfully tended had come to depend on us. They were no longer the stroppy, half-wild creatures they had been in Bagamoyo, especially young Speke who brayed excitedly when he heard our voices. Stanley still preferred Christine's attentions, though would put up with Andy and my administrations as a poor second. They were so used to us they viewed us as part of the vegetation.

On the KSPCA open day we milled around the grounds with our donkeys, talking to visitors interested in our expedition.

'I really admire what you've done,' said a whiplash-faced David Evans, an import/export representative. He paced around the donkeys. 'Tell you what, why don't you bring the donkeys to me, I've got plenty of land and you can stay there too.' Evans owned an import/export company and he seemed to love the idea of having the donkeys on his land. I couldn't believe our luck. I offered to sign the donkeys over to him, but he wanted me to remain the owner. We rebuilt the stable and fencing. There was lots more grazing land! We slept in large safari tents Evans had erected out back of his house and moved the donkeys onto his land.

And now we could go home too.

Arrival in Ujiji

*

The romantic quest of one tenacious white man's search for another in the Dark Continent was and ever will be Stanley's tale. It therefore seems to me fitting that this account should end with Stanley's words, which speak to the three of us across over a century:

> *'At this grand moment we do not think of the hundreds of miles we have marched, of the hundreds of hills that we have ascended and descended, of the many forests we have traversed, of the jungles and thickets that annoyed us, of the fervid salt plains that blistered our feet, of the hot suns that scorched us, nor the dangers and difficulties, now happily surmounted...'*

Epilogue

This book should have been written many, many years ago. But Christine and I didn't come back from Africa at the end of our expedition in 1986, when we had planned to return. I couldn't face it. I knew it would be a big task and was exhausted.

From what we had seen Tanzania was in a state of flux, attempting desperately to forge a unique African identity for itself in the face of twentieth-century pressure. *Ujamaa* was a noble experiment which, if it had been successful, would have provided a shining example to the rest of Africa.

Immediately after *Uhuru* ('Independence') Tanzania's neighbour Kenya had chosen an easier route. Despite rejecting British rule, it began adopting Western methods and retained British advisers to help run the country. Black Kenyans copied the English language; meanwhile in Tanzania under President Julius Nyerere the Kiswahili language joined all tribes in communicating with each other and provided a national identity. But there was a conflict of views. Many Tanzanians said they preferred English; it was the language of progress.

Epilogue

While Europeans busily forged forward and planned ahead, Tanzanians lived for today, in the present moment. They respected their ancestors, believed in their spirits, and observed and obeyed nature's dictates. And who were we to say this was wrong? In the West there seemed to be something missing in our lives. We searched for guidance, self-improvement courses, wise-sounding gurus. And there was no need! In Africa, as far as we saw it, everyone was their own guru; answers were within every person's reach. In a Kenyan youth hostel we met a motorcyclist who with a sidecar to carry essential goods had casually travelled four times around the world. In the Lake District I had befriended a fellow student named Dave Shell, who had kayaked the whole of the River Nile from its source to the sea, a long and perilous journey. No one had heard of these major endeavours as they hadn't been written up. There were many such notable expeditions which remained unrecorded, and it was my modest hope that our expedition would draw attention and give hope to these unsung journeys.

The donkeys were settled outside Nairobi with David Evans. And out of the blue we were then invited to the Seychelles by their tourist board. Apparently, Stanley, travelling back to England after finding Livingstone, had to return via Zanzibar, the Seychelles and India. The Suez Canal did not then exist. The tourist board obviously wanted to glean possible publicity from our expedition. This was too good an opportunity for us to miss. We could never afford the Seychelles by any other means.

We stayed seven months in the Seychelles, attempting to recuperate, recover our equilibrium and keep our minds off the donkeys. We were hoping to rest but had to work, writing a walking tour of its capital, Victoria, and the botanical gardens. Also a promotional hotel article and a weekly eating-out guide in the local newspaper. While there, Andy disappeared; I found a handwritten note from him saying he couldn't cope and had returned to England. The Seychelles, after all our tribulations, was heavenly. But our paradise was upset by a brief telex from Evans in Nairobi. He wrote that he wanted to castrate the youngest donkey, Speke.

The donkeys were threatening to become a saga!

I briefly replied with a telex, 'Hold on!', and Christine and I flew to Nairobi to find a much-changed David Evans. It was as if we had never met! He wanted to castrate the donkey, he said, because it brayed and kept him awake. I explained that castration would not solve the problem, but to mollify him I did arrange the castration through a vet, and every morning travelled by native bus to the donkeys – though whites were not supposed to travel on native buses.

Soon after we arrived in Nairobi from the Seychelles, we heard from Andy. He'd suffered a nervous breakdown after our time in the Seychelles and been flown back to England by the British High Commission. He told us that our expedition had featured in all the UK newspapers, the *New York Times* and the *Philadelphia Enquirer*, and we had been due to appear on TV – *Blue Peter* and *The Terry Wogan Show* – while two publishers had expressed interest in the prospect of publishing a book on our expedition.

At this stage, 1987, I was disinclined to contact either publisher because I was suffering from stress and couldn't even *think* about Africa, let alone write about it. And it wasn't long after this that the donkey-hosting arrangement with David Evans came to an end by mutual agreement, and it was up to us to take the donkeys from his land.

Mr Don Vear of the *Sunday Telegraph*, with whom Andy had been in touch while staying with his brother in London, kindly sponsored him to fly out to Kenya to assist me. I was ecstatic that Andy had returned, as I truly needed his help to move the donkeys from Evans and once again dismantle the stable and fences.

Andy had changed considerably in the short time he had been away. He looked lost and meek, like a younger, quieter shadow of himself. He'd been working steadily as a telephone clerk. 'I've joined the rat race,' he said.

I was horrified to discover at Evans's place that Livingstone had trapped his front hoof, fallen and broken his leg. We speedily removed the donkeys to the temporary care of the KSPCA (there was nowhere else) who surprisingly charged us hefty stabling fees, cleaning out what we had collectively saved, and at last we found a permanent home for the donkeys at the Giraffe Manor in Karen, Langata, a European suburb of Nairobi. It was abundantly clear that the Giraffe Manor was hoping to glean publicity from housing the donkeys and that I would have to write for Kenyan wildlife magazines in order to recoup money. Andy said he'd make an attempt at sponsorship. But he disappeared again, leaving for London.

The property at the Giraffe location was, we were told, originally built by the Mackintosh toffee king to resemble his stone-built Scottish manor. An American lady and her British husband had bought the property and organised

Epilogue

it as a sanctuary for Rothschild giraffes, an endangered subspecies with lighter-coloured decorative patches less jagged in shape than the main species. She had written a successful book, *Raising Daisy Rothschild*. 'Daisy' was a giraffe which was supposed to suffer epileptic fits and the manor had become an established feature on the tourist route. Tourists (usually from America) stayed in the main house and African school groups regularly visited to feed the giraffes.

Having rebuilt stable and fencing, also including a noticeboard detailing the donkeys' intrepid expedition, it was time to recruit a good vet for Livingstone.

There was a list of vets in the phone book. I chose the first good English name, John Sercombe. He came out to examine Livingstone.

He was brisk: 'I'm afraid I'll have to put your donkey down, this is a serious break.'

I explained that I wanted to keep my donkey alive.

'With all due respect,' he said, 'this is merely a donkey. At the racecourse we put horses down with this kind of break.'

'Livingstone survived an arduous expedition,' I said. 'He's one of the first donkeys to have achieved this. To me he's not just a donkey but a fully-fledged personality. He has a broken leg which I'm asking you to fix. If he had been a human being you wouldn't put him down.'

Sercombe bristled. 'Are you telling me how to do my job? I'm not prepared to treat him. Either you have him put down or I leave, it's your decision.'

'I want to keep him alive.'

'OK then.' Sercombe stormed off to his car. Looking

back he shouted, 'Don't bother to contact other vets. They will think the same way I do.'

I contacted a long line of Nairobi vets and eventually found a Mr Varma, who was prepared to come out and examine Livingstone.

'Your story sounds fascinating,' he said, then added, 'I'm the official vet at the Nairobi racecourse.'

Mr Varma was a marvel. The broken leg, it seemed, had remained untreated for two days. He injected Livingstone, curetted the bone and plastered it in place. 'You'll have to replaster and tend to the donkey yourself from now on,' he said. 'I can't afford to be coming out here all the time.' He looked into my eyes. 'This is going to take a while to heal if at all. If it doesn't take, we'll have to put the donkey down, OK?'

Under the circumstances I had to agree.

Christine and I pampered Livingstone, building up his strength with antibiotics and masses of powdered calcium interspersed with treats of cassava, pawpaw, corn kernels and oats. African donkeys are unused to carrots. We changed his newly bought plaster of Paris every month (the original Chinese-made plaster didn't last for more than a week) and I devised wooden splints incorporated into the plaster with a rubber tyre rocker at the end so Livingstone could put his weight on the bone and walk like Pegleg Pete. We made sure that in the stable he was isolated away from Stanley and Speke and had an unimpeded space for himself. Donkeys when kept together tend to playfully bite and kick each other.

A film team arrived to use Giraffe Manor as a location intending to shoot a feature film, *Shadow on the Sun*, directed

Epilogue

by Tony Richardson, and stars of the film eventually appeared: Stefanie Powers, Claire Bloom, James Fox, Peter Bowles. The film team had a problem. They wanted a Rothschild giraffe (for the epileptic Daisy) to poke its head in at the front door of the manor when James Fox opened it. There was no animal trainer. I heard them openly discussing the difficulty, and encouraged by my donkey-caring, promptly said, 'I can do that!' With a bucket of horse nuts which I deliberately rattled, I trained Daisy to follow me and eventually to look around inside the manor door on hearing the rattle. This secured me a role in the film.

Nine months passed looking after Livingstone. Varma was right; the leg was certainly taking time to heal. It was now 1988. Each time he arrived with his portable X-ray machine there was a visible gap in the bone.

'Surely,' I asked, 'after all this time feeding Livingstone calcium the bone should have joined together?'

'We won't know until the plaster finally comes off and Livingstone puts weight on his leg. X-rays are not infallible. And Livingstone is not a young donkey. You'll have to risk it!'

I brought Livingstone forward, and Mr Varma cut off the plaster. With heart choked in my breast, I watched Livingstone tentatively at first put his weight on his front leg, then gradually with confidence stride off strongly across the field. The bone had healed!

*

We returned to Dar es Salaam by sponsored flight in the summer of 1988 to hand in the reports to which we had been so faithful and which various bodies had asked for:

the exact location of Kisabengo's lost city of Morogoro for the University of Dar es Salaam; changes in ecology, crops grown and reasons why fishermen were not catching more fish on Lake Tanganyika for the Ministry of Agriculture; location of genetic mutants seen (see *Daily Mail*, 25 September 1998), poaching trails and locations of caches of buried elephant tusks for the Game Department; and successful *Ujamaa* villages for the Prime Minister's Office.

The report on why fishermen were not catching more fish in Lake Tanganyika was undertaken while we lived for six months in Ujiji, and it has always provided me with a knowing smile. There had already been two thick UN reports written on the subject – multimillion-dollar aid projects. Lake Tanganyika had been shown to be saturated with fish, and it was thought that fishermen were not catching more fish because they couldn't sail into deeper waters. They were given engines for their simple boats. They sold these across the water in Zaire. Then it had to be the string fishing nets which broke and caused fishermen to spend much time fixing them by hand. Nylon nets were distributed. These they also sold.

Living with the fishermen we gradually gained their confidence and discovered that the reason they didn't deliberately catch more fish was that they were afraid that, having increased the supply, the price would drop!

We handed the report on poaching trails and buried caches of tusks to the Minister for Natural Resources in Dar es Salaam. He asked in perfect English, 'Would you help us end elephant poaching?'

'I thought our report was a contribution toward that end.'

Epilogue

He continued, 'If you went back into the bush posing as gemstone smugglers, you would get to know the poachers as allies.'

'But why ask us?' I questioned. 'We're white. And not from this country.'

'In only ten years 55,000 of our elephants have been killed for their tusks. We still have 55,000 left, but it won't take another ten years to decimate them all. Aid agencies have threatened to cut our financial aid if we don't do something to stem the losses from our elephant population.' Aha, now we were getting to it.

'You are white and the aid agencies are white, you speak fluent Kiswahili, you have travelled in the bush and met poachers. They will trust you. Do you know why else I am asking you?'

'Because the anti-poaching unit is poaching,' I said.

'Ah, so you know.'

The anti-poaching unit was disbanded. Operation Uhai was launched, comprising police, army and rangers from the Wildlife Department who cracked down on the poachers with a vengeance. In Nairobi at the same time they burned a mountain of tusks, which made headline news all over the world.

During this time many local newspapers and magazines provided income for us – for descriptive articles for the Tanzania Tourist Corporation and the *Tanzanian Daily* and *Sunday News*. Christine and I, though, felt caught in a time warp that seemed to descend around our bodies – and that was to keep us trapped in Africa for a total of eight and a half years!

I was happy with Giraffe Manor as a long-term home for

the donkeys, had fenced off a suitable area of land, prepared the notice board as at the Bagamoyo Museum and beside it a collection box to assist Giraffe Manor with funds. But I felt definite guilt at abandoning them, particularly young Speke as I had grown particularly fond of him. We gave the donkeys a final brush-down, whispered in their long velvety ears that we were going to England and scurried quietly away. To tell the truth, at that time I was relieved to be shedding this great responsibility – but I felt a total coward.

When visiting Giraffe Manor from Tanzania a year later in 1989, Speke heard my voice from miles away and began braying. It melted my heart. I would have liked the three of them with me. But it was not to be.

*

Our expedition was an education. For me, it was like attending three seats of university learning at the same time: anthropology, history, veterinary science, and there were many more subjects. I learnt much about wild animal behaviour and lore, changing ecology, detection, aid projects.

But many of the poor Tanzanians whom I've criticised – they never stood a chance. I felt great guilt. They were definitely impoverished and struggling to survive with no hope in view. And I had abandoned them as well as the donkeys.

But finally, with borrowed money, we flew home to England. It was that easy. And I felt nothing about going home – no anticipation or feeling of relief. Nothing.

Epilogue

And so back in London in 1991 and the greatest dangers of life now seemed almost pathetically inconsequential. Africa had dragged us into its morass and had seemed reluctant to relinquish its grip. It had tossed us like rag dolls into a roaring windspout of emotion-consuming events that threatened to spin for ever. I had given myself up to it like a sacrificial victim. I believe not doing so is why Andy had his breakdown. He believed there was a choice and could not conceive of being entirely helpless. You sometimes had to give yourself up to events in order to be allowed to emerge at the other end. There was no question of choice.

At home in Camden, north London in 1991, we established ourselves again in our ramshackle house which over the years had suffered severe subsidence. We had begun our journey in 1982, the actual expedition in 1984, so long ago now. We fervidly checked bank accounts for *Telegraph* article payments for our tax return and caught up on our missed eight and a half years of news: the Falklands War, Mrs Thatcher's regime, Arthur Scargill… Cyclists sped past wearing helmets and smog masks like SAS men; the new Sainsbury's in Camden Town was chock-full of goods. Twenty varieties of toothpaste and soap, varieties of everything imaginable, mounds of mangoes, star fruit and papaya out of season. The choice after Tanzania was obscene! For a while I mainly hid away.

Since Africa I had been living in a permanent winter. Life in London was tedious, without substance, a repetitive continuation of the past. Everyday living destroyed me. I belonged nowhere. A numbness and spiritual emptiness mirrored my outer world.

Epilogue

While Christine was not affected at all, I began to have bad dreams. And I suffered great guilts: I hadn't taken up either of the publisher offers as I couldn't write the book; I had abandoned the donkeys, particularly young Speke. In my dreams I wept and begged forgiveness. The dreams got much worse. I sweated profusely at night and cried out, waking to find myself entwined in damp sheets.

One minute I was restless and in a state of feverish excitement – a rekindling of the African experience, the magical excitement about being near to danger, a passing into another existence. The next minute I was lethargic, completely frozen. I was constantly irritable, with a tendency to be argumentative and inflexible in my views, with a readiness for physical aggression. And now this emptiness was all there was. I didn't belong here. I felt in a pit of despair. I wanted to die. I was just marking time, treading water until I was finally extinguished. I had no feelings, no passion. It had all been drained into the bush. For the first time in my life I seriously considered psychiatric help.

On a routine visit to my GP about blocked breathing problems which had begun almost immediately on our return to England, she questioned me about my sleeping habits. 'I want you to see this specialist,' she said, making a quick referral to his office.

The specialist, I believe, attended to Falklands returnees.

'You have post-traumatic stress,' he announced. I let that sink in for a while. It didn't really mean anything to me.

'But I haven't been in a war,' I said.

'No, you haven't, but you have spent over two years

Epilogue

in the African bush, and eight years in Tanzania without a break, some of that time potential prey to carnivorous animals and humans attempting to rob and kill you.' He explained that in order to personally survive and ensure the survival of my group I had discarded all my emotions and had always been on alert. My adrenalin count was presently way off the chart. Now that I was back in a safe normal environment, such precautions were not necessary. I was definitely emotionless and out of place! I could readily understand this. In Africa I had allowed myself to become madder than the mad circumstances I was surrounded by in order to survive.

I didn't see the specialist again. I thought I could sort myself out. I was wrong. Mental health issues often do need professional help, and there is no shame in admitting so. Then I came upon an advert for a part-time drama course at the City Literary Institute. I signed up.

One of the acting exercises was to tell a story about an incident in your life to the rest of the class that you had never told anyone before. You would think that the students could choose a funny incident from their life but no, the students chose the most harrowing of experiences. One girl described how she had spent time in an insane asylum. She believed she could fly and was always attempting to jump out of windows. Old Cockney Tom – he was much older than me – was unliked in the class. He was solitary and mean with money. In the pub after class he never stood anybody a drink. But he told a painful story about his abandonment as a child. As he spoke, I could feel internal tickles in my lower stomach, like fluttering butterflies, slowly creeping up to my heart and chest. I thought, *You poor, poor old sod. I'll buy you a drink any day.* I realised suddenly that I was finally allowing myself to *feel* again. Wowee! I then mistakenly thought my post-traumatic stress was banished for good.

Since then I have got older and experienced more injustices. I have tried, really I have tried my best to escape my predicament by extensive travel. I nearly died in the Boxing Day tsunami (2004) in Thailand. I've yet to get over my fear of the sea and I'm still marking time. Perhaps writing this book is the final cure.

*

Our unawareness led us to make our expedition. If we had not been so naive and idealistic, innocent of the ways of Africa, we would have realised just how difficult, if not impossible, was the task we were attempting. Above all, it had been a personal journey. We did it for ourselves and nobody else. Most Europeans we had met in Kenya and Tanzania had thought our journey laughable, foolhardy, an extended holiday. I suppose it was a search for honour which moved further away from us the more we travelled towards it. And having started something, we felt we had to finish it. We wanted to believe desperately but discovered that society's way was a series of deceptions.

In Africa I had to become a much worse person in order to survive. This did not lie well with me. At the end of the trek, I was *wiser* but not necessarily *nicer*.

I had never felt in step with the metropolitan way of life. For the sake of my shrinking soul I desperately needed to find a niche where beings were still human and practised

Epilogue

the old-fashioned virtues of generosity, truth, loyalty and honour. Somewhere they had to exist. I wanted to just once sit with the Knights at their Round Table (for all its warp and knot-holes) and then set off on a mad, jubilant, impossible quest for my ideals.

Such was my Holy Grail when undertaking the expedition I have described, and I believe it to have been shared at least to some extent by my companions. It seems inseparable from a state of mind which remains with me to this day, in which I still imagine the shimmer of endless tawny plains stretching and entering the room, the heart-cracking sizzle of cicadas, and smell the baked, hot breath of Africa – blankets of moving heat – the musk of sun-dried plants, cloying fragrance of smoking wood, and catch drumming sounds out of the earth, the ever-cooing mourning doves, a clop of fragile hooves, the tearing out and munching of grass…

And Sergeant-Major Burton happy at the end of the day's trek, hiccupping and braying as if his heart would burst.

Glossary of Terms in Swahili

The prefix *m* denotes a single person, as in *mtoto* – a child; *mtu* – a person. The prefix *wa* denotes more than one person, as in *watoto* – children; *watu* –people.

askari – soldier or guard

bahati – luck
balozi – ambassador
bamia – okra
bao – a game like draughts played on a long piece of rough-hewn polished wood with carved hollows to hold pebbles
biltong – sun-dried lean meat
binadamu – human
boma – enclosed home space; also fort or protected building
bure – free/useless
Bwana – Mr

dagaa – small sprats
debe – tin container for commonly four gallons

dik-dik – very small antelope
doum palm – bears small orange-coloured, pineapple-shaped fruit
duka – shop

fundi – craftsman

gellabia – full-length white robe worn by Arabs in Egypt and Sudan and on the African east coast
gonga – a cheat

hamna – there is none
hayupo – he is absent
hondo hondo – hornbill
hongo – bribe

jeshi – army
jiko – charcoal brazier

kamchape – exorcists
kanga – gulnea fowl
karibu – welcome; nearby
Katibu – a CCM party secretary. There is one in every village
kesho – tomorrow
kiboko – hippopotamus
kidogo – small/little
kikoi – knee-length piece of striped cloth wound round the waist
kitenge/kikoi – patterned sheet worn wrapped around the body

Glossary of Terms in Swahili

konyagi – gin from Holland; or any spirit often made in Tanzania
kugalagala – to roll about in excitement

masika – the long rains
masikini – impoverished/poor
matobolwa – boiled slices of sweet potato
matoke – plantain bananas
mawesi – cattle
mbege – local beer
mchawi – wizard or witch
mchicha – kind of spinach
mchwa – white ants
mdulele – shrub providing food; also with medicinal uses
mganga – doctor or healer
mgude – sycamore tree
mihama – palm trees
miombo – dwarf acacia woodland
mizimu – spirits/ghosts, usually of ancestors
mkoche – doum palm
mpani – tiny flies that invade every orifice seeking liquid
mtama – millet
mtemi – chief
mto – river
Mungu – *God*
mwalmu – *teacher*
mwenyekiti – village chairman, whom we would always ask to organise an area for us to camp
mwezi – moon
mwizi – thief
mzee – an older person; often a term of respect
mzungu – white man

nati – buffalo
ndorobo – tsetse fly
ngambo – voluntary civil militia attached to the CCM
nini? – what? Also meaning 'thing'
nyoka – snake, with positive or negative symbolism for healing or danger

panga – heavy curved knife used as a tool or weapon
papai – papaya fruit
pombe – alcohol

safari – journey
salama – peace
shamba – piece of land for cultlvation/allotment
sheitani – devil/demon
shenzi – barbarous/rubbish; term of insult
shikamoo – term of respectful greeting (meaning 'I hold your feet')
shuka – blanket
siafu – soldier/safari ants
simba – lion
subiri – wait
SunguSungu – vigilante group from the Wasukuma tribe

tembe – traditional Wagogo house design
tembo – palm wine; also elephant
toka – go away
tu – only
twanga – to heavily pound dried cassava, millet or corn
twiga – giraffe

uchawi – black magic
ugali – staple food, a kind of porridge made from maize meal
uhuru – freedom/independence of a nation
Ujamaa – collectivised village community formed in Tanzania on Independence in 1961
upupu – buffalo bean

wachawi – witches/black magicians
wadudu – insects/pests
wakimbizi – runaways/refugee South Africans
wamumiani – bloodsuckers
wapi? – where? (exclamation)
wazungu – white men
weh – exclamation, abbreviation of *wewe* (you)

ziwani – large pool of water
zizi – stockade made of thorn branches

Abbreviations in English

ANC – African National Congress
CCM – Chama Cha Mapinduzi, the Party of the Revolution, the dominant political party in Tanzania
DNR Officer – District National Resources Officer
FAO – Food and Agriculture Organisation
NORAD – administrative body for development co-operation linking the Tanzanian Office of Foreign Affairs with Norwegian sustainability policy
PAC – Pan-African Congress
RTC – Regional Trading Company: the main supplier of goods in Tanzania, with a warehouse in each town, though without access for most people
TTC – Tanzania Tourist Corporation

Bibliography

The author's recommendation of books about East Africa, in the editions he used himself, some of them in suggested comparison or contrast with his own experience

Africa on the Cheap – Geoff Crowther (Lonely Planet 1980)
An Ice-cream War – William Boyd (Penguin 1986)
A Walk Across Africa – J.A. Grant (W. Blackwood & Sons 1864)
Battle for the Bundu – Charles Miller (Westland Sundries 1976)
Burton and Speke – William Harrison (Star 1984)
Captain Speke, Zanzibar – Richard F. Burton (John Murray 1872)
David Livingstone: His Life and Letters – George Seaver (Lutterworth Press 1957)
Donkeys – M.R. De Wesselow (Centaur Press 1973)
English–Swahili Dictionary – (Oxford University Press 1981)
Green Hills of Africa – Ernest Hemingway (Grafton Books 1982)
How I Found Livingstone in Central Africa – H.M. Stanley (Sampson Low, Marston, Low & Searle 1872)

I Presume: Stanley's Triumphs and Disasters – Ian Anstruther (Geoffrey Bles 1956, and also New English Library 1973)

Larger Mammals of Africa – Jean Dorst & Pierre Dandelot (Collins 1980)

Livingstone – Tim Jeal (Penguin 1985)

Lovers on the Nile – Richard Hall (Random House 1980)

My Reminiscences of East Africa – General Von Lettow-Vorbeck (Hurst & Blackett and many further editions)

New Light on Dark Africa – Dr Carl Peters, trans. by H.W. Dulcken Ward (Locke & Co. 1891)

Out of Africa – Karen Blixen (Penguin 1984)

Quest – Sue Newson Smith (Arlington Books 1978)

Richard Meinertzhagen – Mark Cocker (Mandarin 1990)

Sir Henry M. Stanley: The Enigma – Emyr Wyn Jones (Gee 1989)

Snakes and Us – H.A. Skinner (East African Literature Bureau 1973)

The Blue Nile – Alan Moorehead (Penguin 1973)

The Ghosts of Africa – William Stevenson (Star 1982)

The Lake Regions of Central Africa – Sir R.F. Burton (Sidgwick & Jackson 1961)

The Last Hero – Peter Forbath (Mandarin 1990)

The Lunatic Express – Charles Miller (Ballantine Books 1976)

The Scramble for Africa – Thomas Pakenham (Abacus 1992)

The Whales in Lake Tanganyika – Lennart Hagerfors (Penguin 1991)

The White Nile – Alan Moorehead (Penguin 1973)

Through the Dark Continent – H.M. Stanley, 2 vols (Sampson Low 1885)

Where There Is No Doctor – David Werner (Macmillan 1979)

Zanguebar – Father Frits Veirsteijnen (*Zanzibar Gazette* 14 April 1897)

Zanzibar – Giles Foden (Faber & Faber 2002)

Zanzibar – Richard F. Burton (Tinsley Brothers 1872)

This book is printed on paper from sustainable sources managed under the Forest Stewardship Council (FSC) scheme.

It has been printed in the UK to reduce transportation miles and their impact upon the environment.

For every new title that Troubador publishes, we plant a tree to offset CO_2, partnering with the More Trees scheme.

For more about how Troubador offsets its environmental impact, see www.troubador.co.uk/sustainability-and-community